Just because people throw it out
and don't have any use for it,
doesn't mean it's garbage.

— Andy Warhol

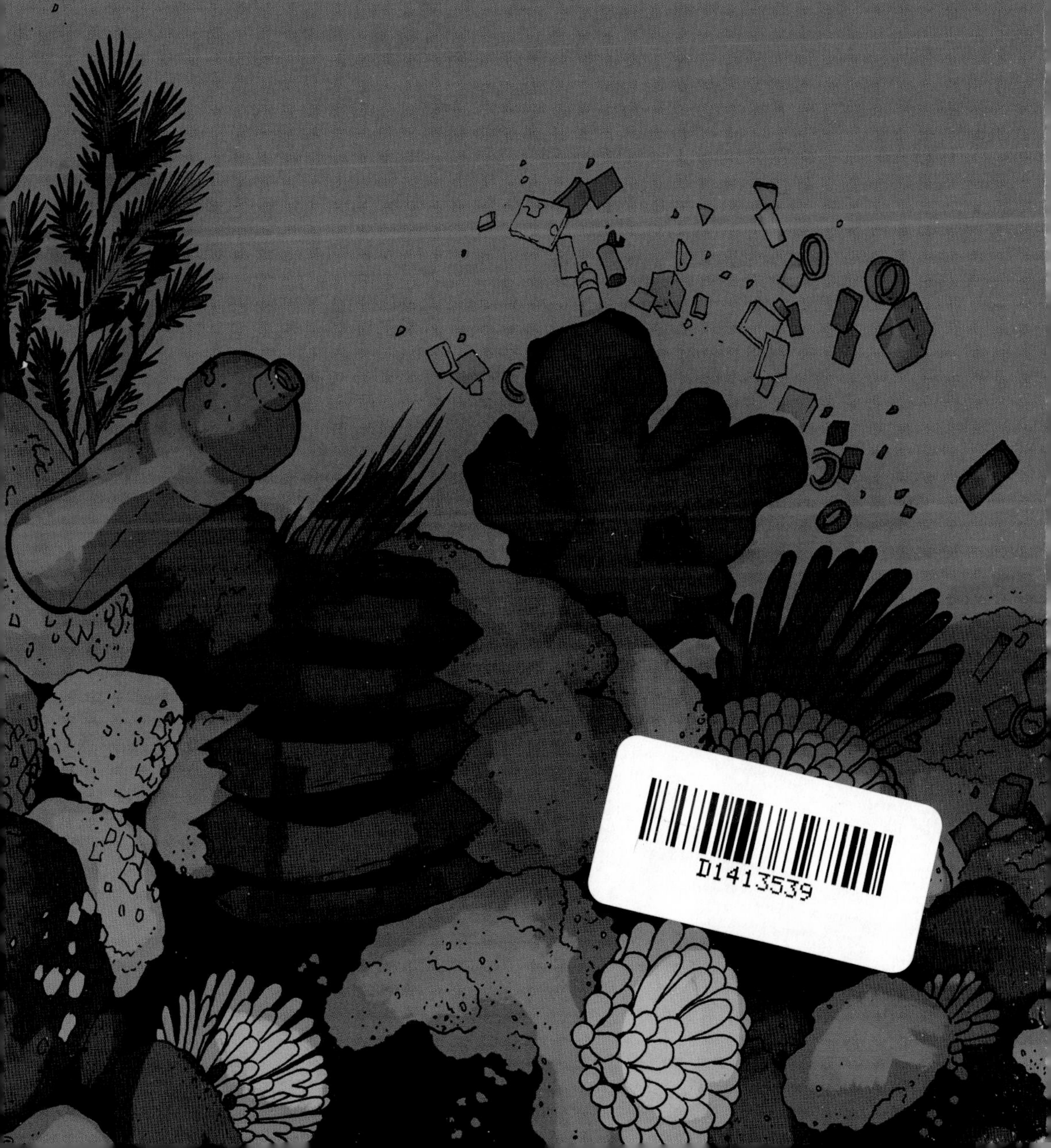

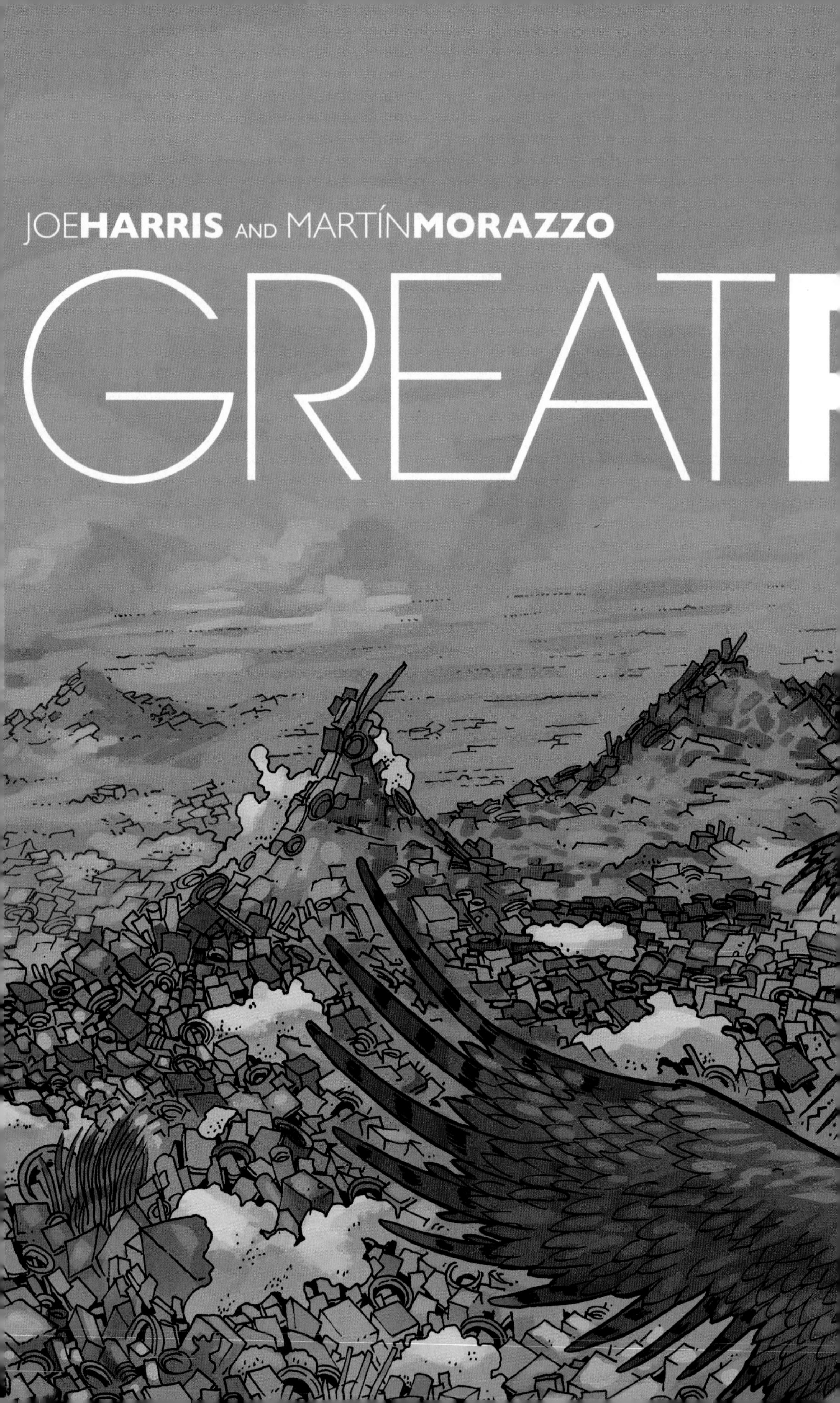
JOE HARRIS AND MARTÍN MORAZZO
GREAT

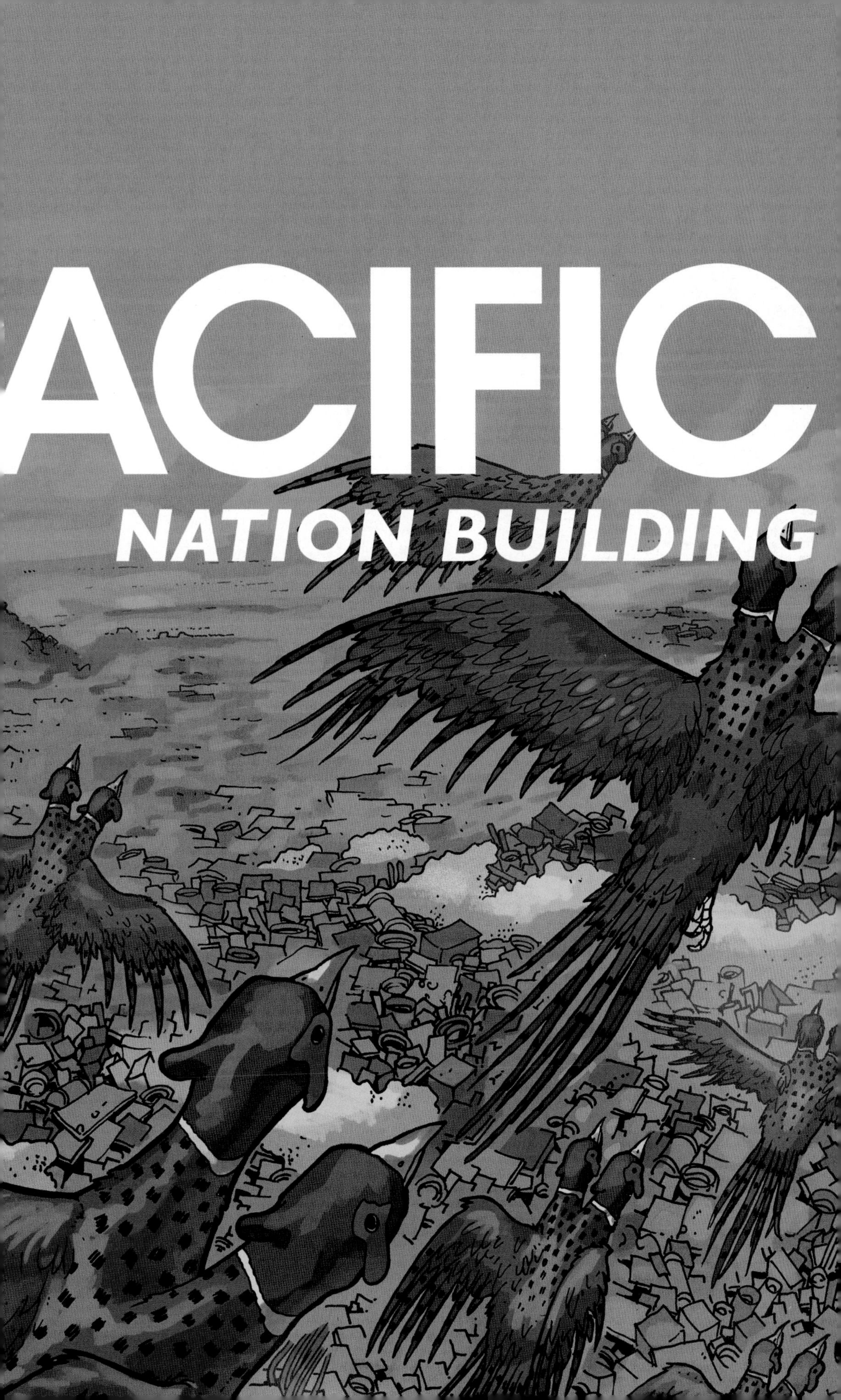
ACIFIC
NATION BUILDING

CREATED BY
JOE**HARRIS** AND
MARTÍN**MORAZZO**

WRITTEN BY
JOE**HARRIS**

ART BY
MARTÍN**MORAZZO**

COLORS BY
TIZA **STUDIO**
& MARTÍN**MORAZZO**

LETTERS BY
MICHAEL DAVID**THOMAS**

DESIGN BY SEAN**DOVE**
EDITED BY SHAWNA**GORE**

WWW. GREATPACIFICCOMICS.COM

WWW.IMAGECOMICS.COM

PUBLISHED BY IMAGE COMICS, INC.

This book collects issues **7-12** of the
Image Comics series GREAT PACIFIC

First edition December 2013
ISBN — 978-1-60706-837-2

IMAGE COMICS, INC.
Robert Kirkman - Chief Operating Officer
Erik Larsen - Chief Financial Officer
Todd McFarlane - President
Marc Silvestri - Chief Executive Officer
Jim Valentino - Vice-President

Eric Stephenson - Publisher
Ron Richards - Director of Business Development
Jennifer de Guzman - Director of Trade Book Sales
Kat Salazar - PR & Marketing Coordinator
Jeremy Sullivan - Digital Marketing Coordinator
Jamie Parreno - Online Marketing Coordinator
Emilio Bautista - Sales Assistant
Braewyn Bigglestone - Senior Accounts Manager
Emily Miller - Accounts Manager
Jaemie Dudas - Administrative Assistant
Tyler Shainline - Events Coordinator
David Brothers - Content Manager
Jonathan Chan - Production Manager
Drew Gill - Art Director
Meredith Wallace - Print Manager
Monica Garcia - Senior Production Artist
Jenna Savage - Production Artist
Addison Duke - Production Artist
IMAGECOMICS.COM

image

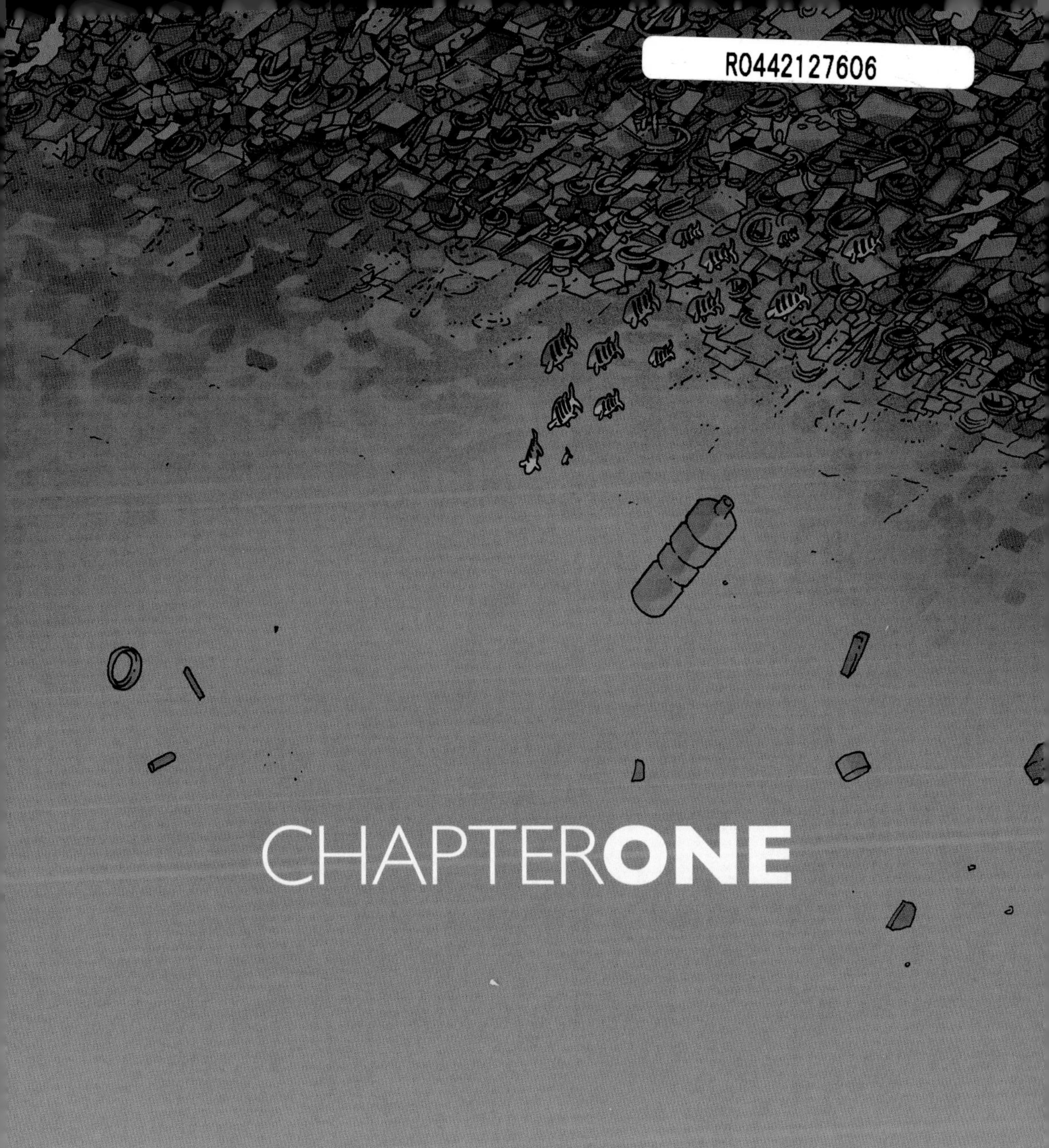

CHAPTER ONE

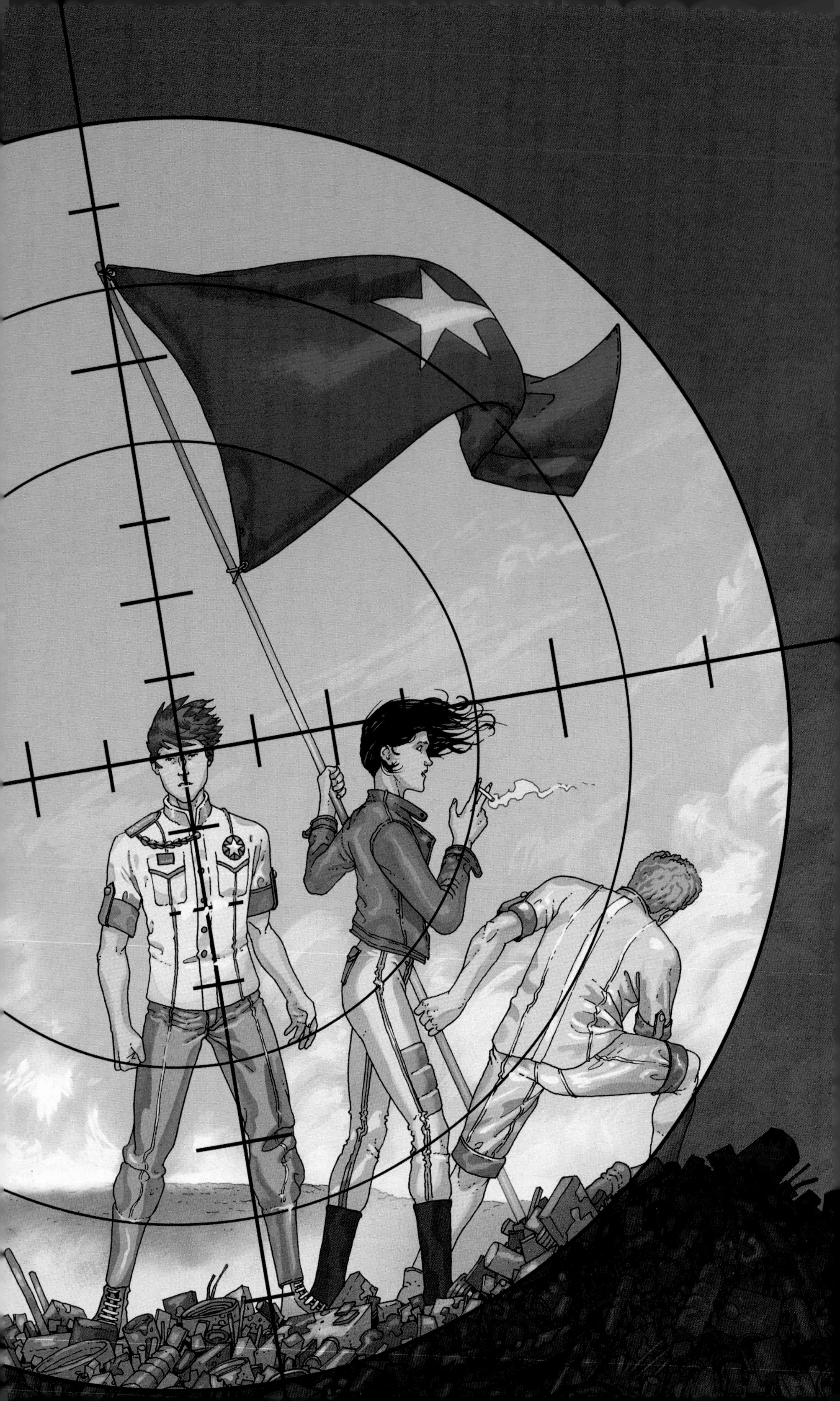

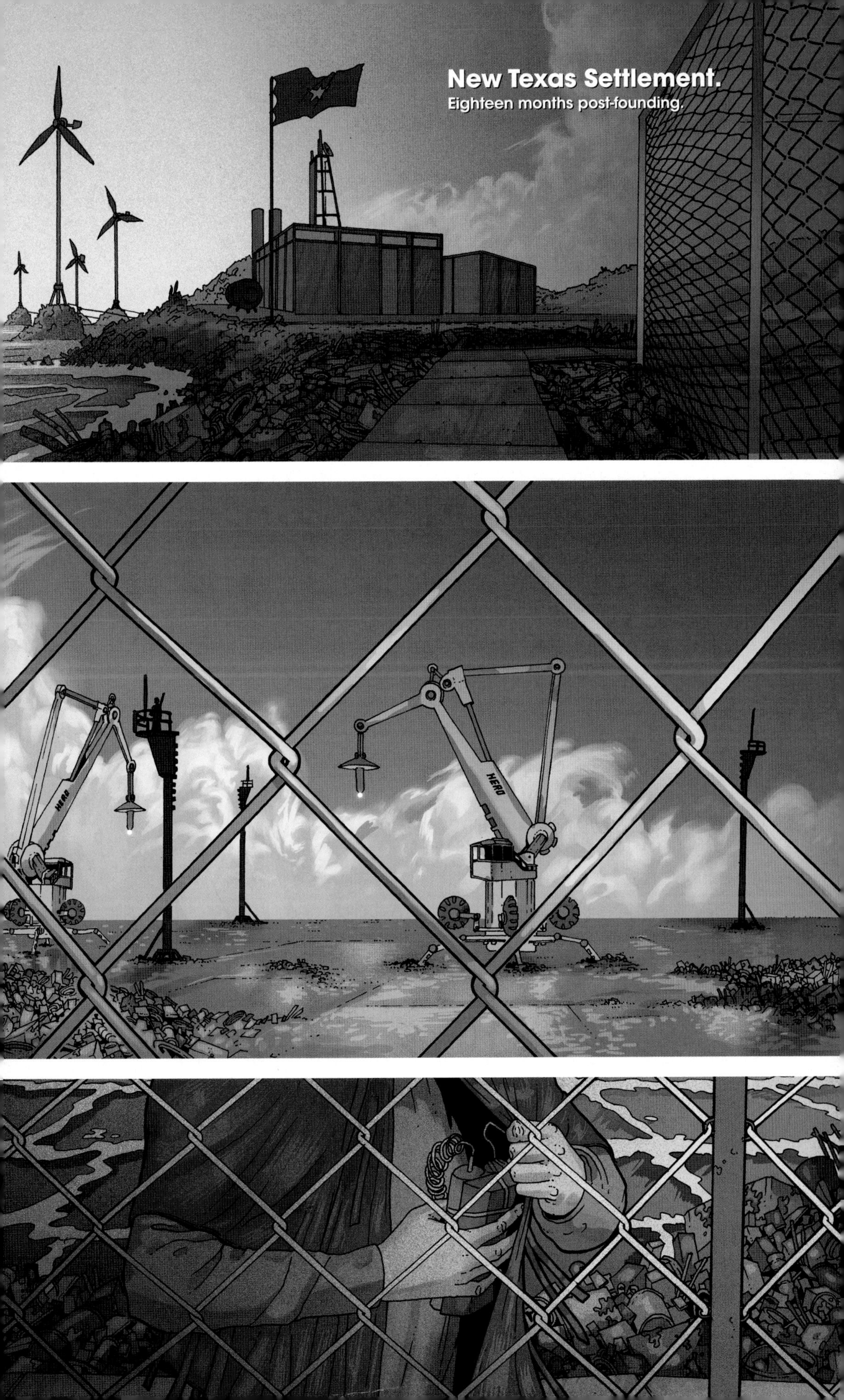
New Texas Settlement.
Eighteen months post-founding.

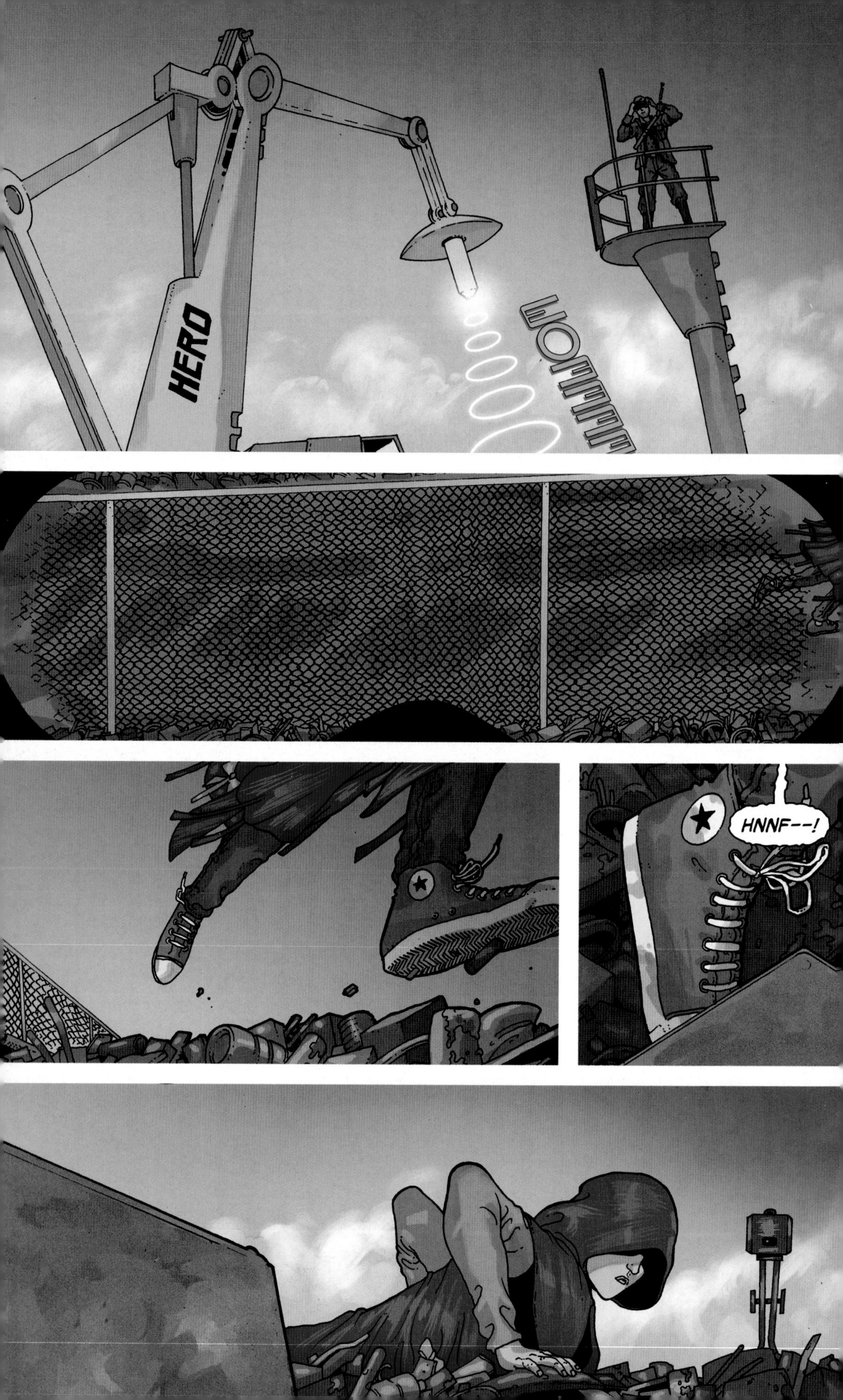
HERO
WOMMMM
HNNF--!

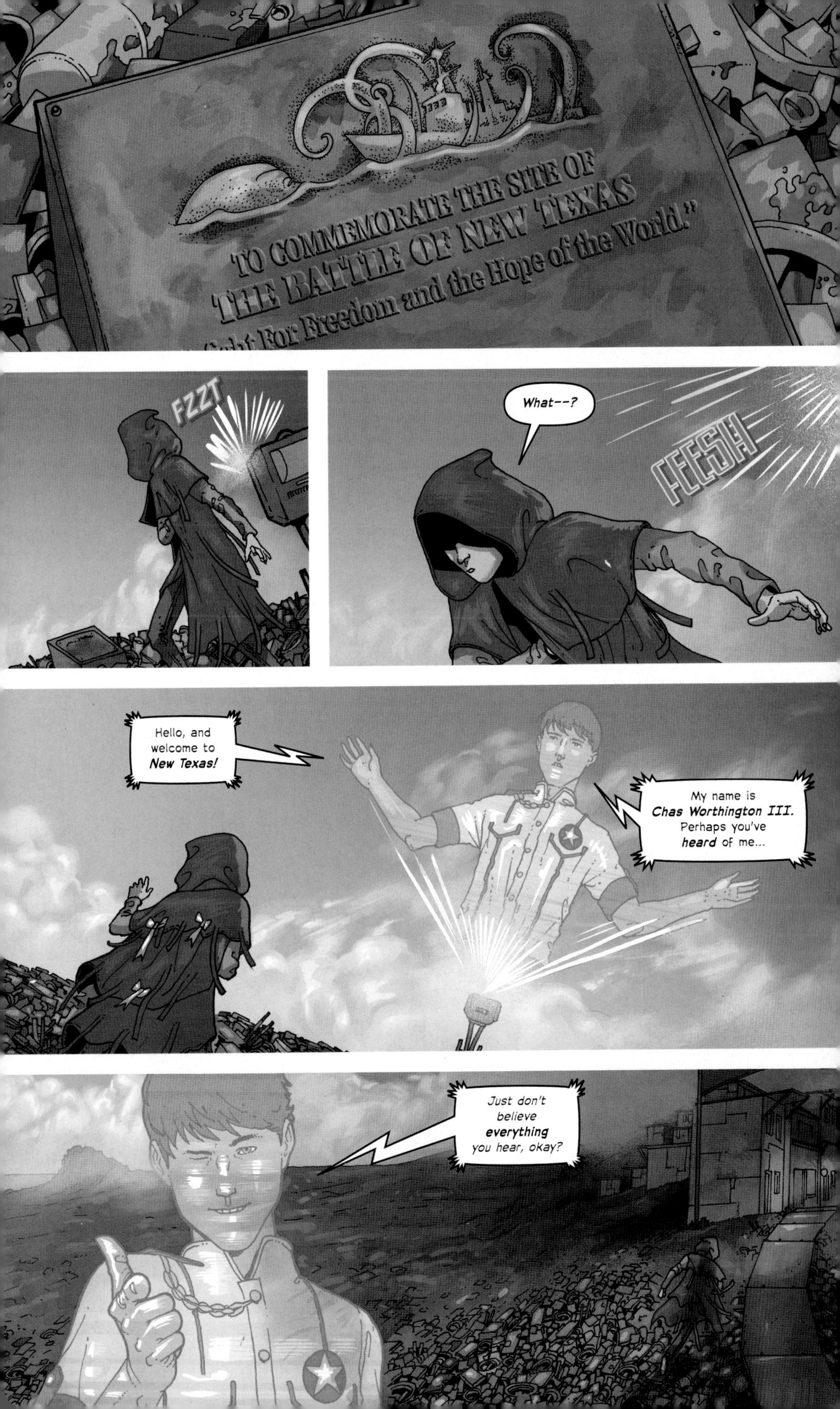
TO COMMEMORATE THE SITE OF
THE BATTLE OF NEW TEXAS
FZZT
What--?
FEESH
Hello, and welcome to New Texas!
My name is Chas Worthington III. Perhaps you've heard of me...
Just don't believe everything you hear, okay?

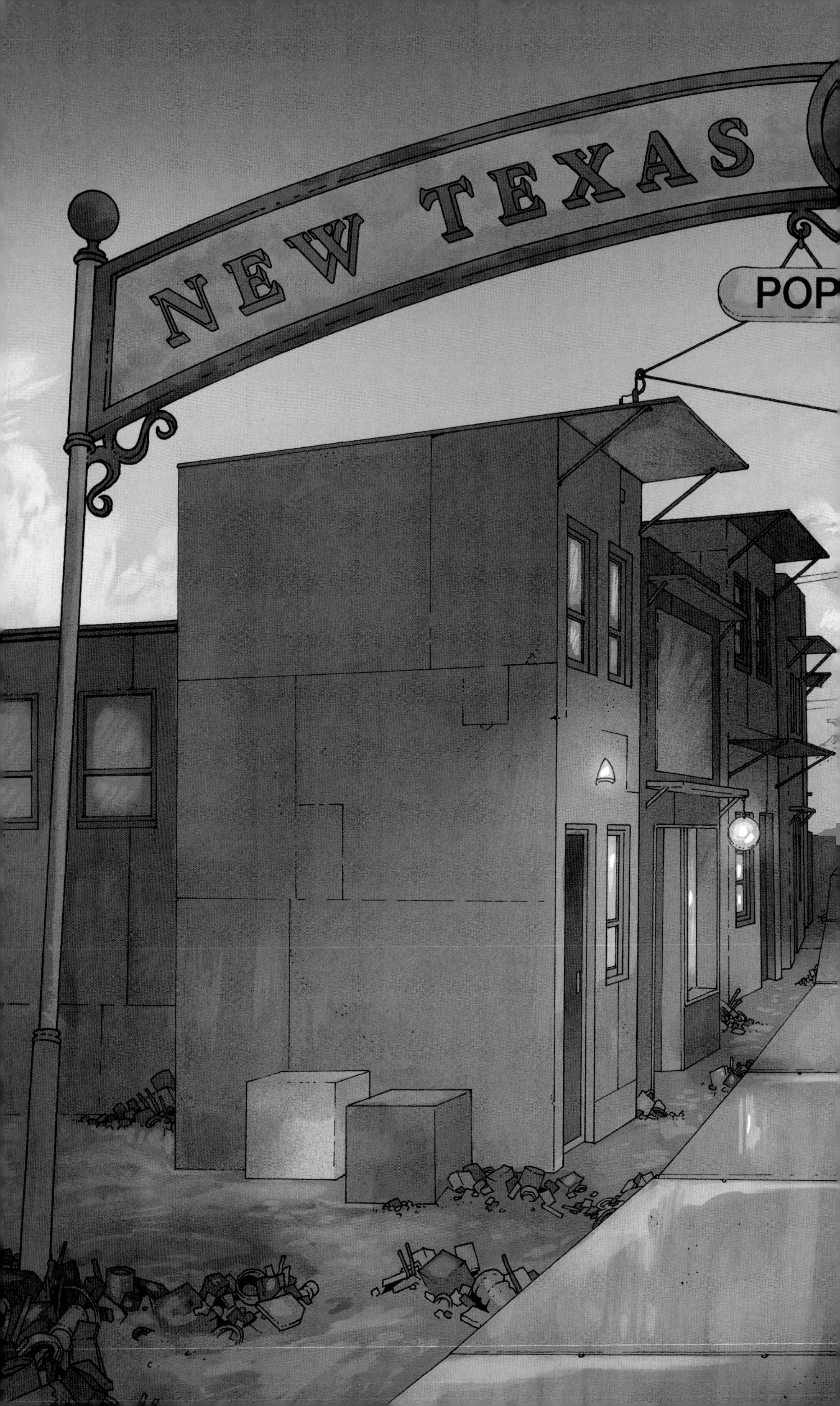

NEW TEXAS
POP

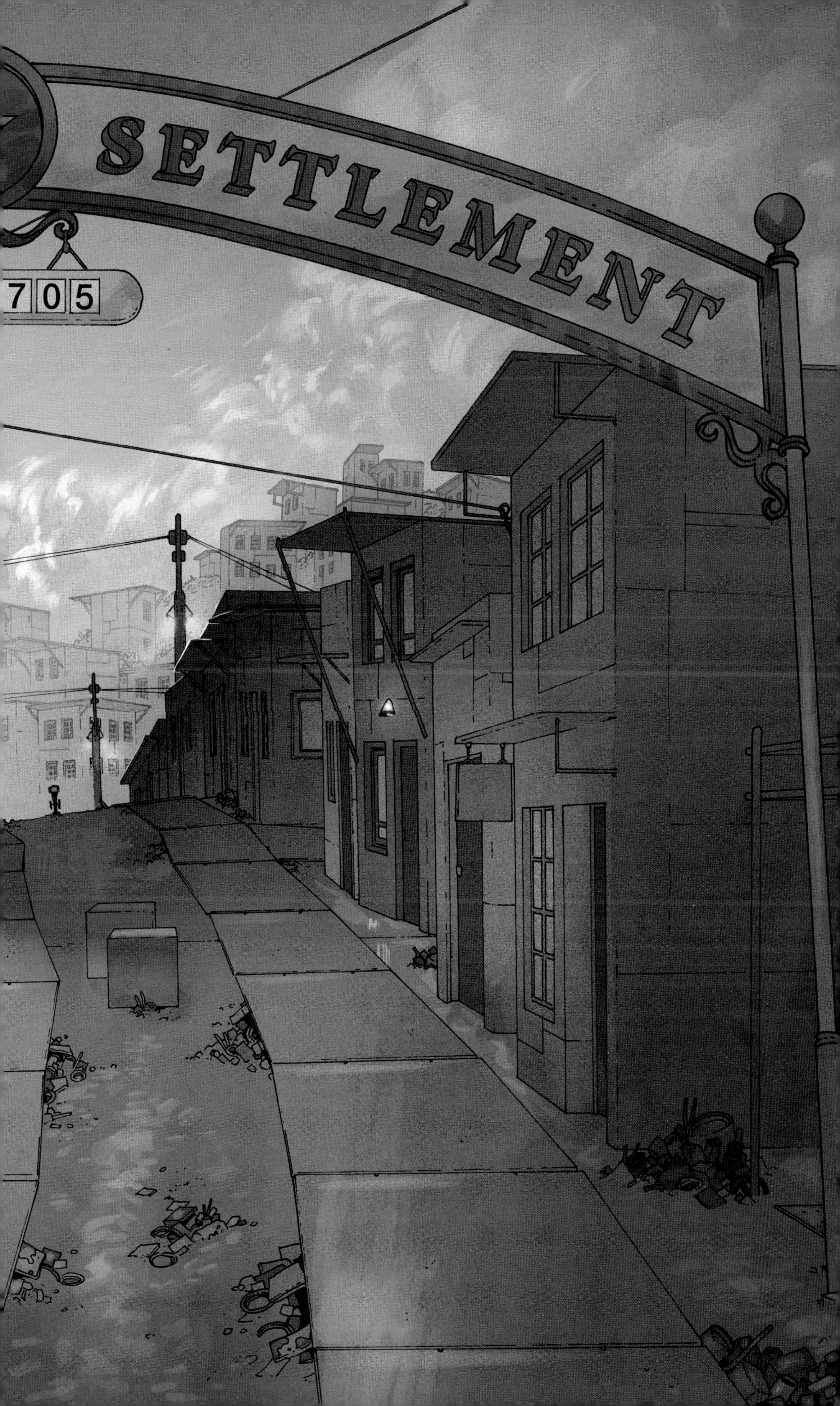
SETTLEMENT
705

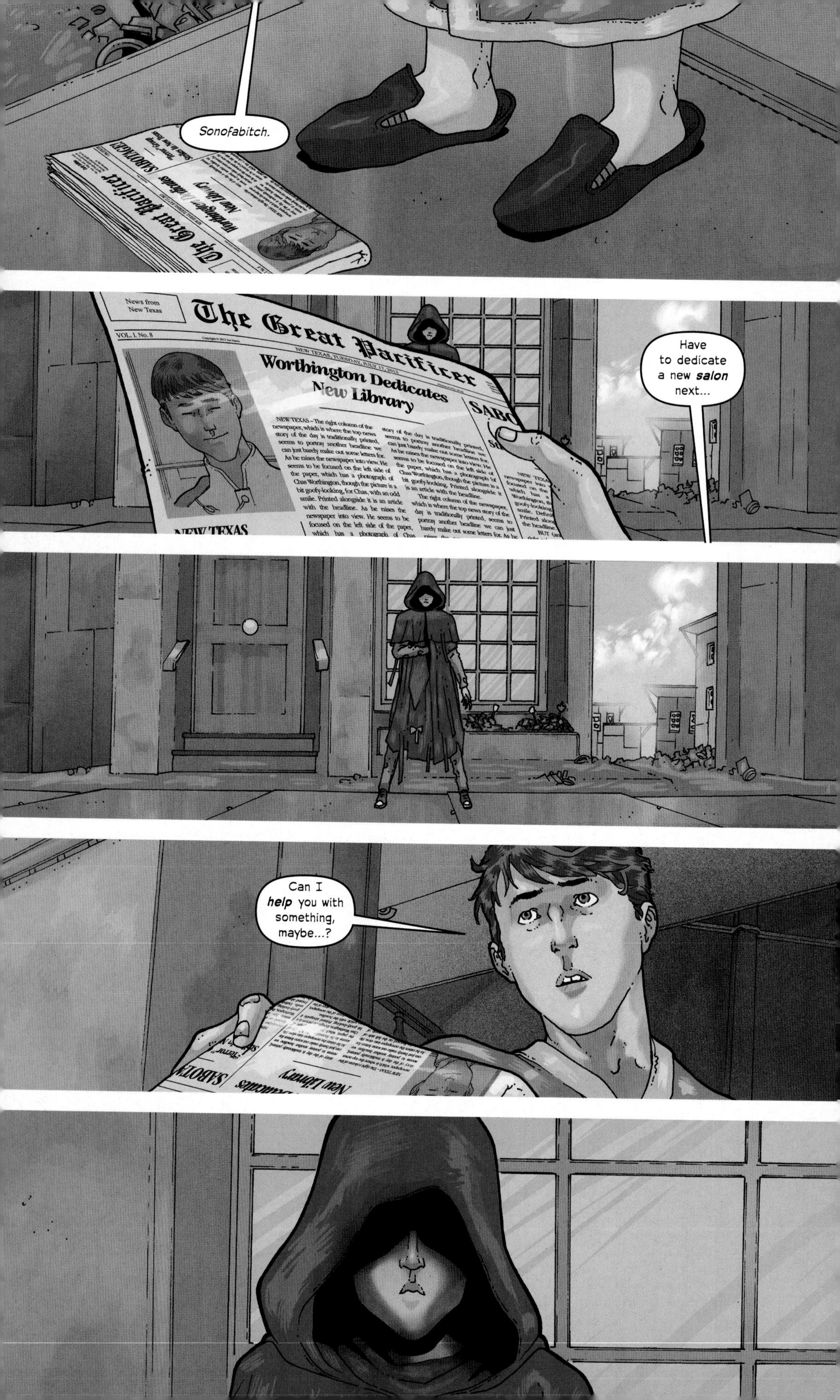

Sonofabitch.
News from New Texas
The Great Pacificer
VOL. I, No. 8
Worthington Dedicates New Library
Have to dedicate a new *salon* next...
Can I ***help*** you with something, maybe...?

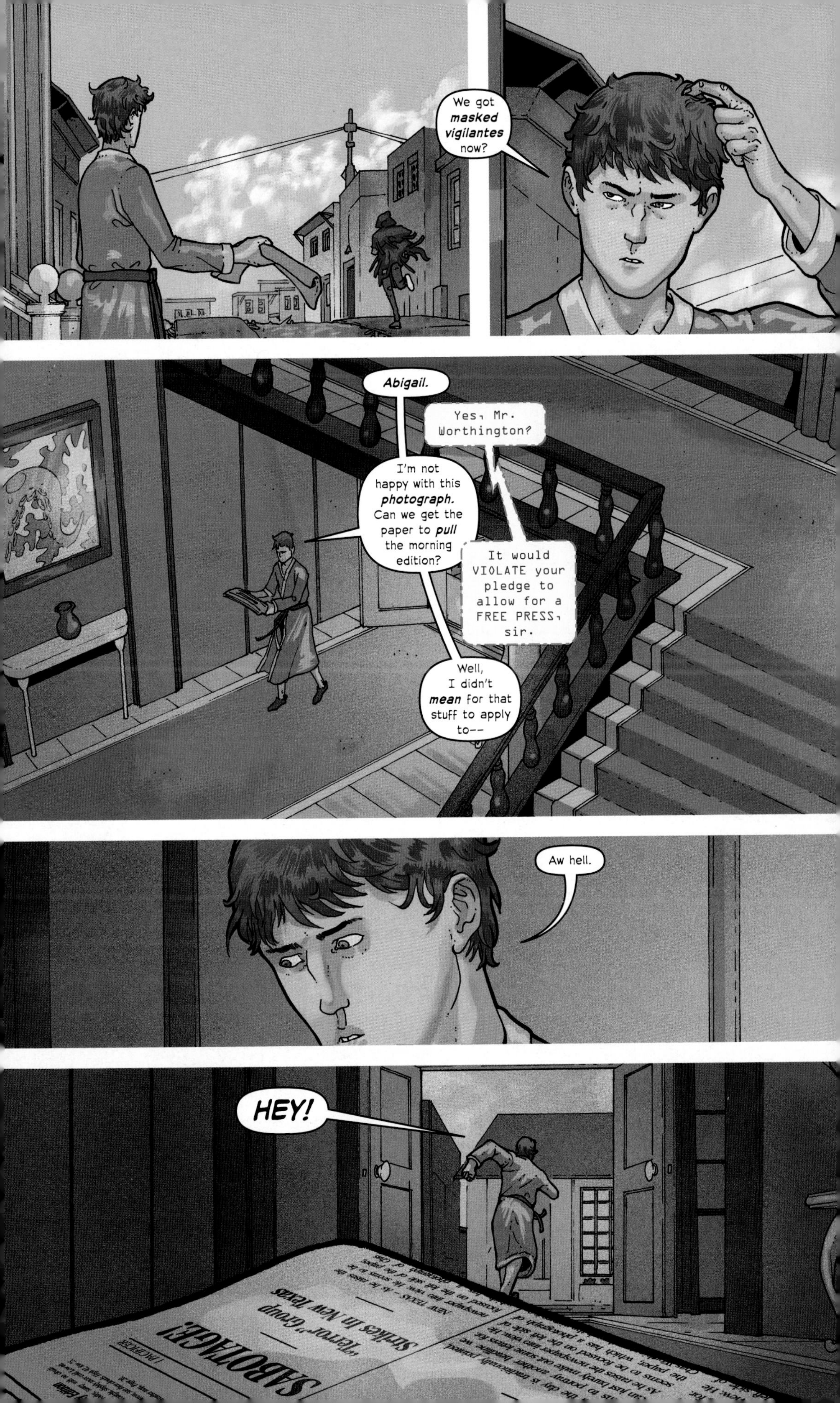

We got *masked vigilantes* now?
Abigail.
Yes, Mr. Worthington?
I'm not happy with this *photograph.* Can we get the paper to *pull* the morning edition?
It would VIOLATE your pledge to allow for a FREE PRESS, sir.
Well, I didn't *mean* for that stuff to apply to--
Aw hell.
HEY!

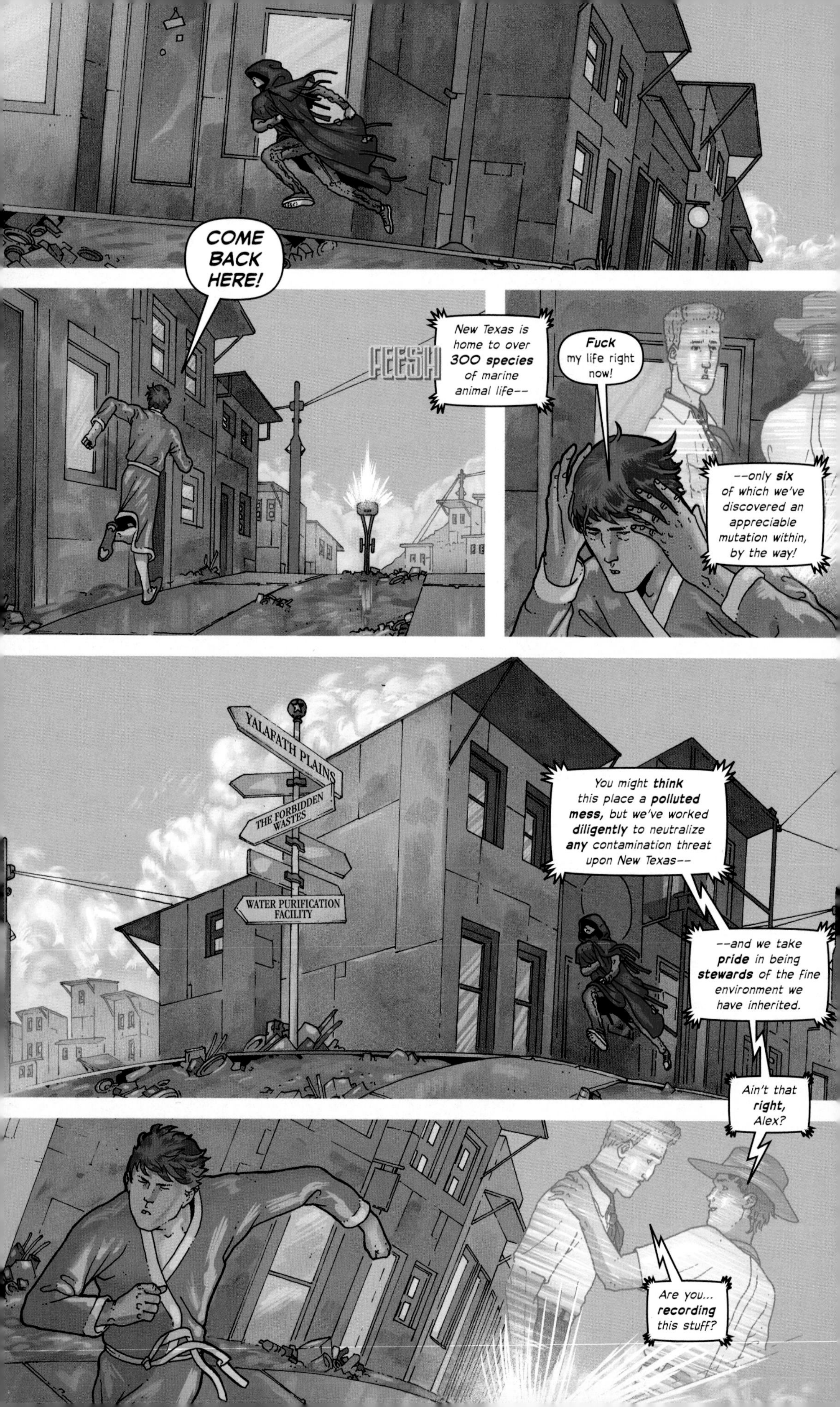
COME BACK HERE!
FEESH
New Texas is home to over 300 species of marine animal life--
Fuck my life right now!
--only six of which we've discovered an appreciable mutation within, by the way!
YALAFATH PLAINS
THE FORBIDDEN WASTES
WATER PURIFICATION FACILITY
You might think this place a polluted mess, but we've worked diligently to neutralize any contamination threat upon New Texas--
--and we take pride in being stewards of the fine environment we have inherited.
Ain't that right, Alex?
Are you... recording this stuff?

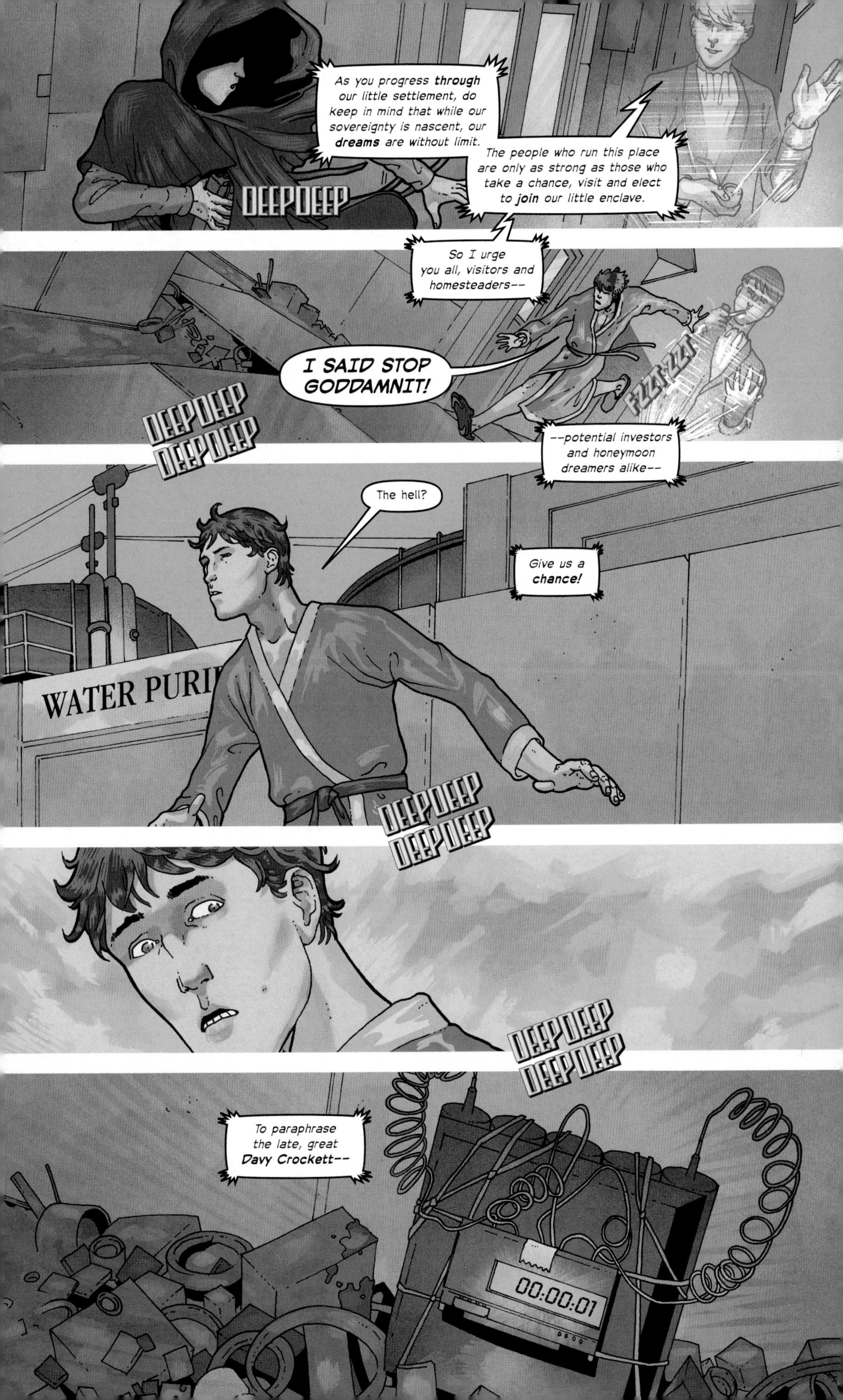
As you progress through our little settlement, do keep in mind that while our sovereignty is nascent, our dreams are without limit.
DEEPDEEP
The people who run this place are only as strong as those who take a chance, visit and elect to join our little enclave.
So I urge you all, visitors and homesteaders--
I SAID STOP GODDAMNIT!
FZZT FZZT
DEEPDEEP DEEPDEEP
--potential investors and honeymoon dreamers alike--
The hell?
Give us a chance!
WATER PURI
DEEPDEEP DEEPDEEP
DEEPDEEP DEEPDEEP
To paraphrase the late, great Davy Crockett--
00:00:01

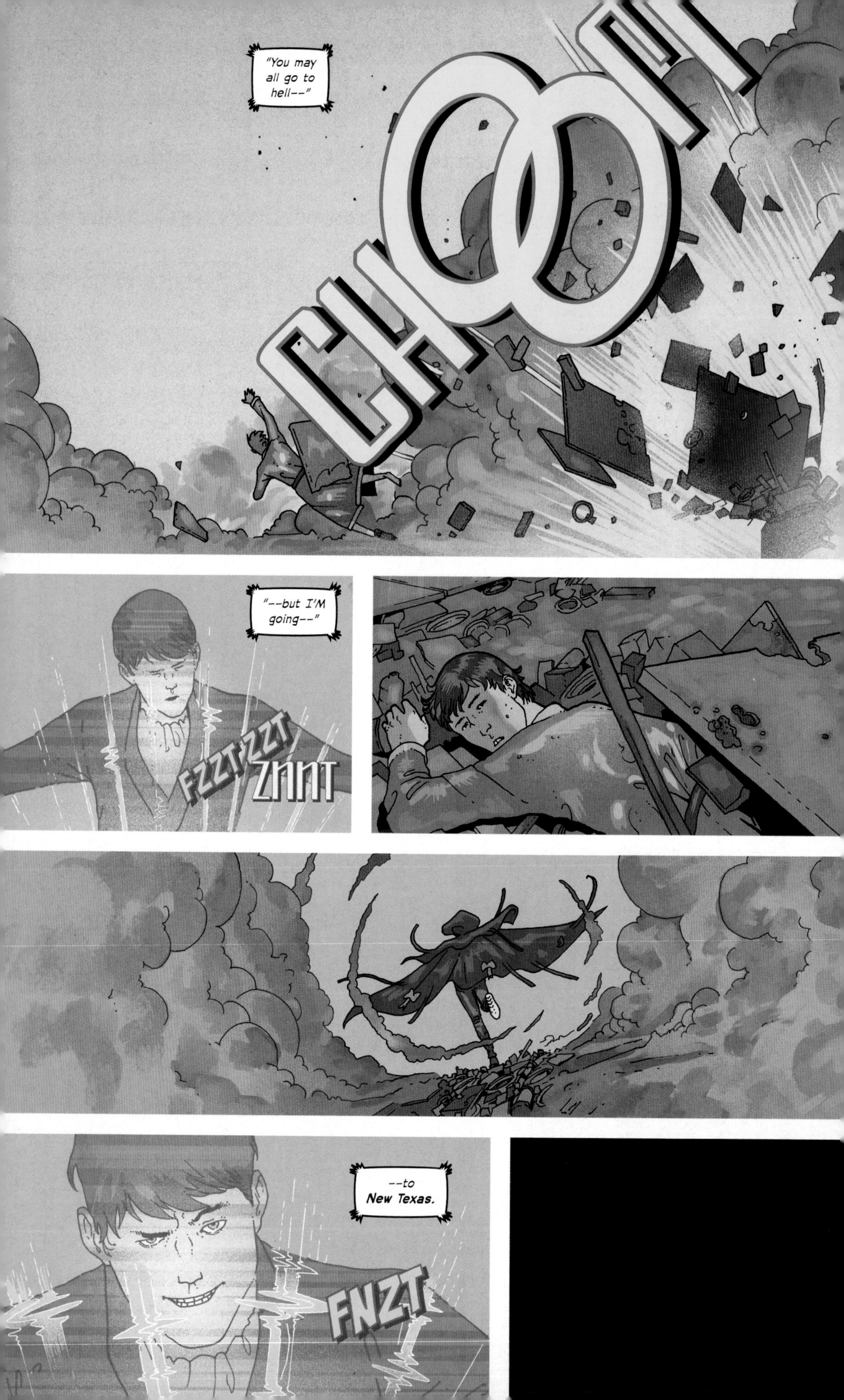
"You may all go to hell--"
"--but I'M going--"
FZZT ZZT
ZNNT
--to New Texas.
FNZT

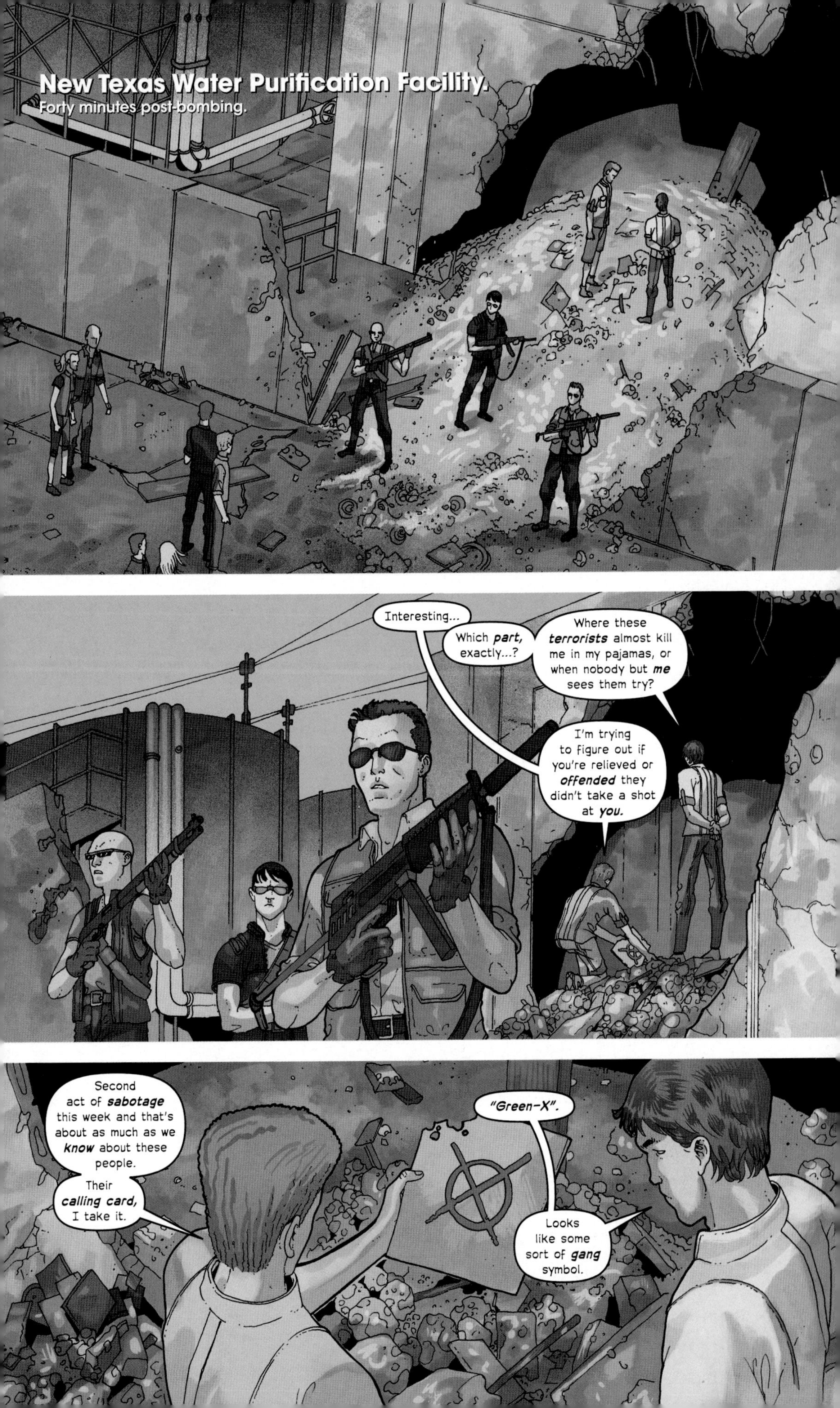

New Texas Water Purification Facility.
Forty minutes post-bombing.
Interesting...
Which *part,* exactly...?
Where these *terrorists* almost kill me in my pajamas, or when nobody but *me* sees them try?
I'm trying to figure out if you're relieved or *offended* they didn't take a shot at *you.*
Second act of *sabotage* this week and that's about as much as we *know* about these people.
Their *calling card,* I take it.
"Green-X".
Looks like some sort of *gang* symbol.

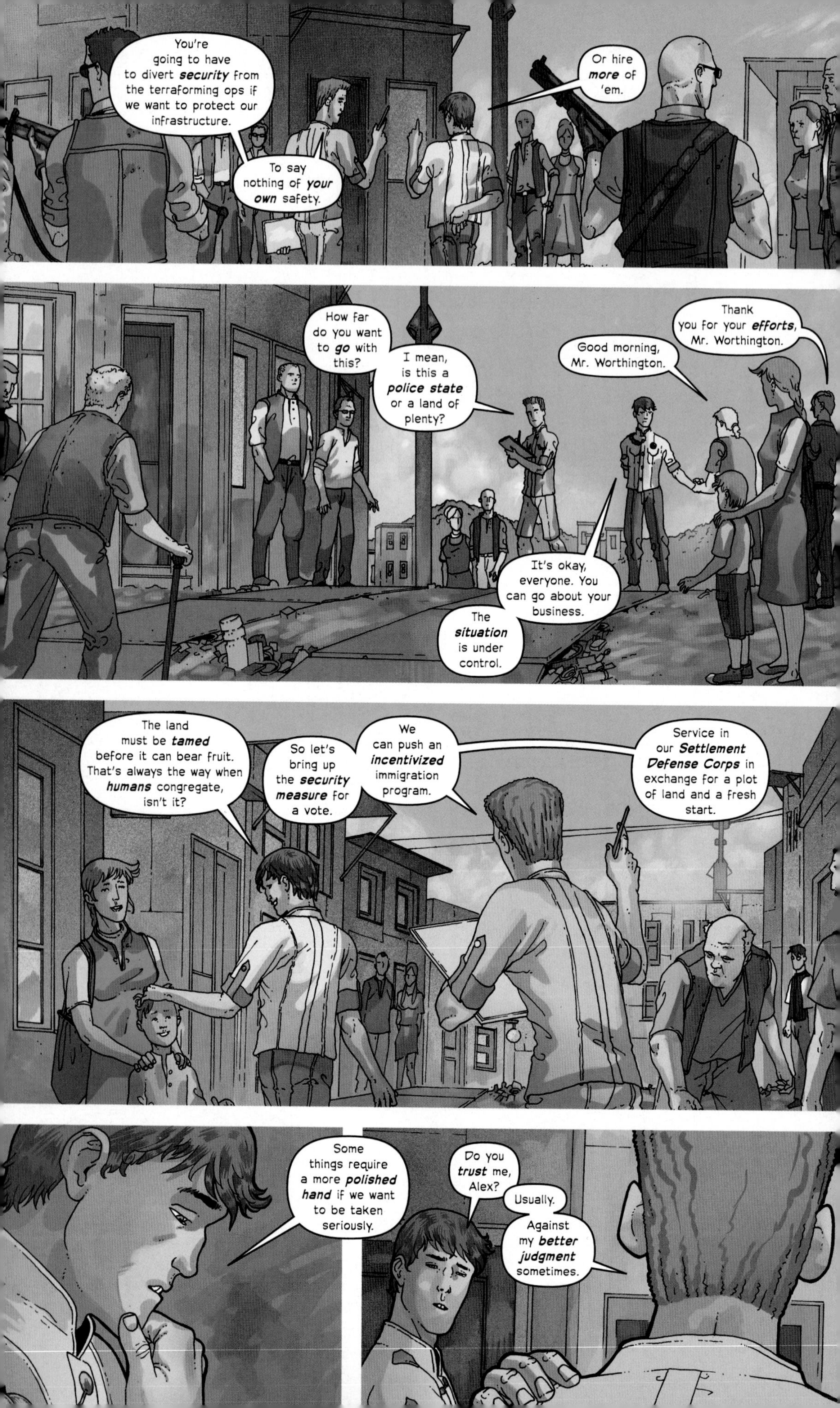
You're going to have to divert *security* from the terraforming ops if we want to protect our infrastructure.
Or hire *more* of 'em.
To say nothing of *your own* safety.
How far do you want to *go* with this?
I mean, is this a *police state* or a land of plenty?
Good morning, Mr. Worthington.
Thank you for your *efforts*, Mr. Worthington.
It's okay, everyone. You can go about your business.
The *situation* is under control.
The land must be *tamed* before it can bear fruit. That's always the way when *humans* congregate, isn't it?
So let's bring up the *security measure* for a vote.
We can push an *incentivized* immigration program.
Service in our *Settlement Defense Corps* in exchange for a plot of land and a fresh start.
Some things require a more *polished hand* if we want to be taken seriously.
Do you *trust* me, Alex?
Usually.
Against my *better judgment* sometimes.

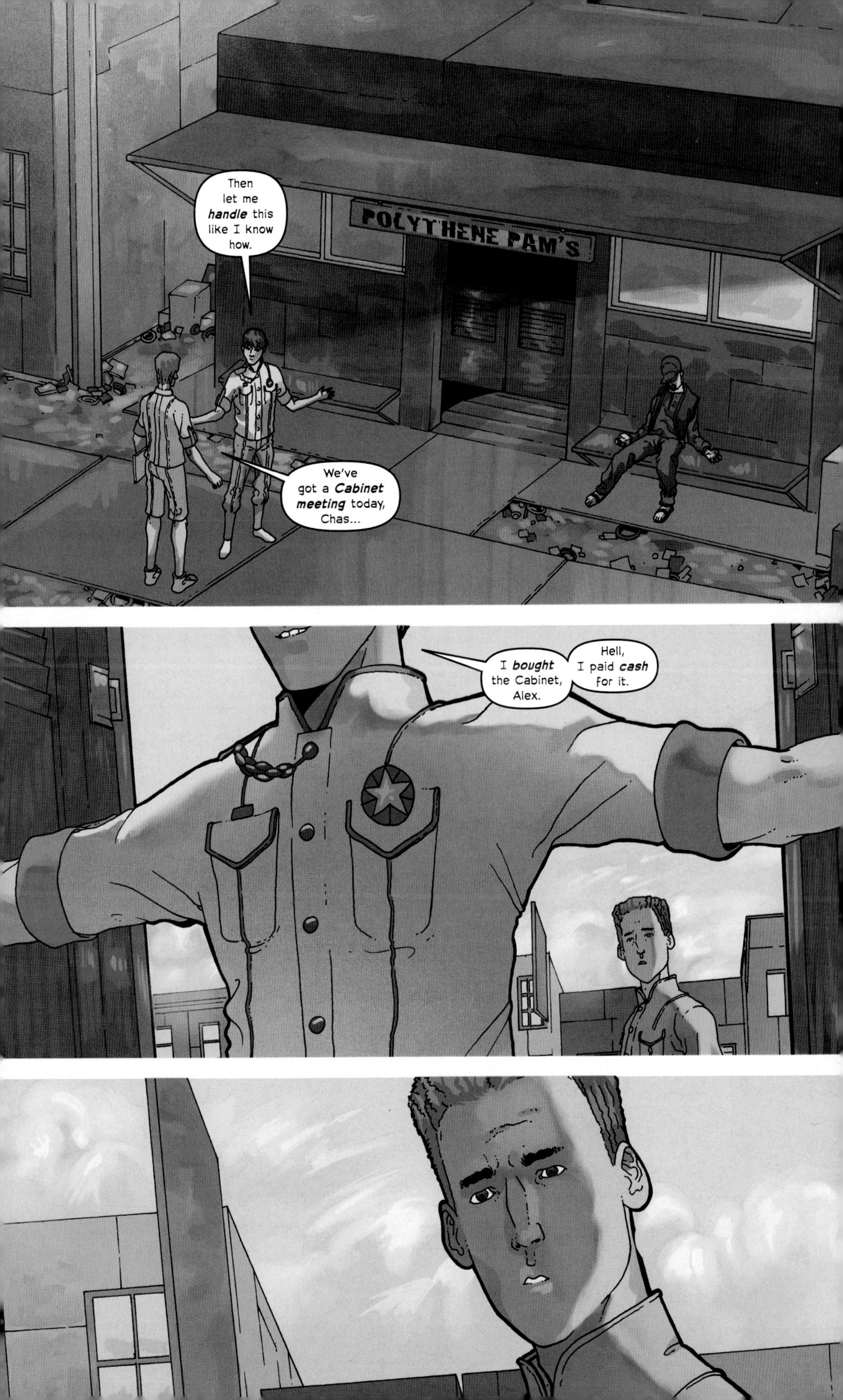

POLYTHENE PAM'S
Then let me handle this like I know how.
We've got a Cabinet meeting today, Chas...
I bought the Cabinet, Alex.
Hell, I paid cash for it.

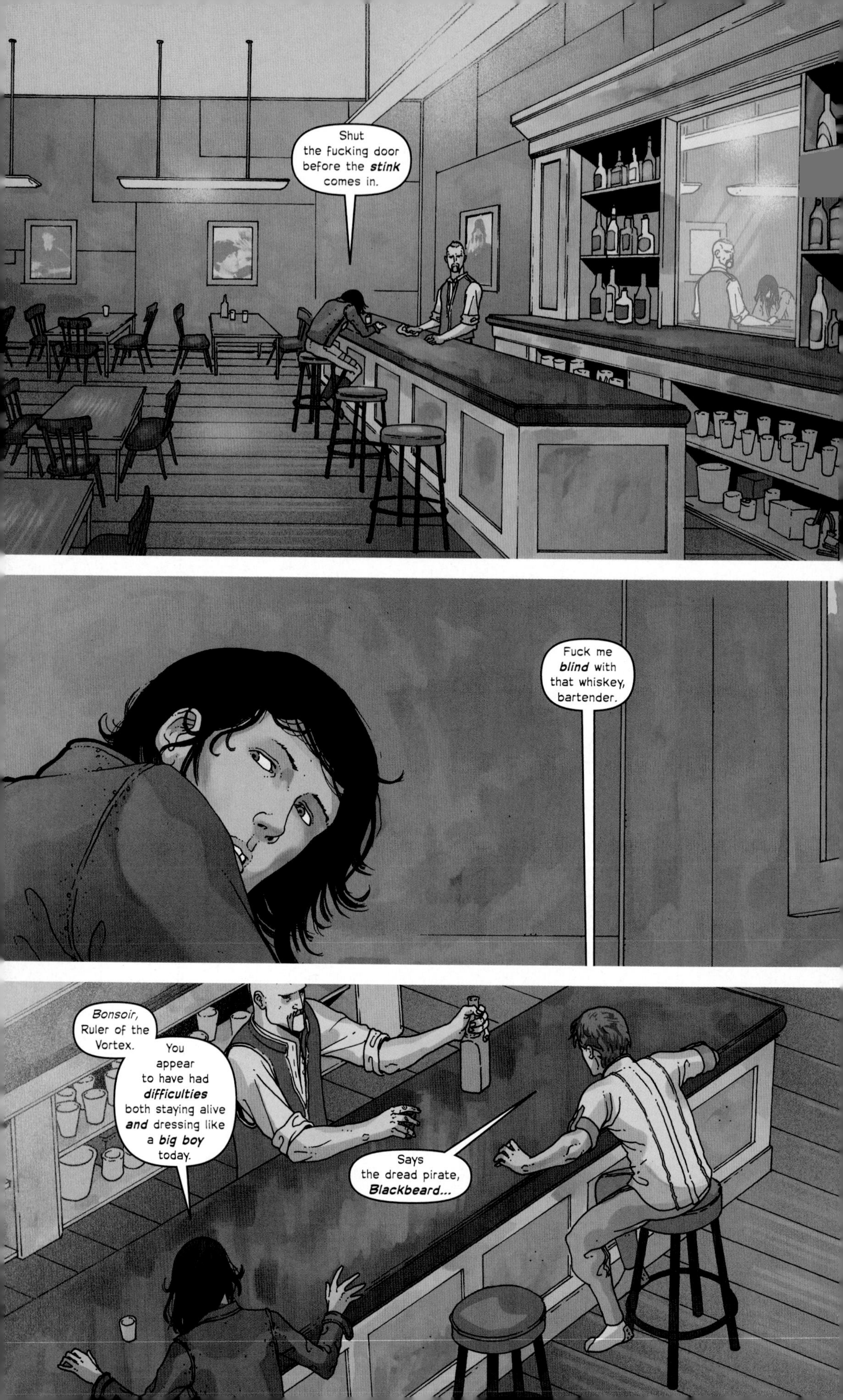
Shut the fucking door before the *stink* comes in.
Fuck me *blind* with that whiskey, bartender.
Bonsoir, Ruler of the Vortex.
You appear to have had *difficulties* both staying alive *and* dressing like a *big boy* today.
Says the dread pirate, *Blackbeard...*

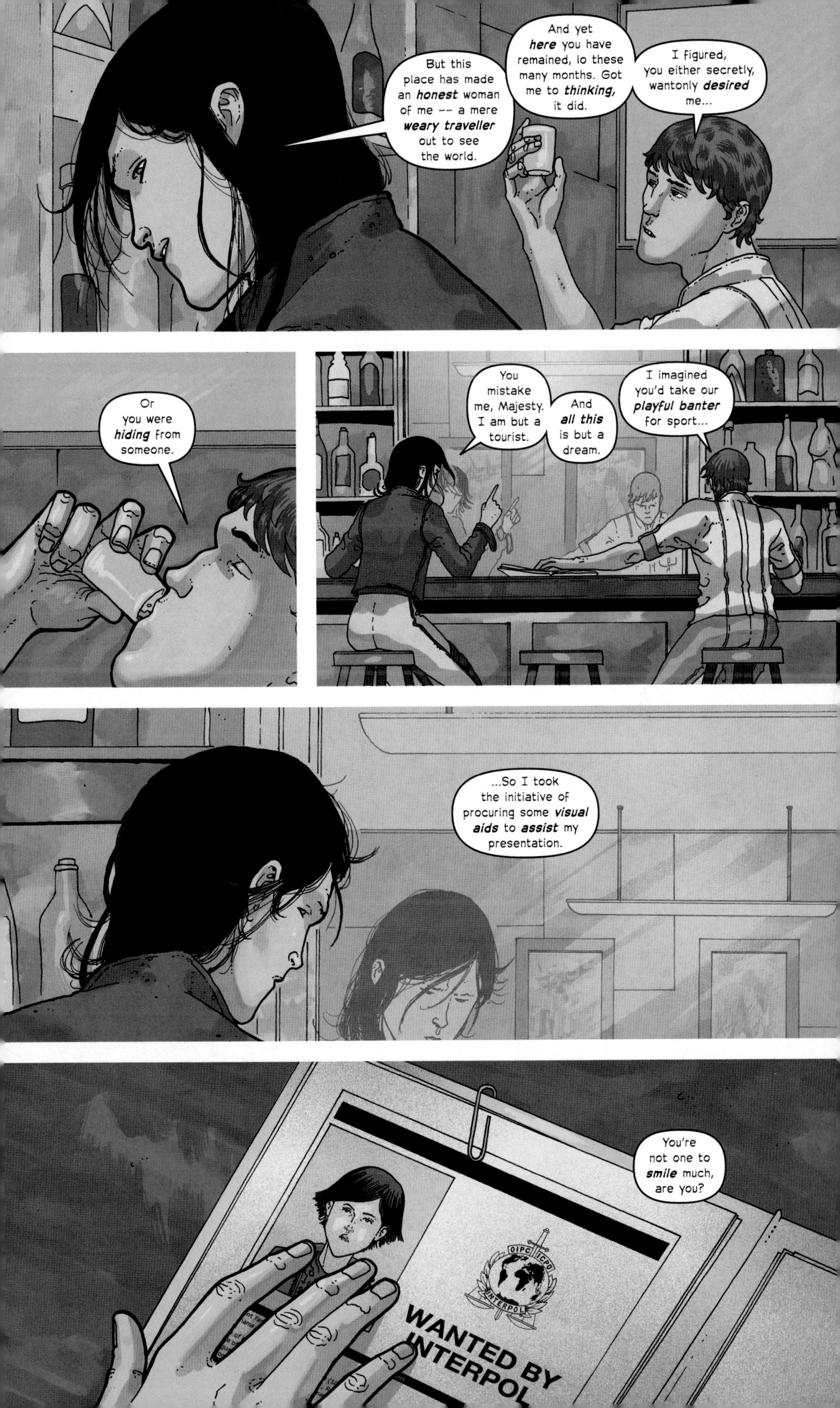

But this place has made an *honest* woman of me -- a mere *weary traveller* out to see the world.
And yet *here* you have remained, lo these many months. Got me to *thinking,* it did.
I figured, you either secretly, wantonly *desired* me...
Or you were *hiding* from someone.
You mistake me, Majesty. I am but a tourist.
And *all this* is but a dream.
I imagined you'd take our *playful banter* for sport...
...So I took the initiative of procuring some *visual aids* to *assist* my presentation.
You're not one to *smile* much, are you?
OIPC ICPO
INTERPOL
WANTED BY INTERPOL

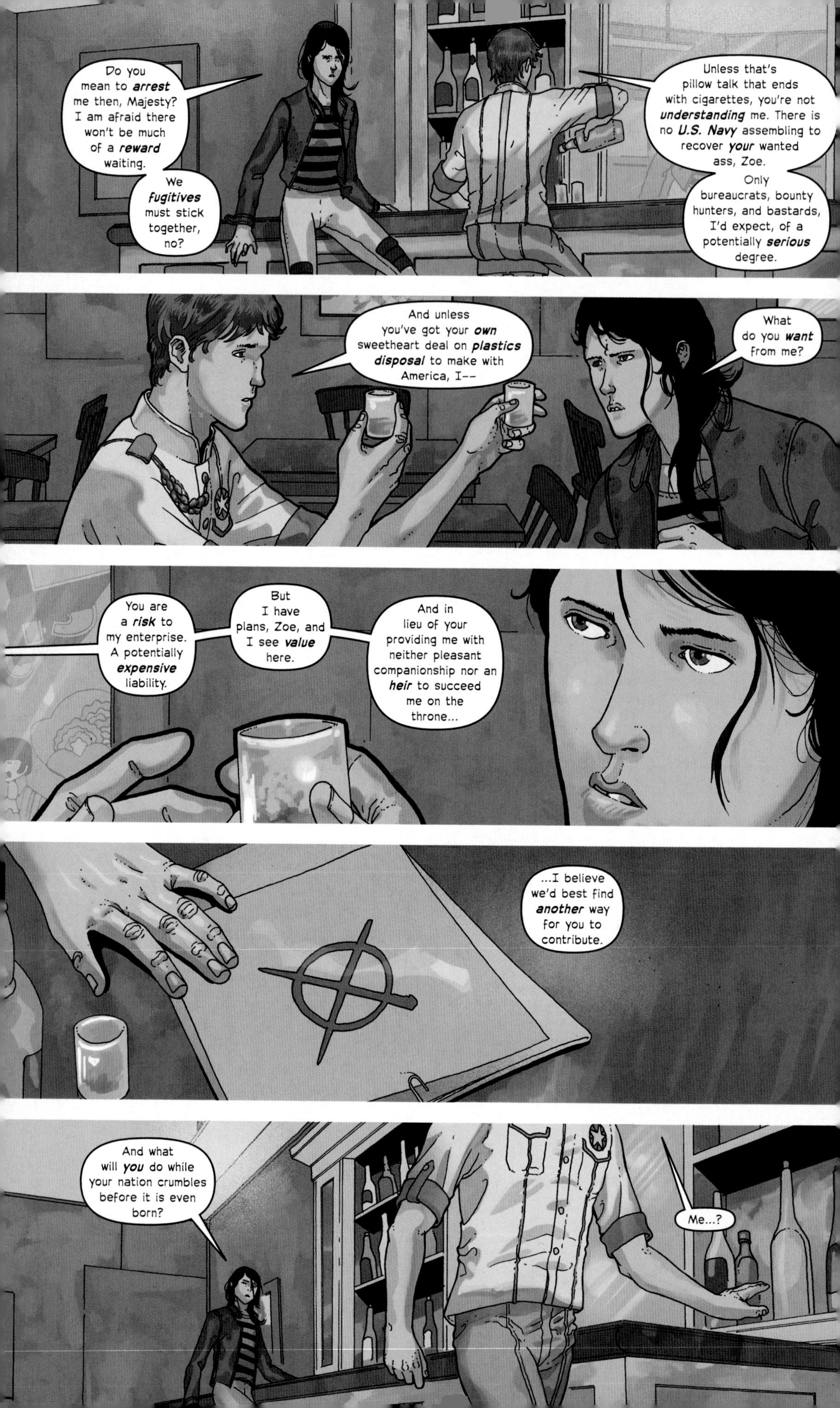
Do you mean to arrest me then, Majesty? I am afraid there won't be much of a reward waiting.
We fugitives must stick together, no?
Unless that's pillow talk that ends with cigarettes, you're not understanding me. There is no U.S. Navy assembling to recover your wanted ass, Zoe.
Only bureaucrats, bounty hunters, and bastards, I'd expect, of a potentially serious degree.
And unless you've got your own sweetheart deal on plastics disposal to make with America, I--
What do you want from me?
You are a risk to my enterprise. A potentially expensive liability.
But I have plans, Zoe, and I see value here.
And in lieu of your providing me with neither pleasant companionship nor an heir to succeed me on the throne...
...I believe we'd best find another way for you to contribute.
And what will you do while your nation crumbles before it is even born?
Me...?

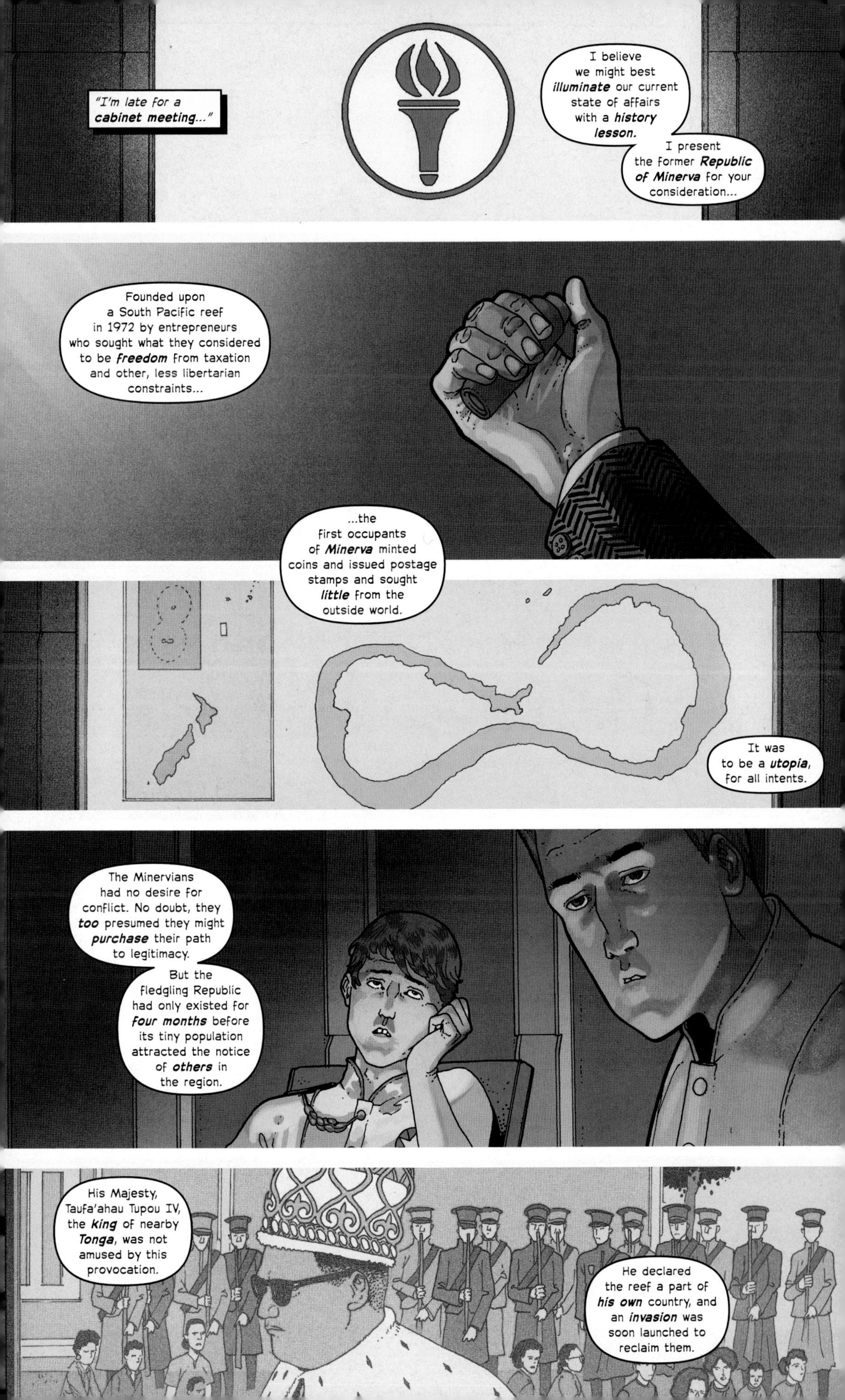
"I'm late for a *cabinet meeting*..."
I believe we might best *illuminate* our current state of affairs with a *history lesson.*
I present the former *Republic of Minerva* for your consideration...
Founded upon a South Pacific reef in 1972 by entrepreneurs who sought what they considered to be *freedom* from taxation and other, less libertarian constraints...
...the first occupants of *Minerva* minted coins and issued postage stamps and sought *little* from the outside world.
It was to be a *utopia*, for all intents.
The Minervians had no desire for conflict. No doubt, they *too* presumed they might *purchase* their path to legitimacy.
But the fledgling Republic had only existed for *four months* before its tiny population attracted the notice of *others* in the region.
His Majesty, Taufa'ahau Tupou IV, the *king* of nearby *Tonga*, was not amused by this provocation.
He declared the reef a part of *his own* country, and an *invasion* was soon launched to reclaim them.

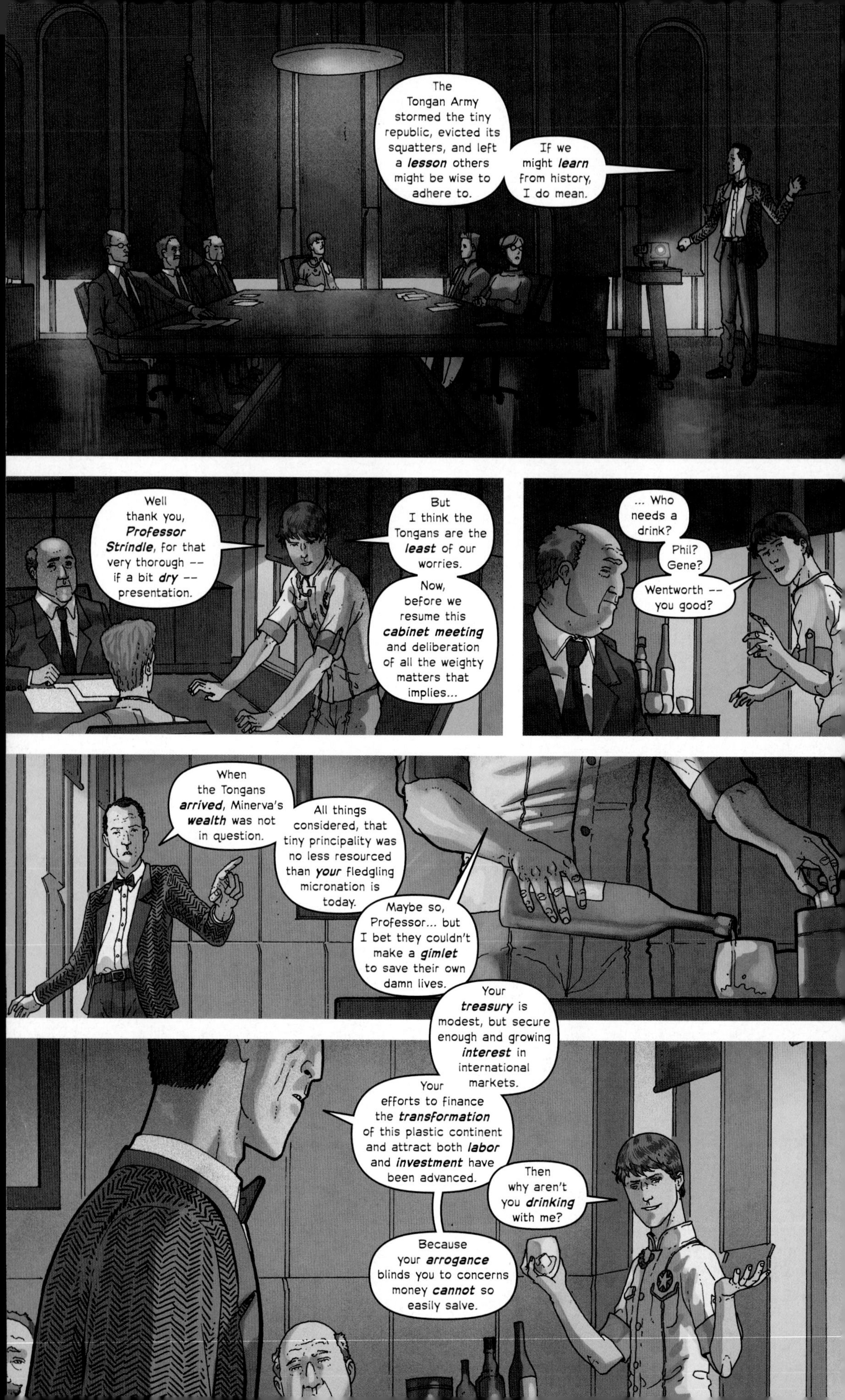
The Tongan Army stormed the tiny republic, evicted its squatters, and left a *lesson* others might be wise to adhere to.
If we might *learn* from history, I do mean.
Well thank you, ***Professor Strindle***, for that very thorough -- if a bit ***dry*** -- presentation.
But I think the Tongans are the ***least*** of our worries.
Now, before we resume this ***cabinet meeting*** and deliberation of all the weighty matters that implies...
... Who needs a drink?
Phil? Gene?
Wentworth -- you good?
When the Tongans ***arrived***, Minerva's ***wealth*** was not in question.
All things considered, that tiny principality was no less resourced than ***your*** fledgling micronation is today.
Maybe so, Professor... but I bet they couldn't make a ***gimlet*** to save their own damn lives.
Your ***treasury*** is modest, but secure enough and growing ***interest*** in international markets.
Your efforts to finance the ***transformation*** of this plastic continent and attract both ***labor*** and ***investment*** have been advanced.
Then why aren't you ***drinking*** with me?
Because your ***arrogance*** blinds you to concerns money ***cannot*** so easily salve.

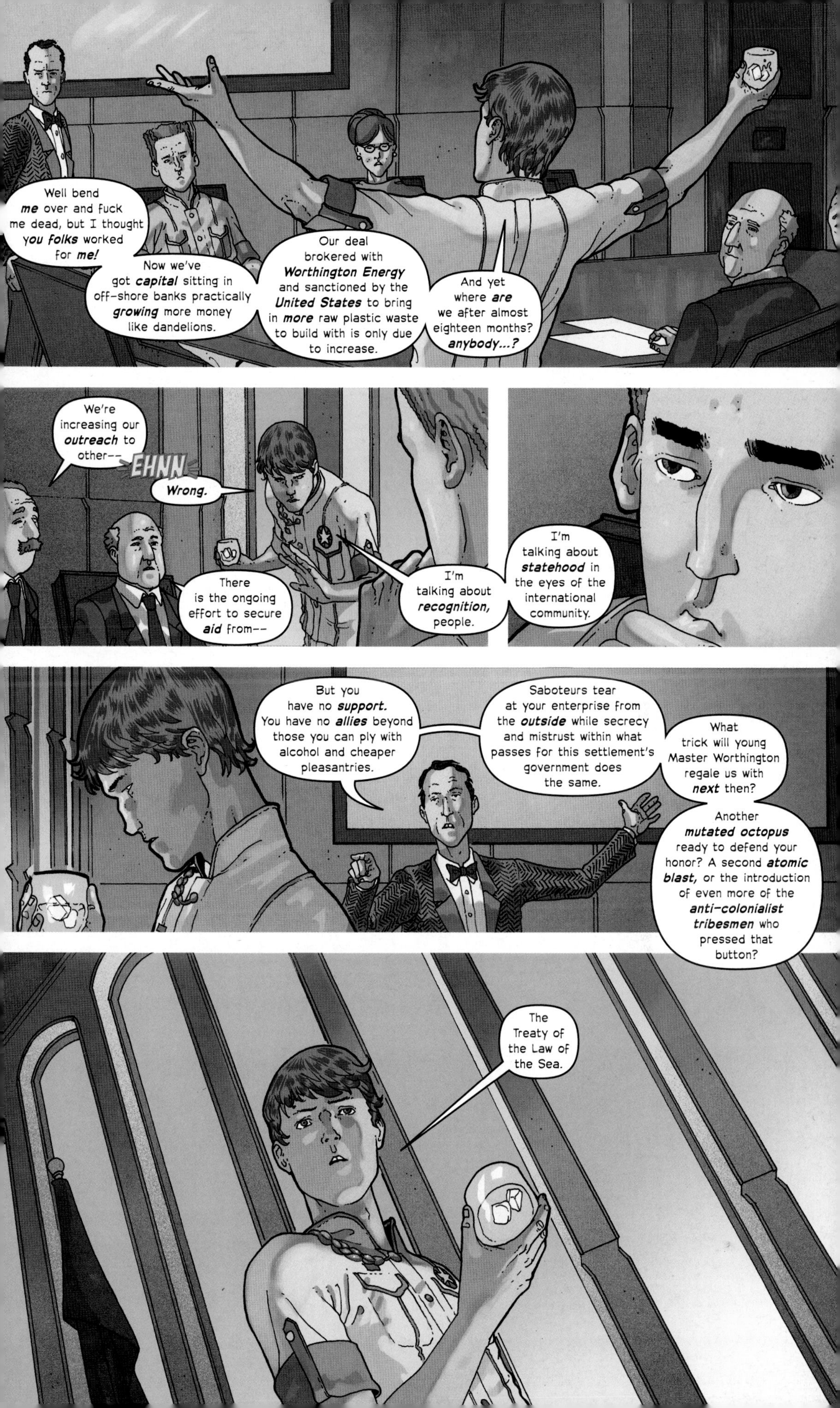

Well bend *me* over and fuck me dead, but I thought *you folks* worked for *me!*
Now we've got *capital* sitting in off-shore banks practically *growing* more money like dandelions.
Our deal brokered with *Worthington Energy* and sanctioned by the *United States* to bring in *more* raw plastic waste to build with is only due to increase.
And yet where *are* we after almost eighteen months? *anybody...?*
We're increasing our *outreach* to other--
EHNN
Wrong.
There is the ongoing effort to secure *aid* from--
I'm talking about *recognition,* people.
I'm talking about *statehood* in the eyes of the international community.
But you have no *support.* You have no *allies* beyond those you can ply with alcohol and cheaper pleasantries.
Saboteurs tear at your enterprise from the *outside* while secrecy and mistrust within what passes for this settlement's government does the same.
What trick will young Master Worthington regale us with *next* then?
Another *mutated octopus* ready to defend your honor? A second *atomic blast,* or the introduction of even more of the *anti-colonialist tribesmen* who pressed that button?
The Treaty of the Law of the Sea.

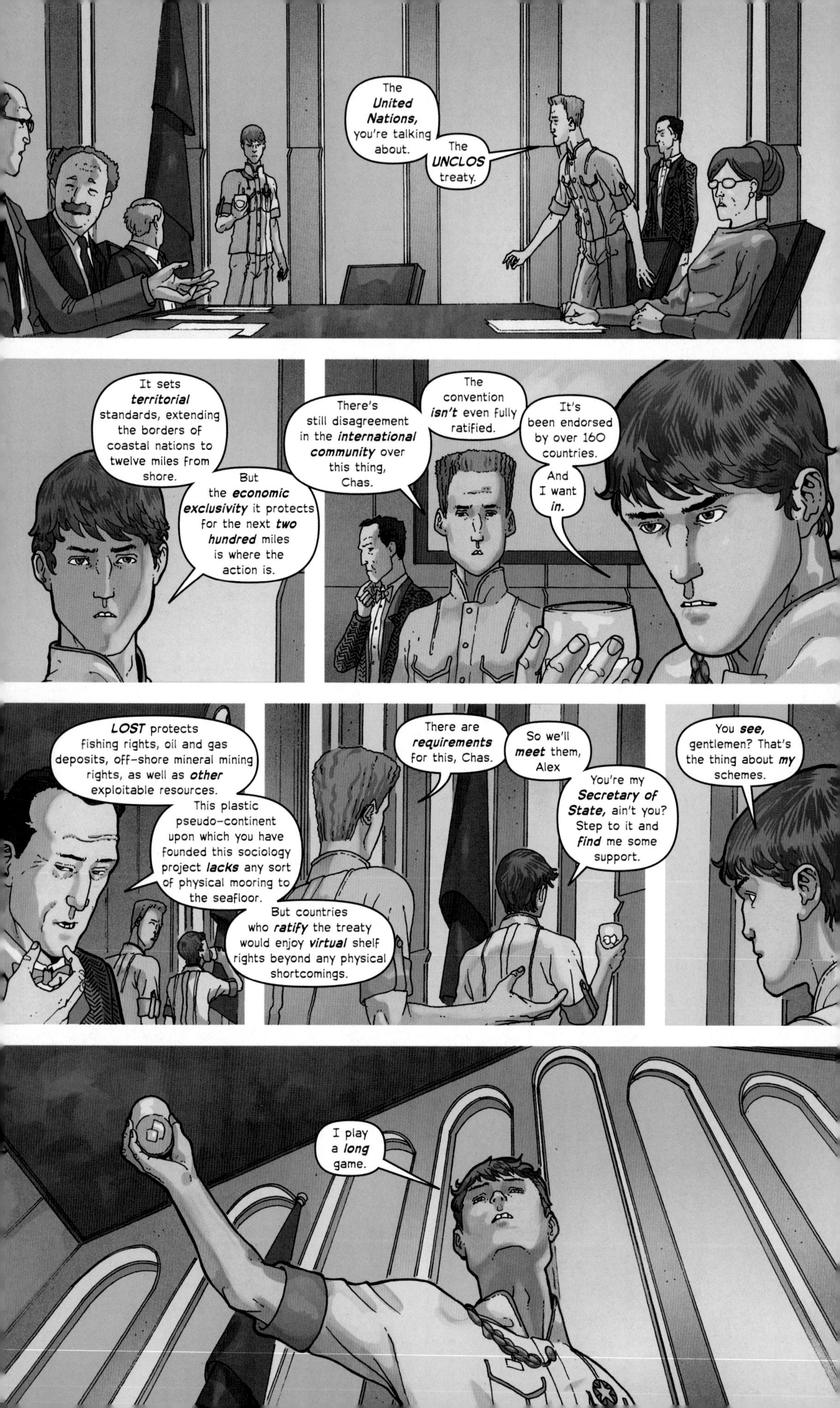
The United Nations, you're talking about.
The UNCLOS treaty.
It sets territorial standards, extending the borders of coastal nations to twelve miles from shore.
But the economic exclusivity it protects for the next two hundred miles is where the action is.
There's still disagreement in the international community over this thing, Chas.
The convention isn't even fully ratified.
It's been endorsed by over 160 countries.
And I want in.
LOST protects fishing rights, oil and gas deposits, off-shore mineral mining rights, as well as other exploitable resources.
This plastic pseudo-continent upon which you have founded this sociology project lacks any sort of physical mooring to the seafloor.
But countries who ratify the treaty would enjoy virtual shelf rights beyond any physical shortcomings.
There are requirements for this, Chas.
So we'll meet them, Alex
You're my Secretary of State, ain't you? Step to it and find me some support.
You see, gentlemen? That's the thing about my schemes.
I play a long game.

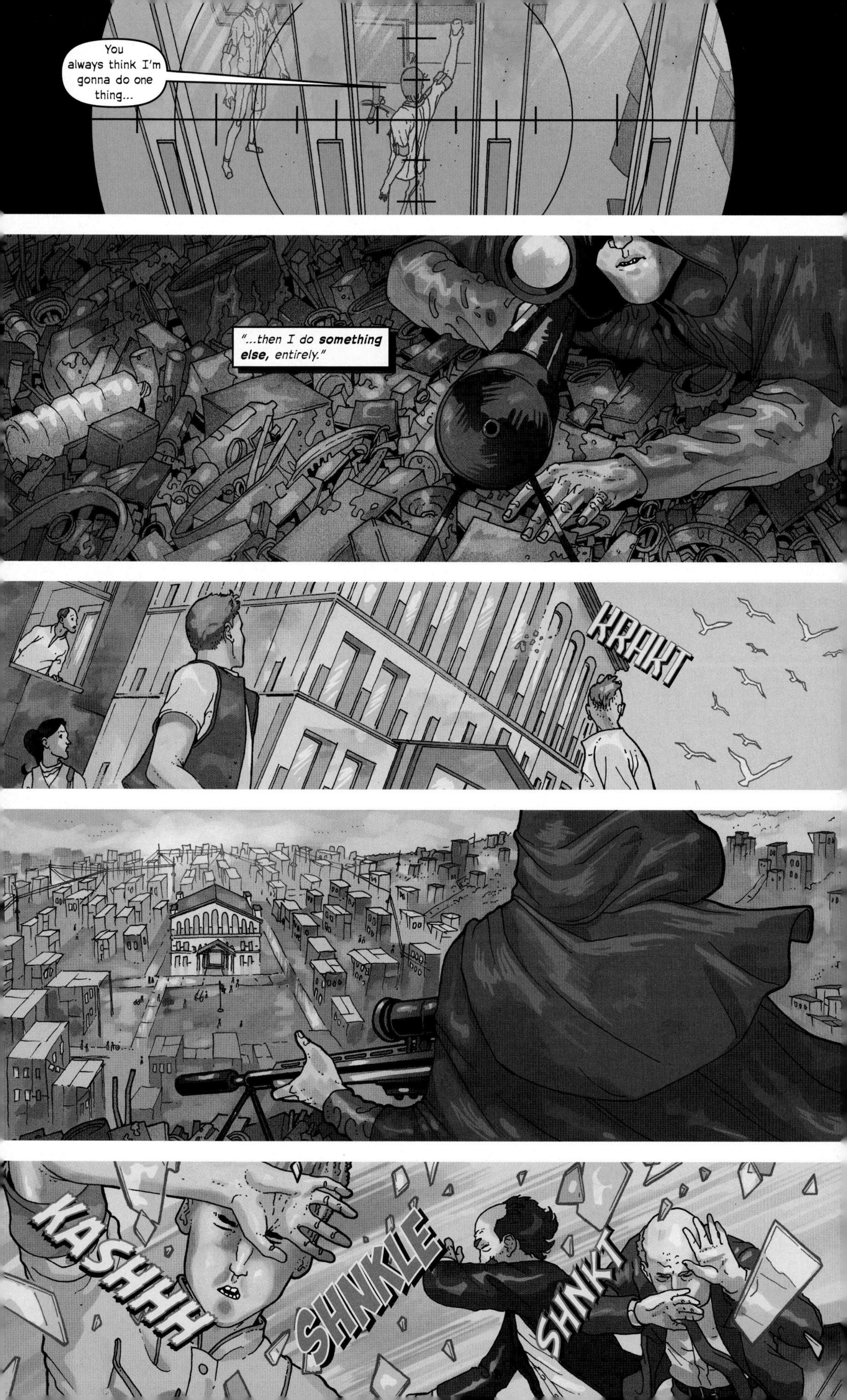
You always think I'm gonna do one thing...
"...then I do **something else,** entirely."
KRAKT
KASHHH
SHNKLE
SHNKT

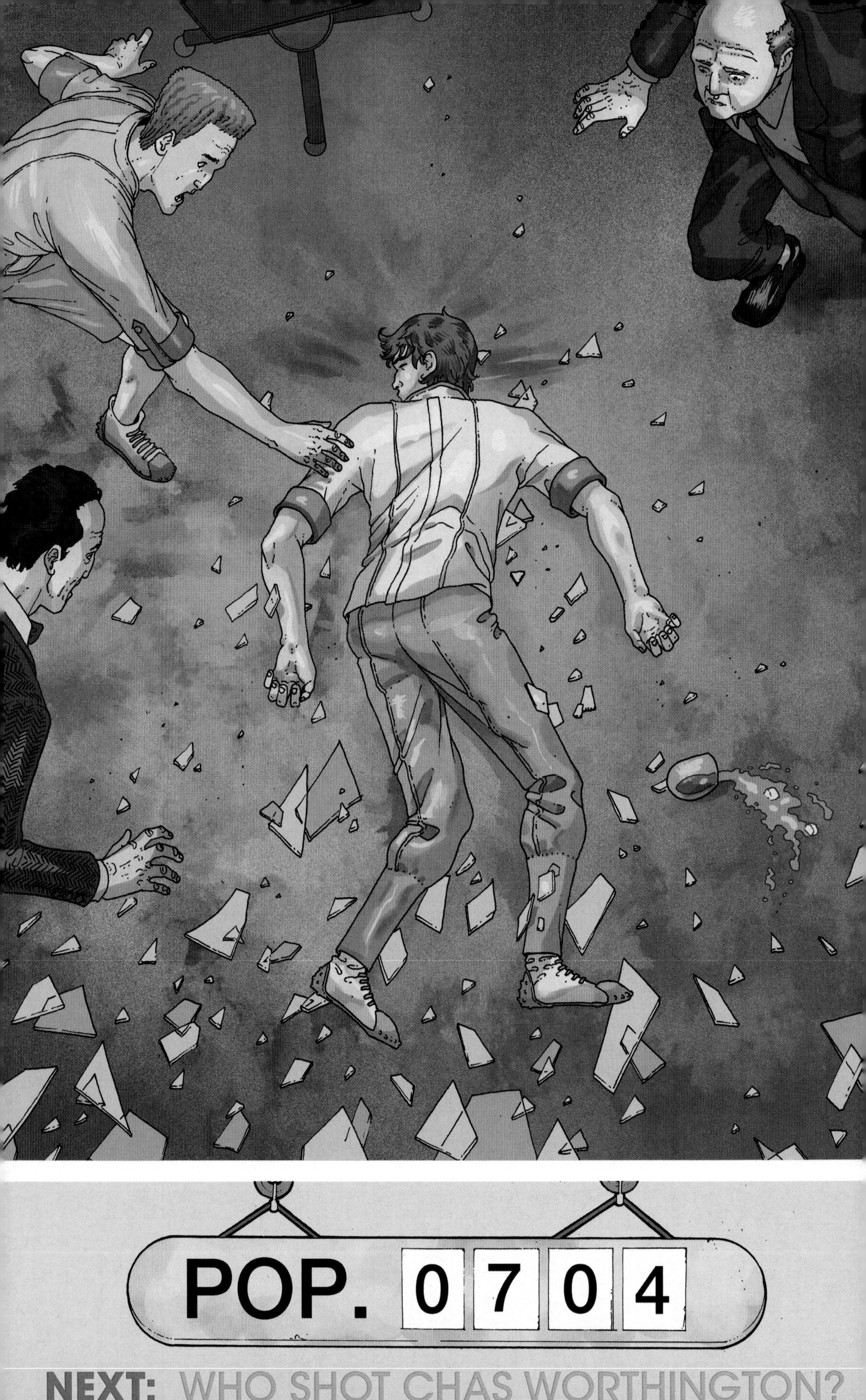
POP. 0704

NEXT: WHO SHOT CHAS WORTHINGTON?

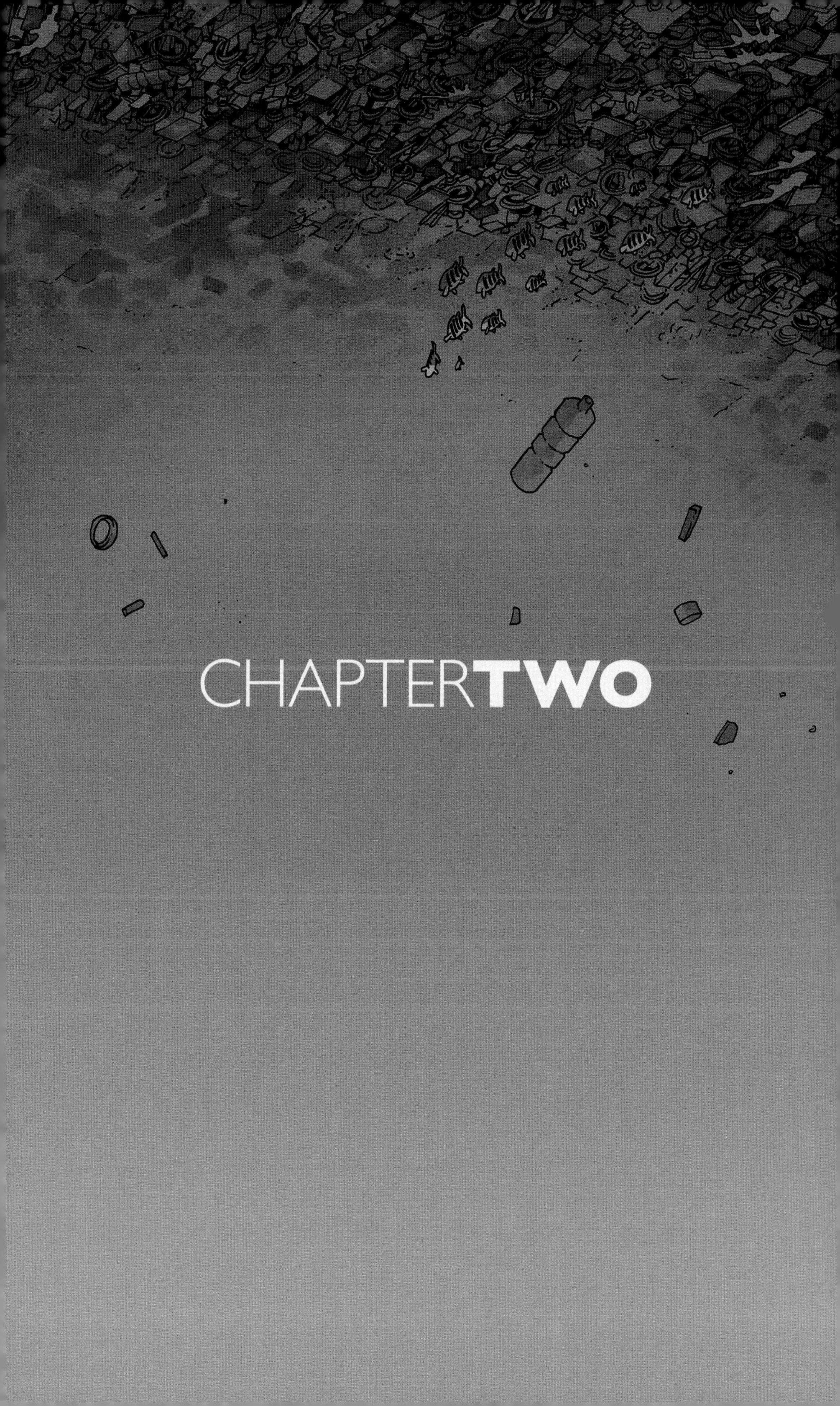

CHAPTER TWO

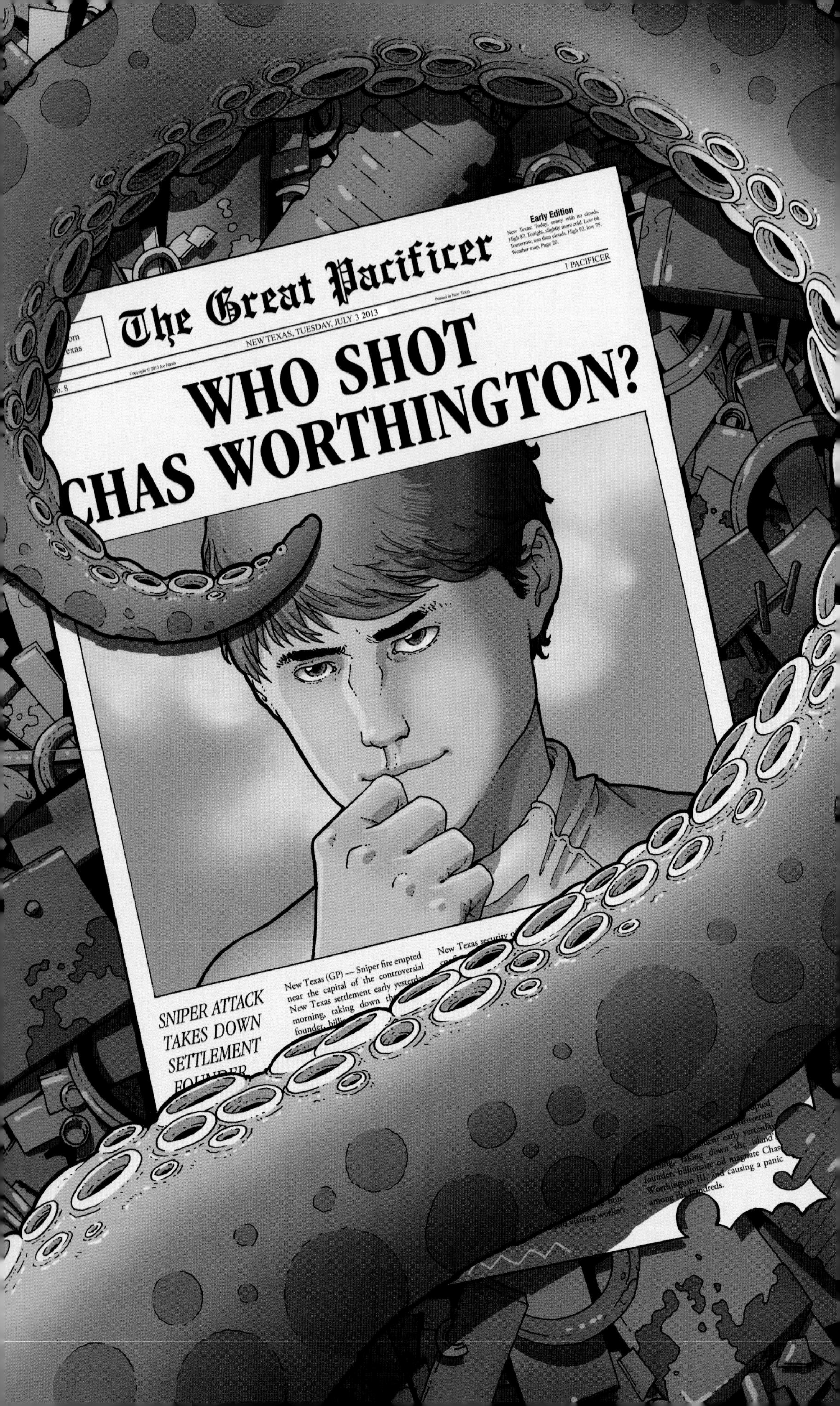

Early Edition
New Texas: Today, sunny with no clouds. High 87. Tonight, slightly more cold. Low 66. Tomorrow, sun then clouds. High 92, low 75. Weather map, Page 20.
The Great Pacificer
1 PACIFICER
Printed in New Texas
NEW TEXAS, TUESDAY, JULY 3 2013
Copyright © 2013 Joe Harris
WHO SHOT CHAS WORTHINGTON?
SNIPER ATTACK TAKES DOWN SETTLEMENT
New Texas (GP) — Sniper fire erupted near the capital of the controversial New Texas settlement early yesterday morning, taking down the
founder, billionaire oil magnate Chas Worthington III, and causing a panic among the hundreds.

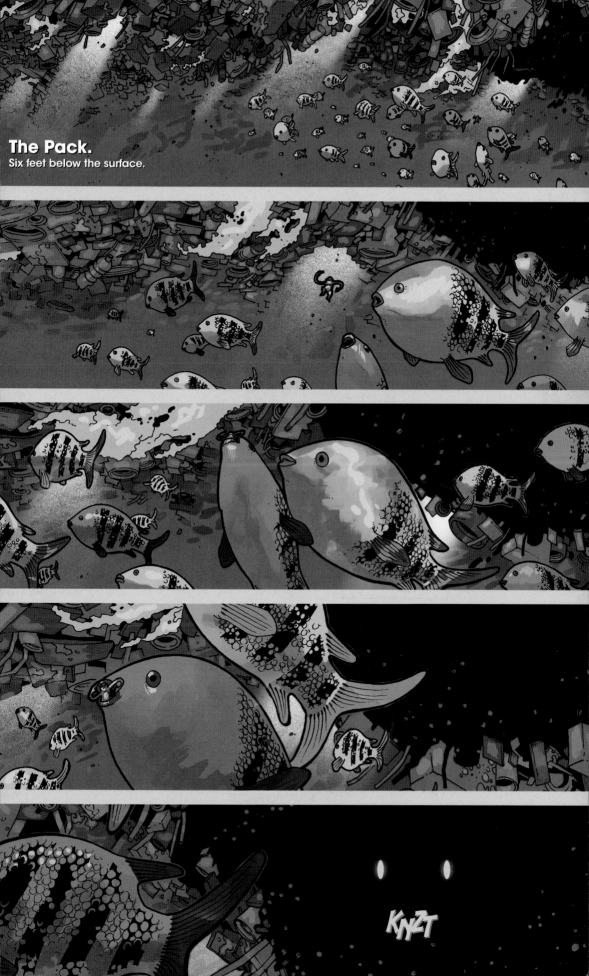

The Pack.
Six feet below the surface.

KNYZT

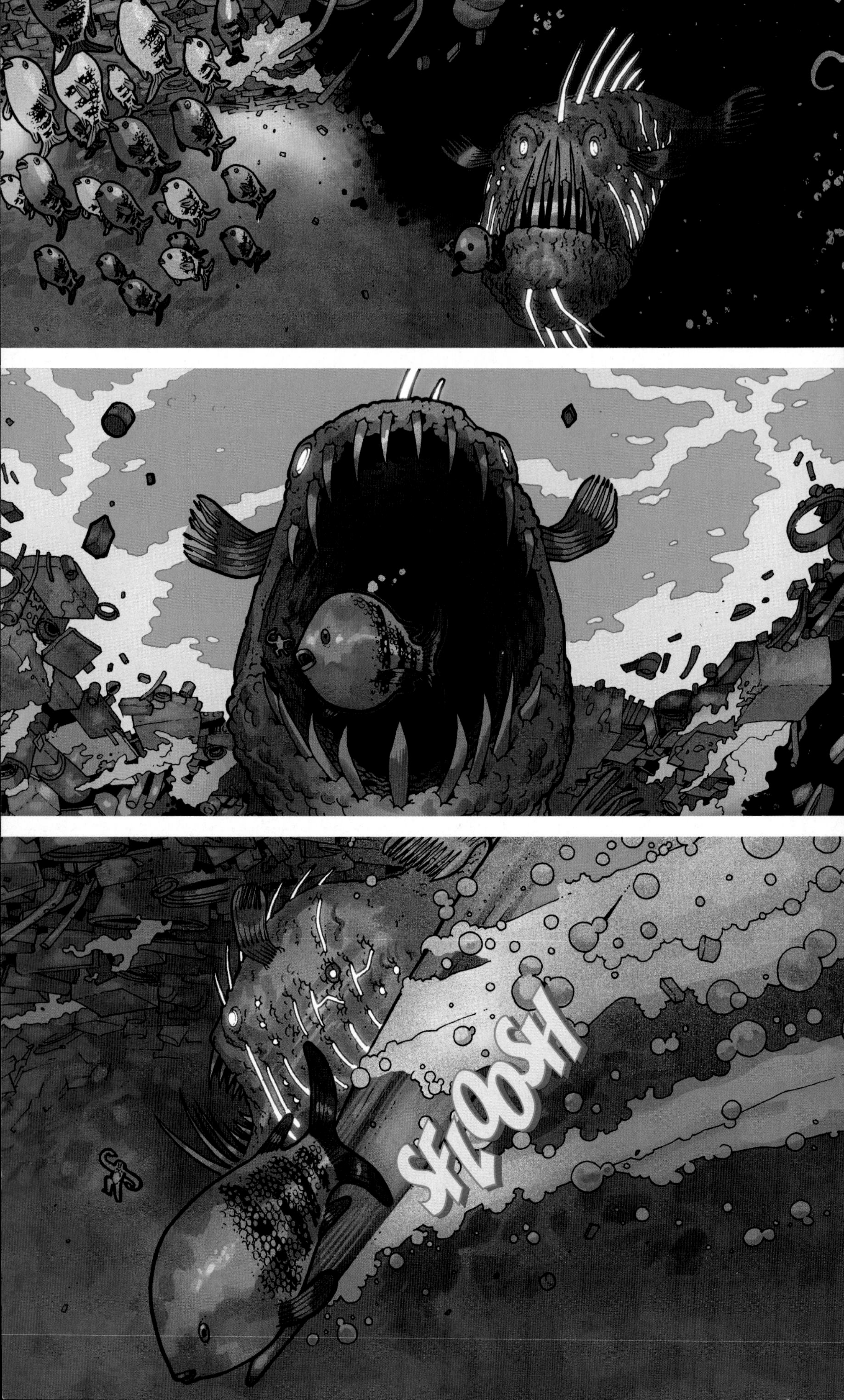
SFLOOSH

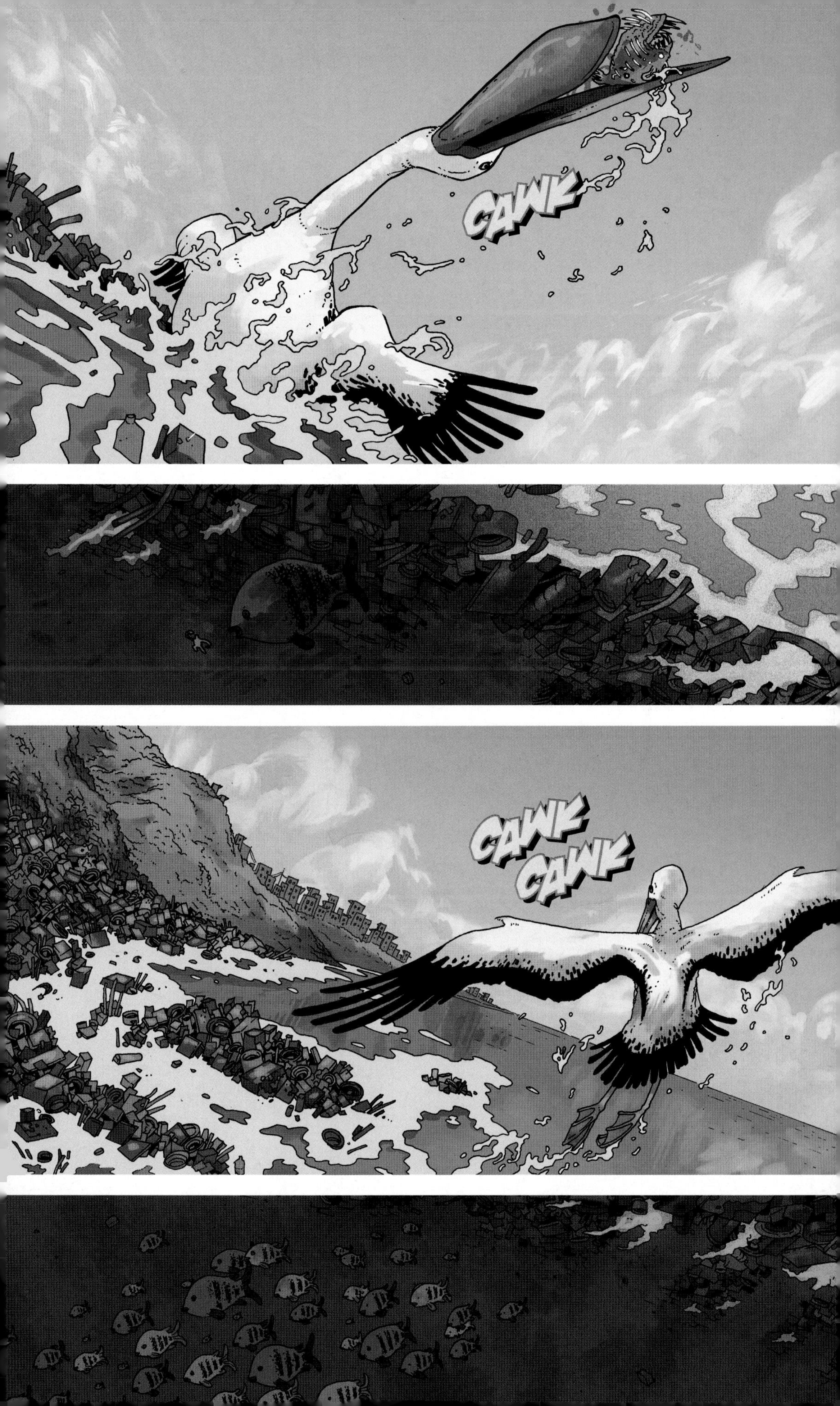
CAWK
CAWK
CAWK

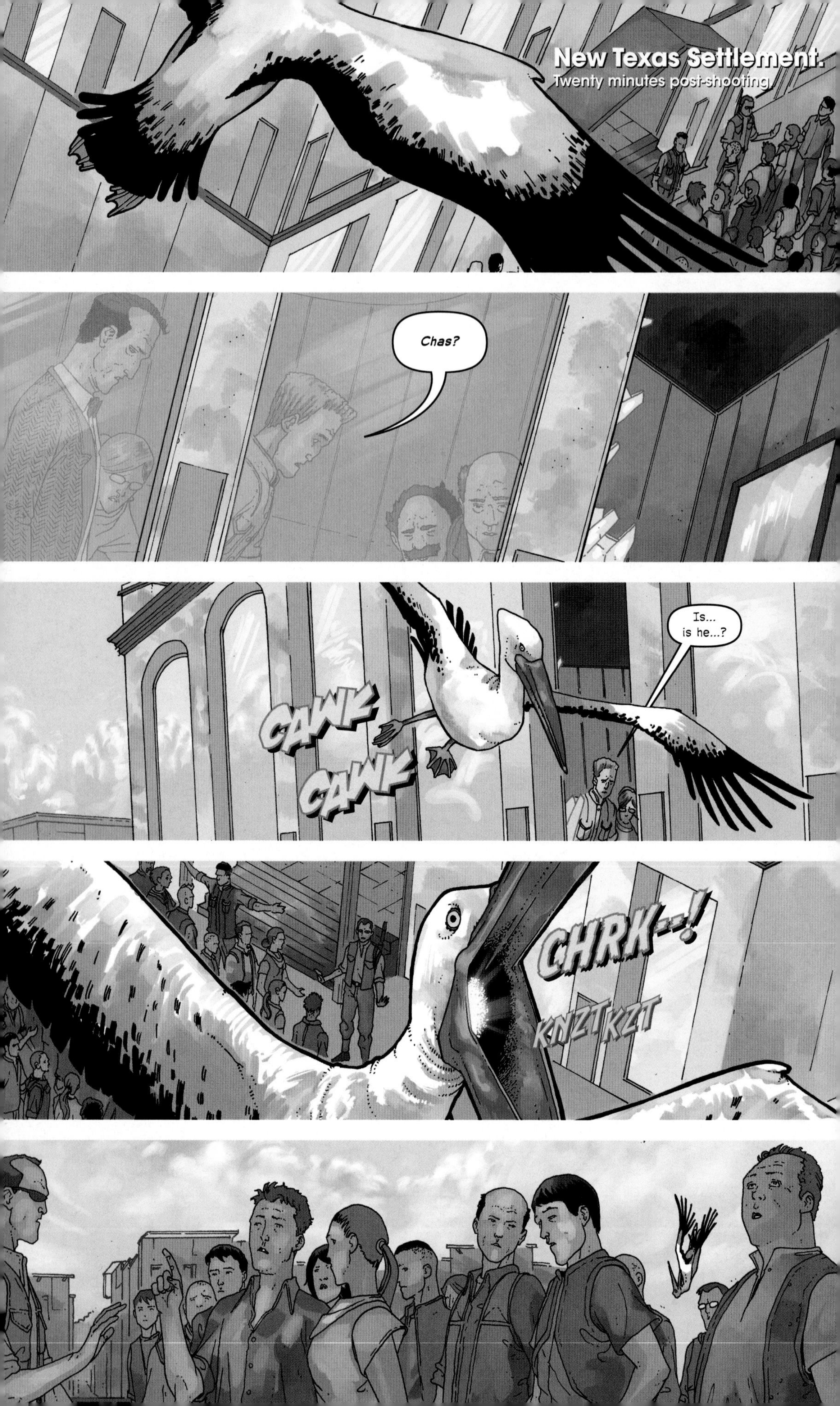

New Texas Settlement.
Twenty minutes post-shooting.
Chas?
Is... is he...?
CAWK
CAWK
CHRK--!
KNZTKZT

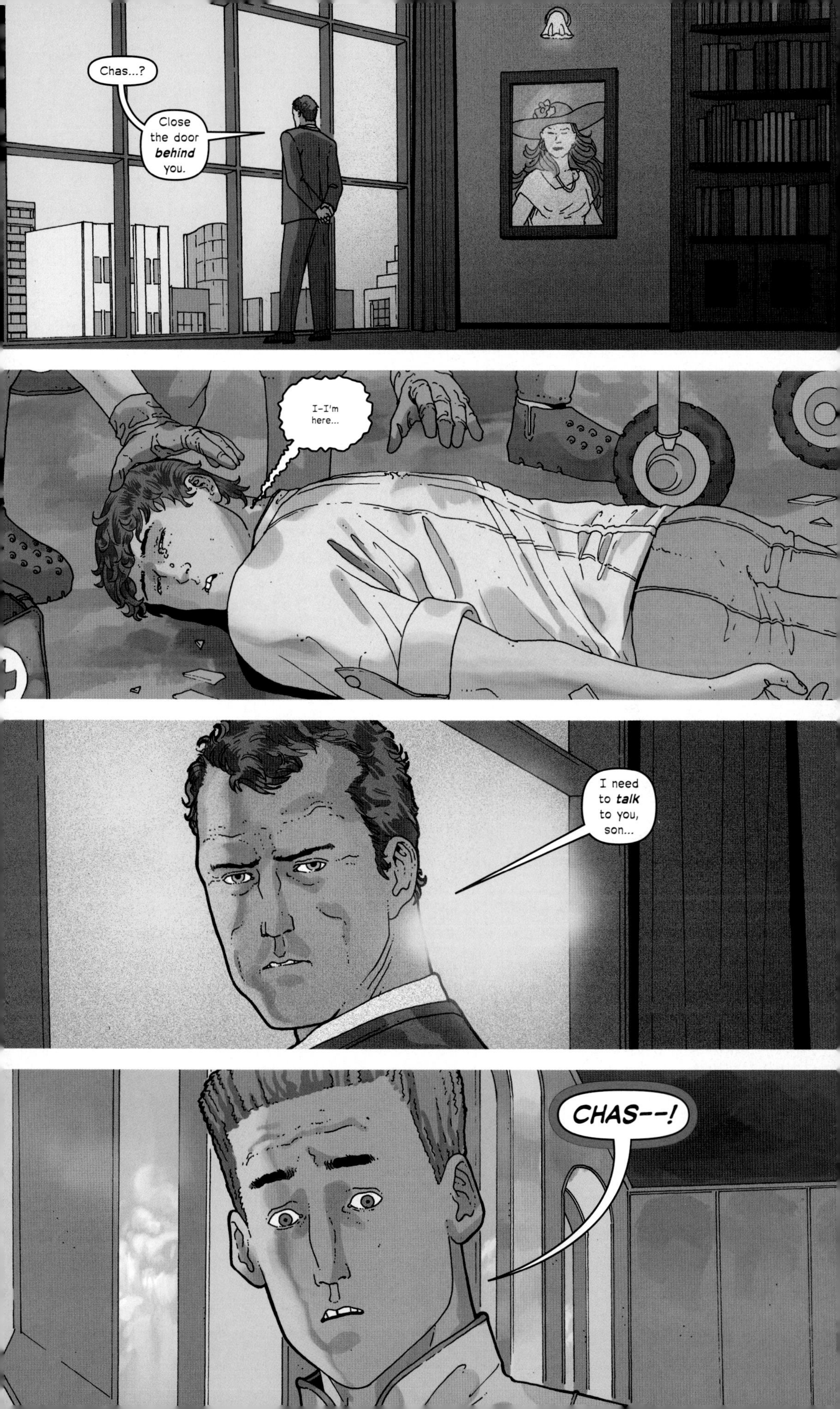
Chas...?
Close the door *behind* you.
I-I'm here...
I need to *talk* to you, son...
CHAS--!

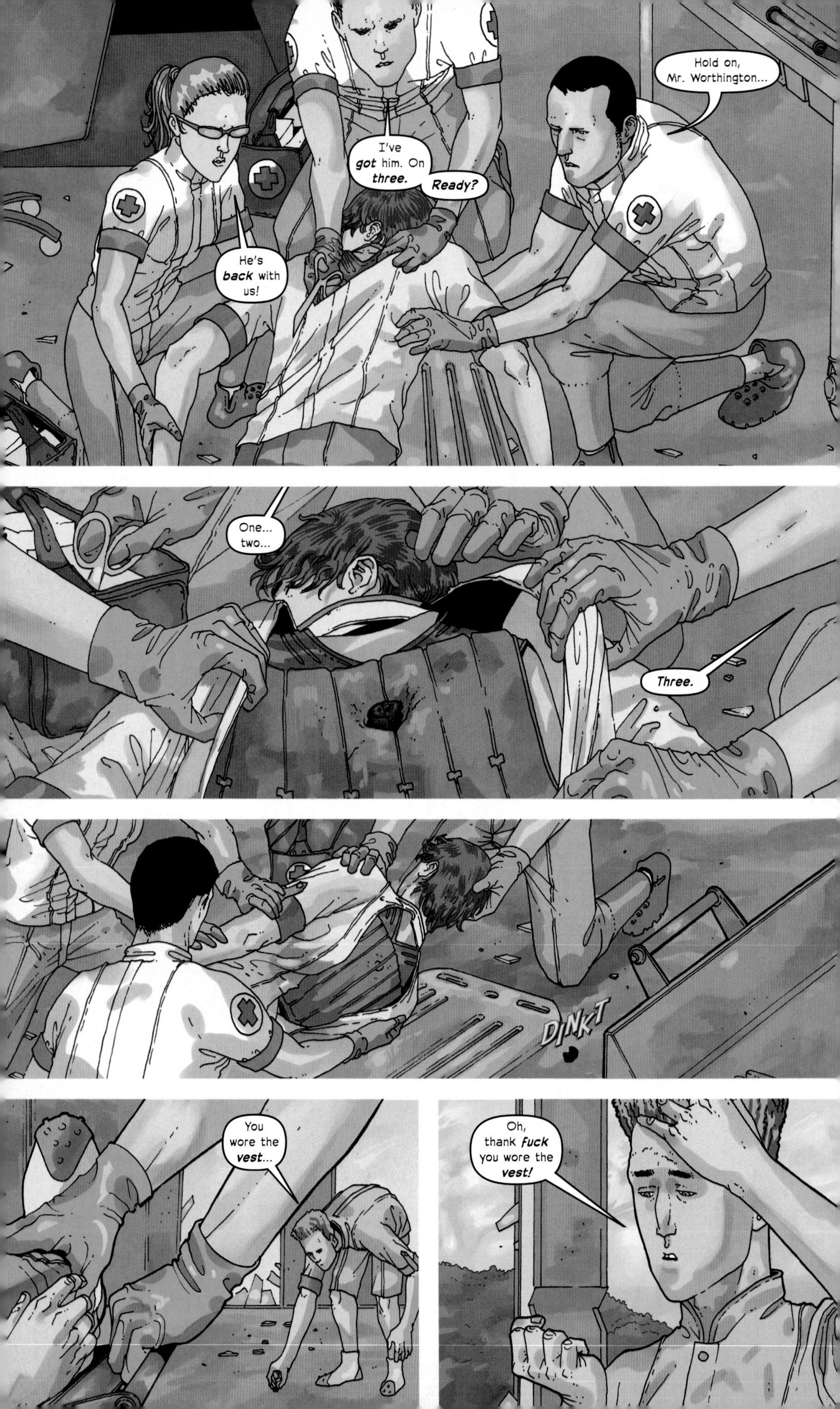
Hold on, Mr. Worthington...
I've got him. On three.
Ready?
He's back with us!
One... two...
Three.
DINKT
You wore the vest...
Oh, thank fuck you wore the vest!

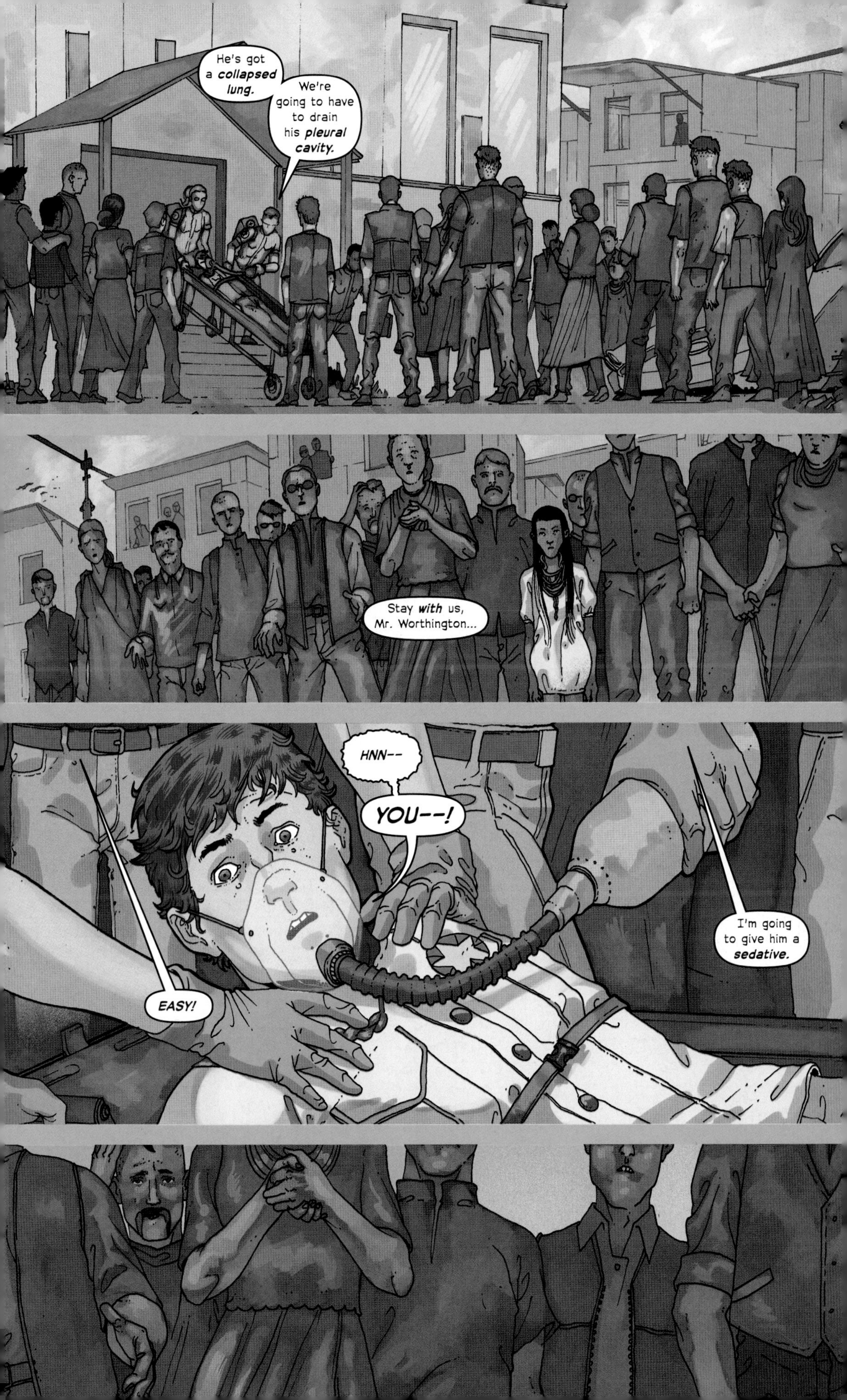
He's got a *collapsed lung.*
We're going to have to drain his *pleural cavity.*
Stay *with* us, Mr. Worthington...
HNN--
YOU--!
EASY!
I'm going to give him a *sedative.*

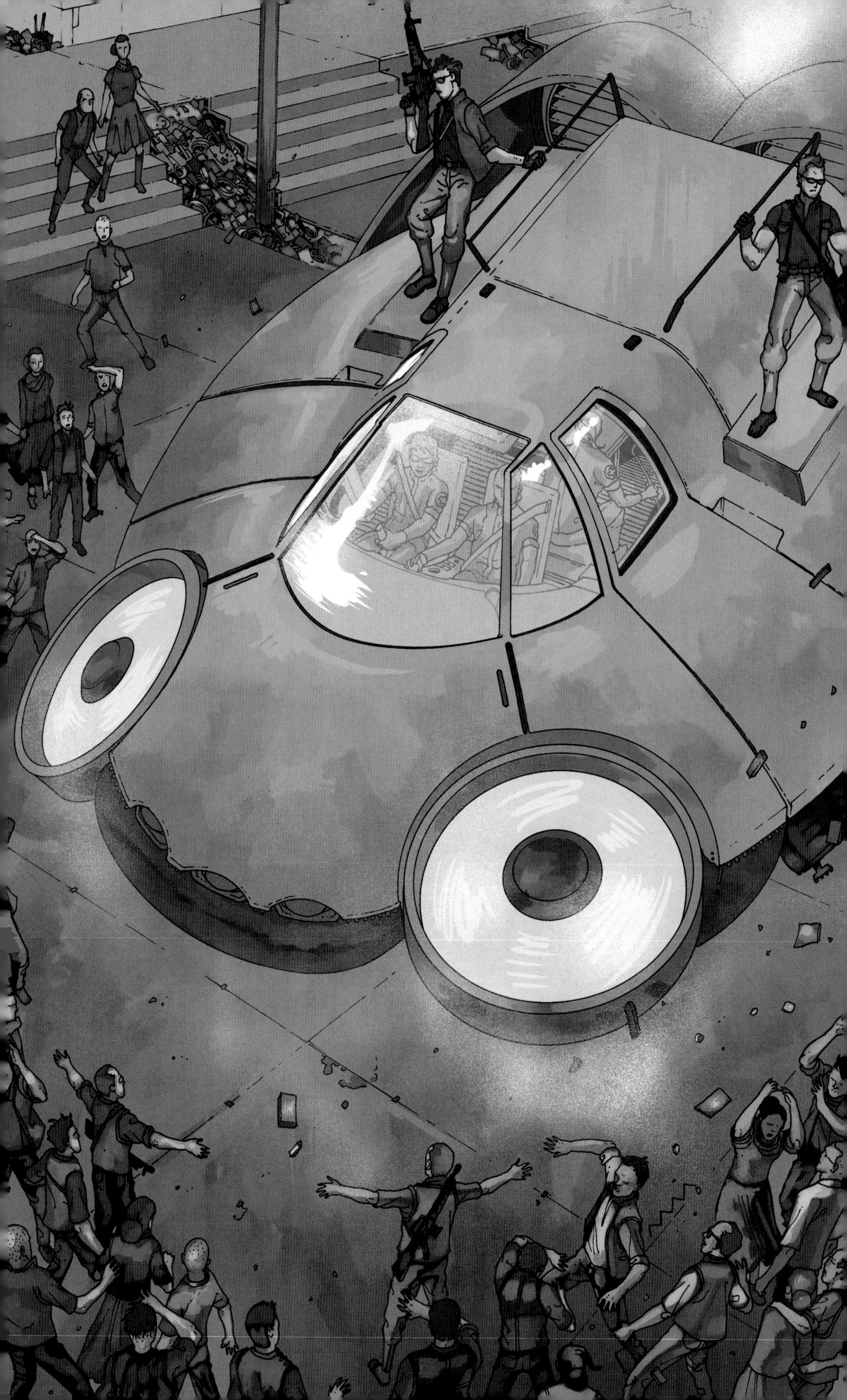

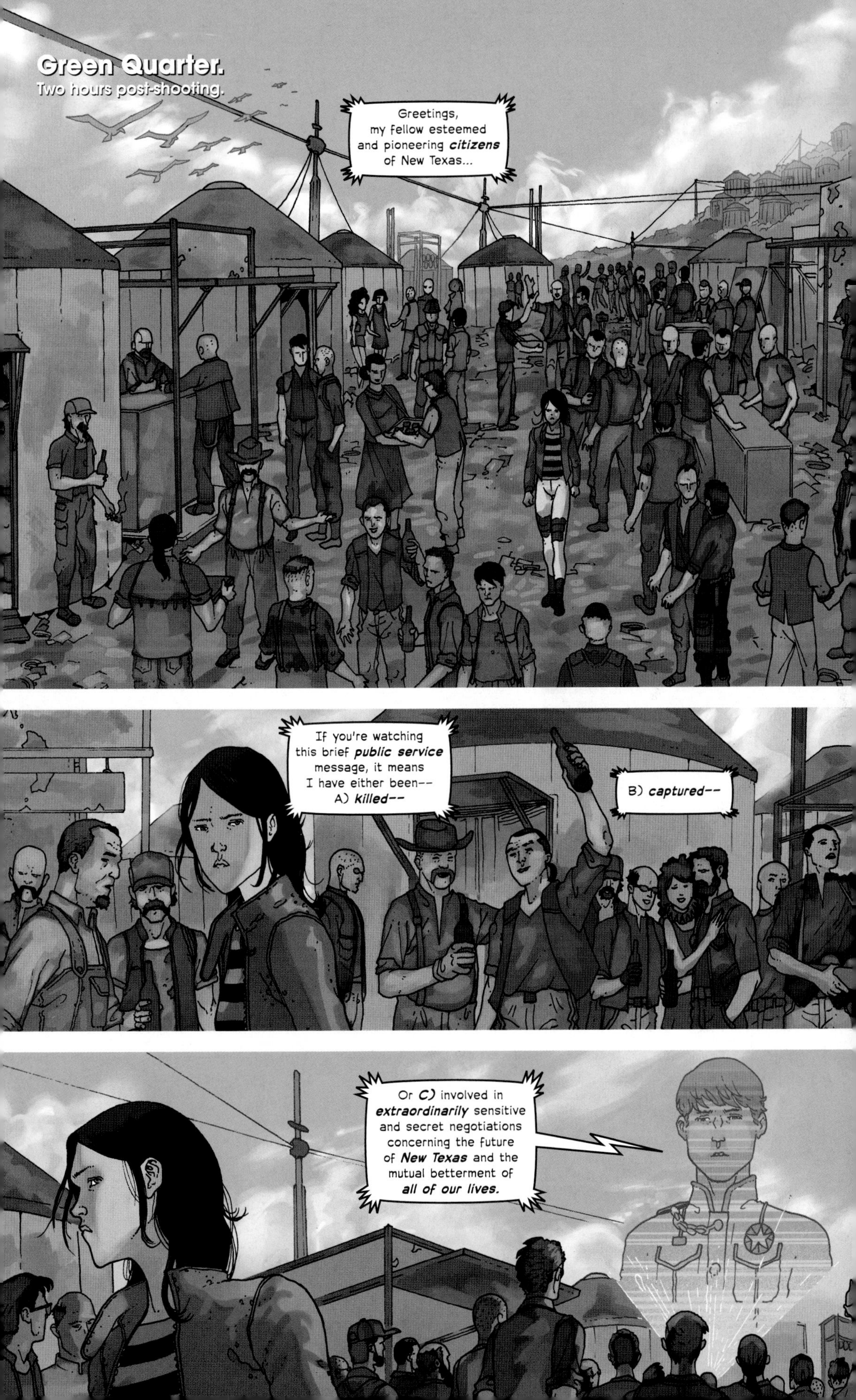
Green Quarter.
Two hours post-shooting.
Greetings, my fellow esteemed and pioneering *citizens* of New Texas...
If you're watching this brief *public service* message, it means I have either been-- A) *killed--*
B) *captured--*
Or *C)* involved in *extraordinarily* sensitive and secret negotiations concerning the future of *New Texas* and the mutual betterment of *all of our lives.*

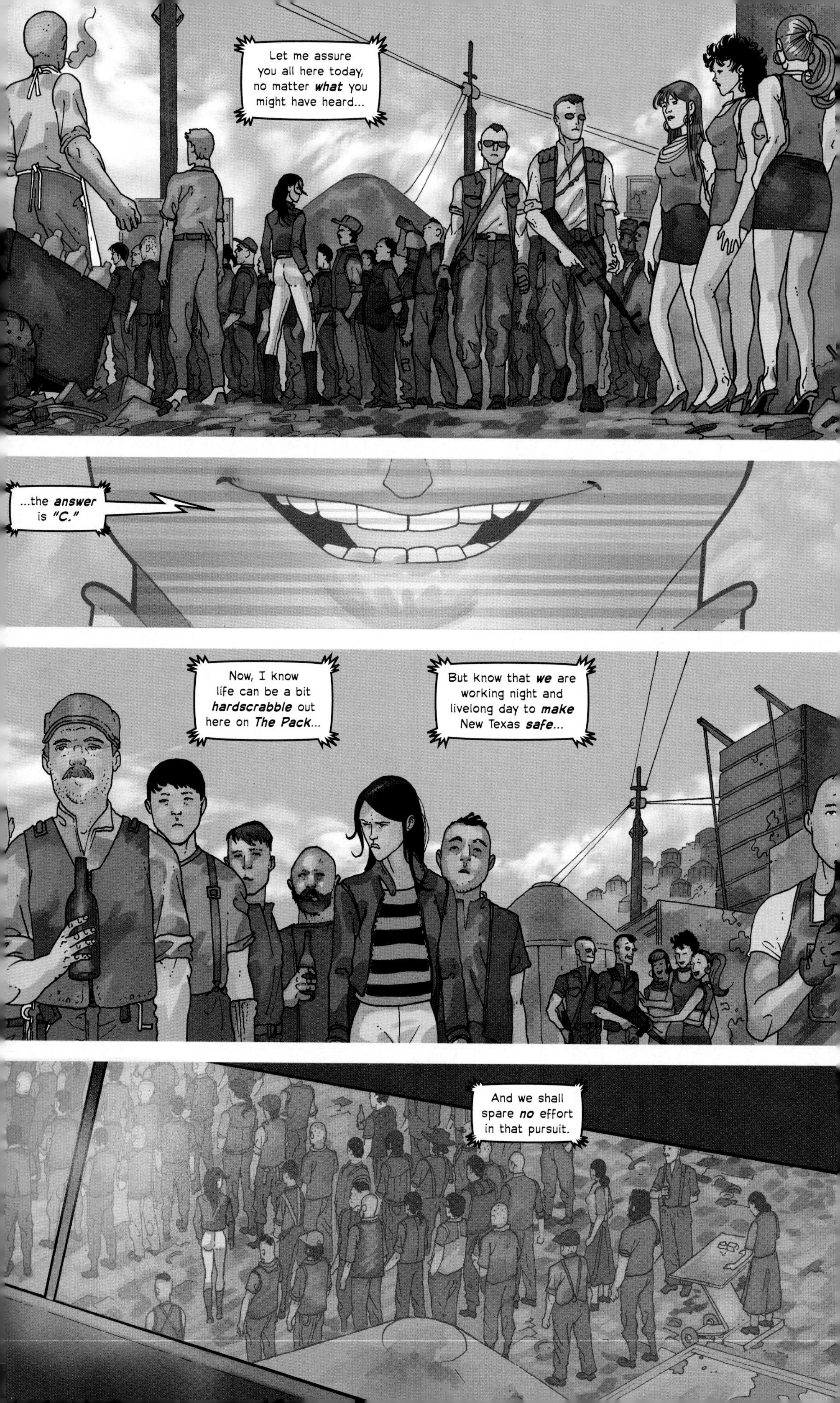
Let me assure you all here today, no matter *what* you might have heard...
...the *answer* is *"C."*
Now, I know life can be a bit *hardscrabble* out here on *The Pack*...
But know that *we* are working night and livelong day to *make* New Texas *safe*...
And we shall spare *no* effort in that pursuit.

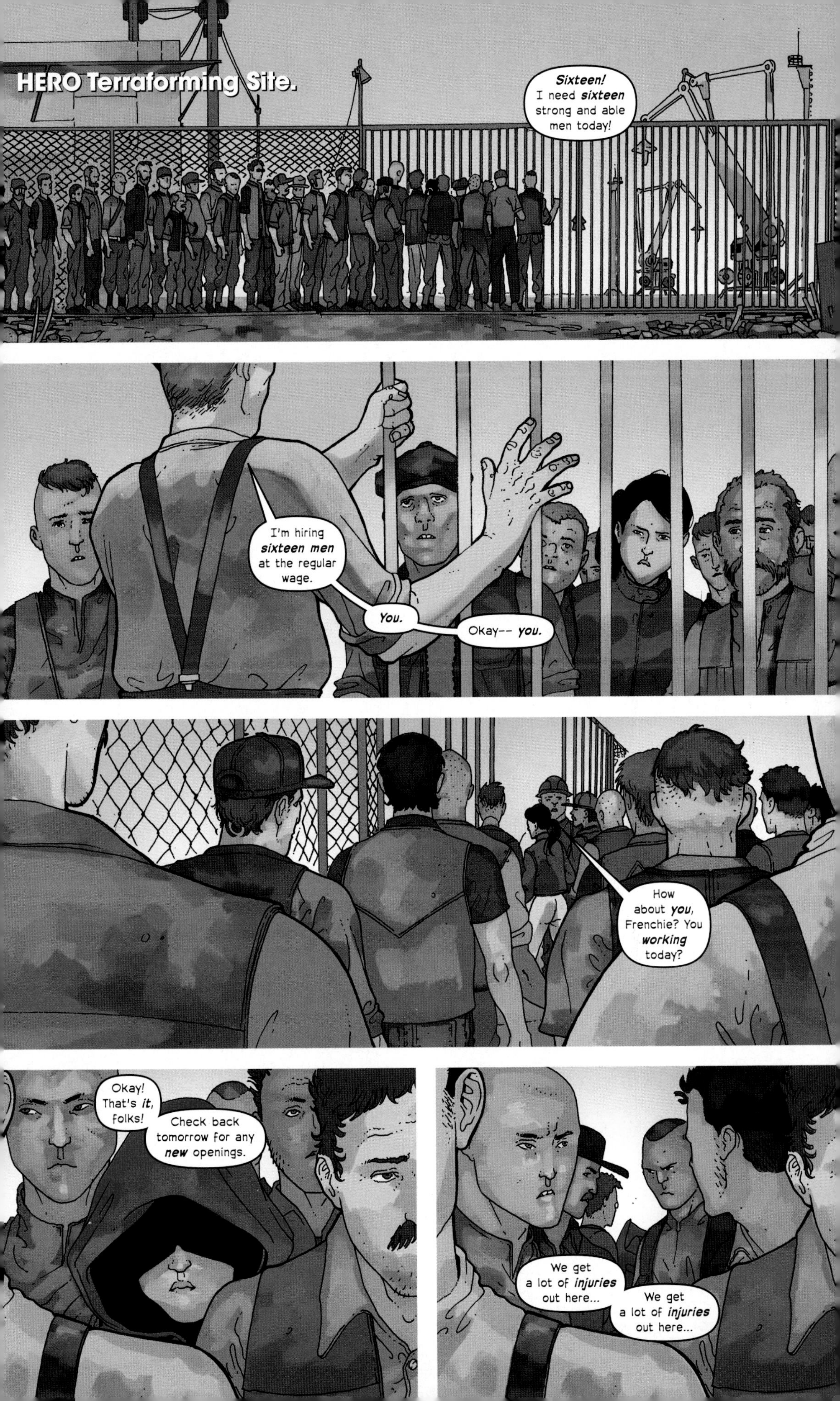
HERO Terraforming Site.
Sixteen! I need sixteen strong and able men today!
I'm hiring sixteen men at the regular wage.
You.
Okay-- you.
How about you, Frenchie? You working today?
Okay! That's it, folks!
Check back tomorrow for any new openings.
We get a lot of injuries out here...
We get a lot of injuries out here...

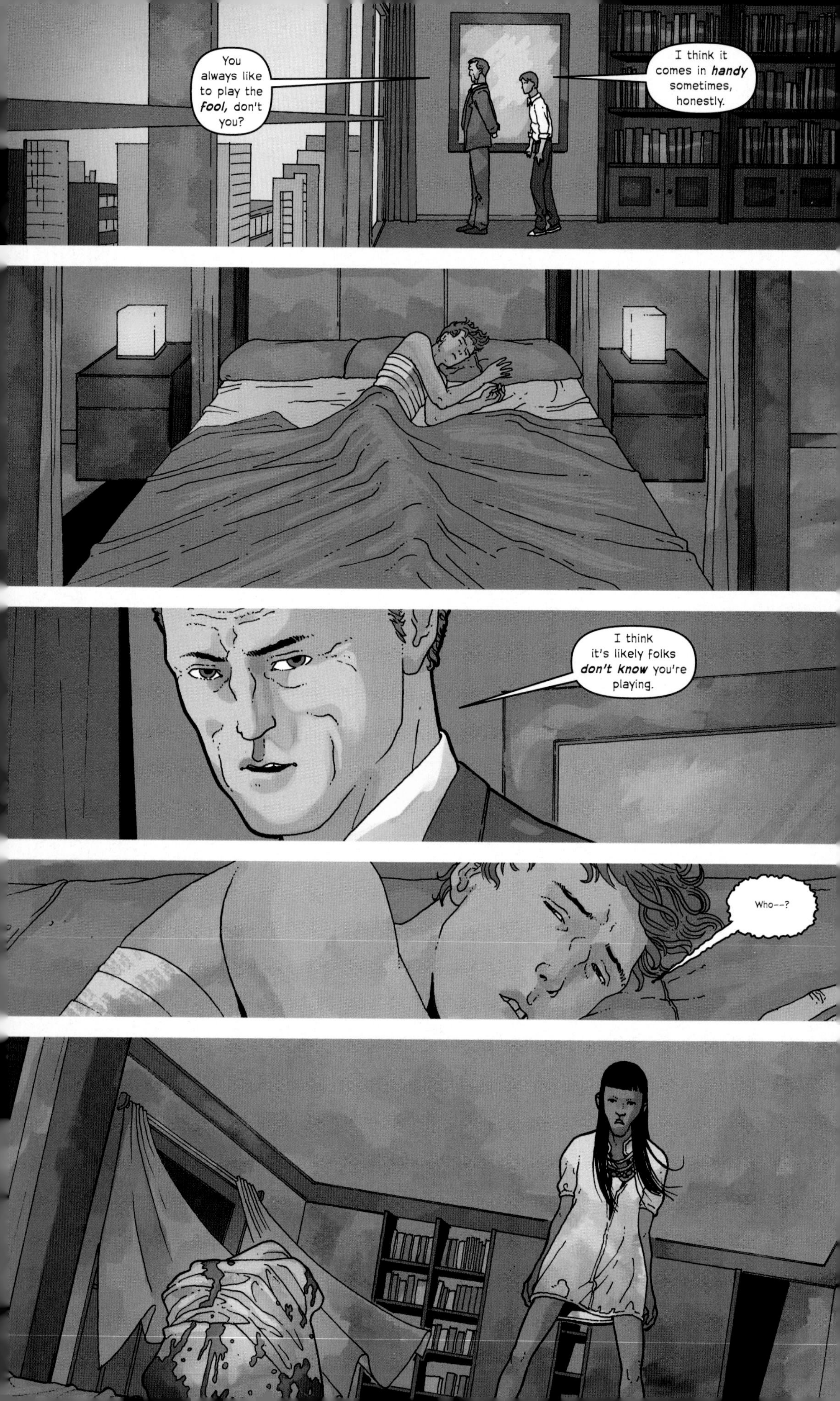
You always like to play the *fool,* don't you?
I think it comes in *handy* sometimes, honestly.
I think it's likely folks *don't know* you're playing.
Who--?

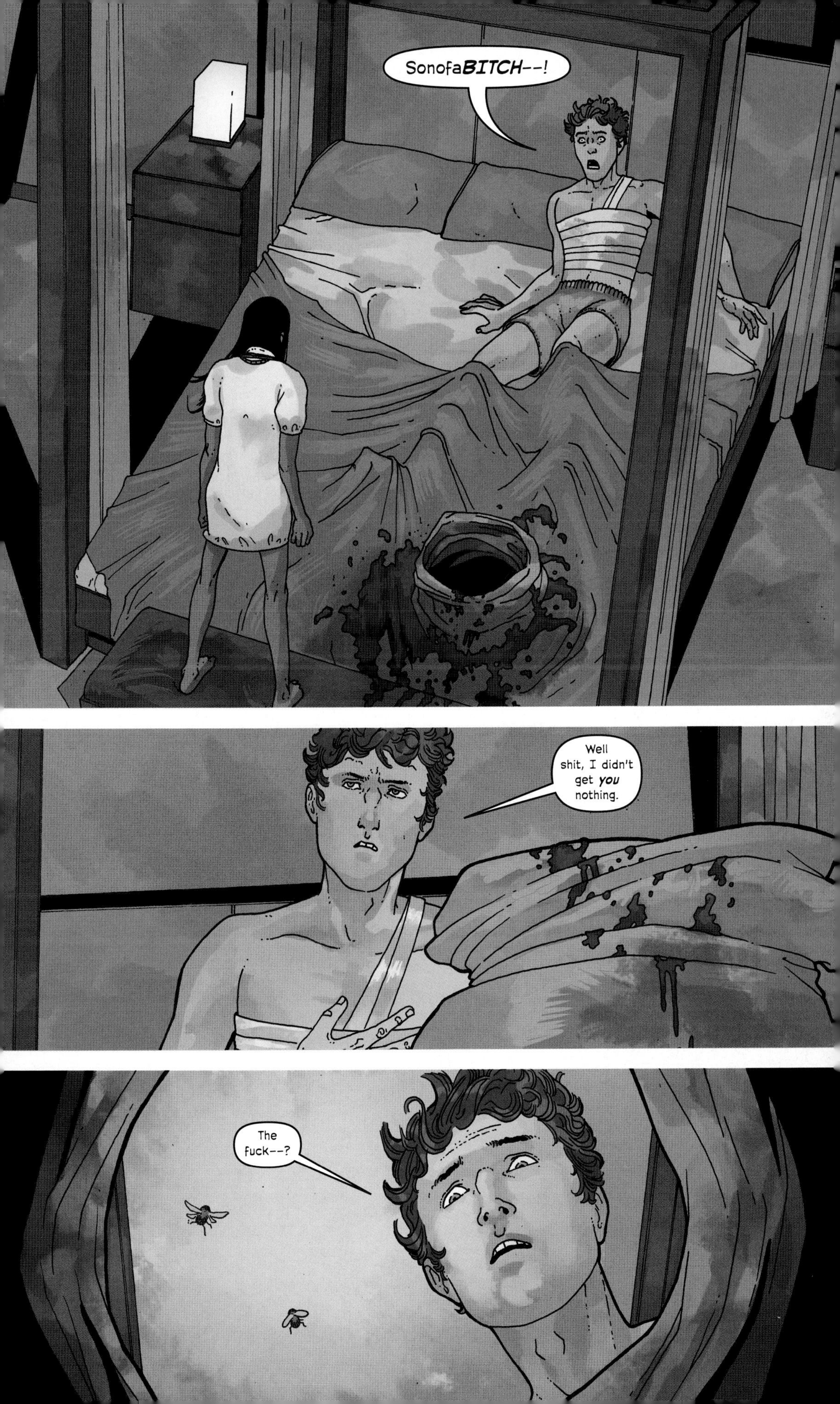
SonofaBITCH--!
Well shit, I didn't get *you* nothing.
The fuck--?

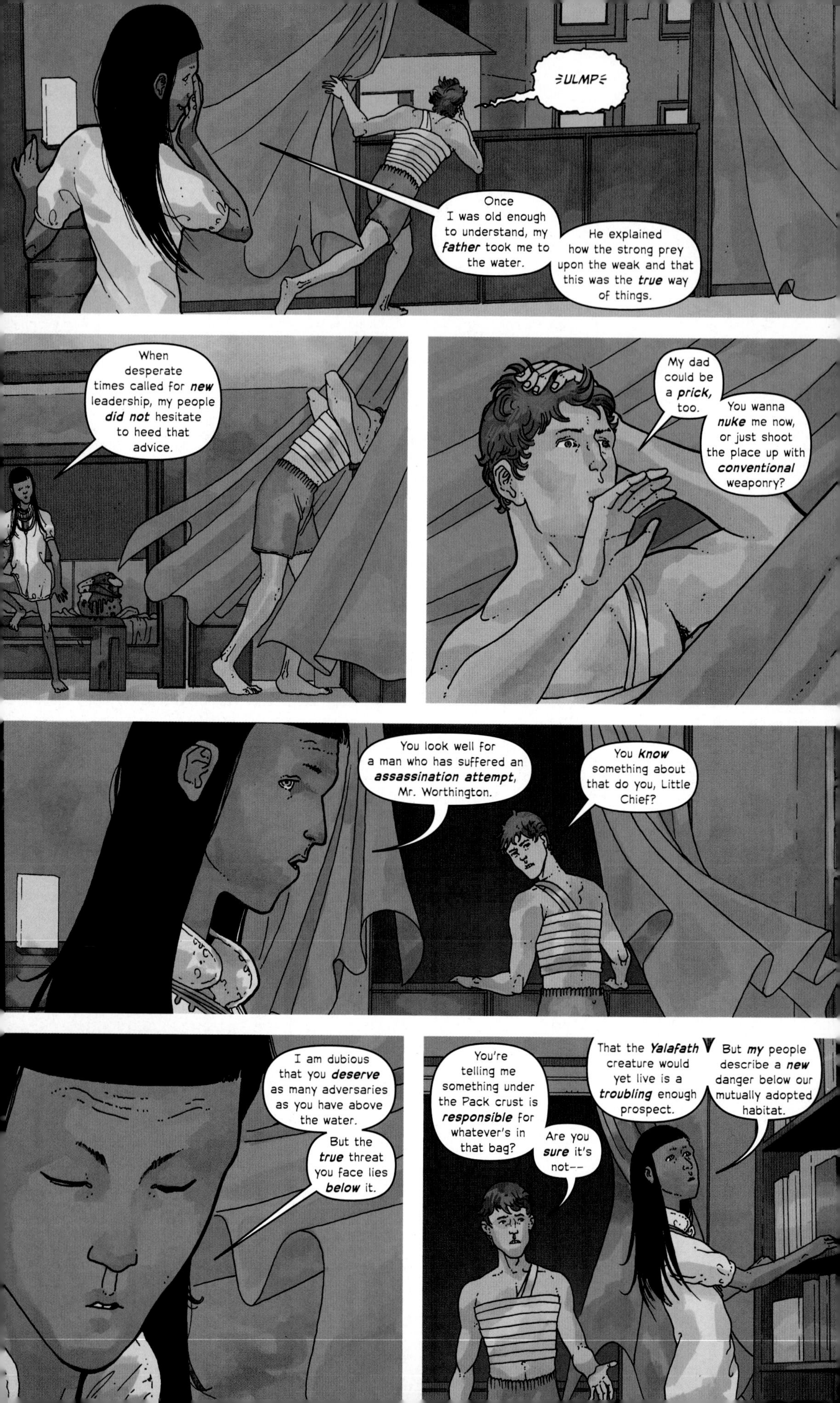

ULMP
Once I was old enough to understand, my *father* took me to the water.
He explained how the strong prey upon the weak and that this was the *true* way of things.
When desperate times called for *new* leadership, my people *did not* hesitate to heed that advice.
My dad could be a *prick,* too.
You wanna *nuke* me now, or just shoot the place up with *conventional* weaponry?
You look well for a man who has suffered an *assassination attempt*, Mr. Worthington.
You *know* something about that do you, Little Chief?
I am dubious that you *deserve* as many adversaries as you have above the water.
But the *true* threat you face lies *below* it.
You're telling me something under the Pack crust is *responsible* for whatever's in that bag?
Are you *sure* it's not--
That the *Yalafath* creature would yet live is a *troubling* enough prospect.
But *my* people describe a *new* danger below our mutually adopted habitat.

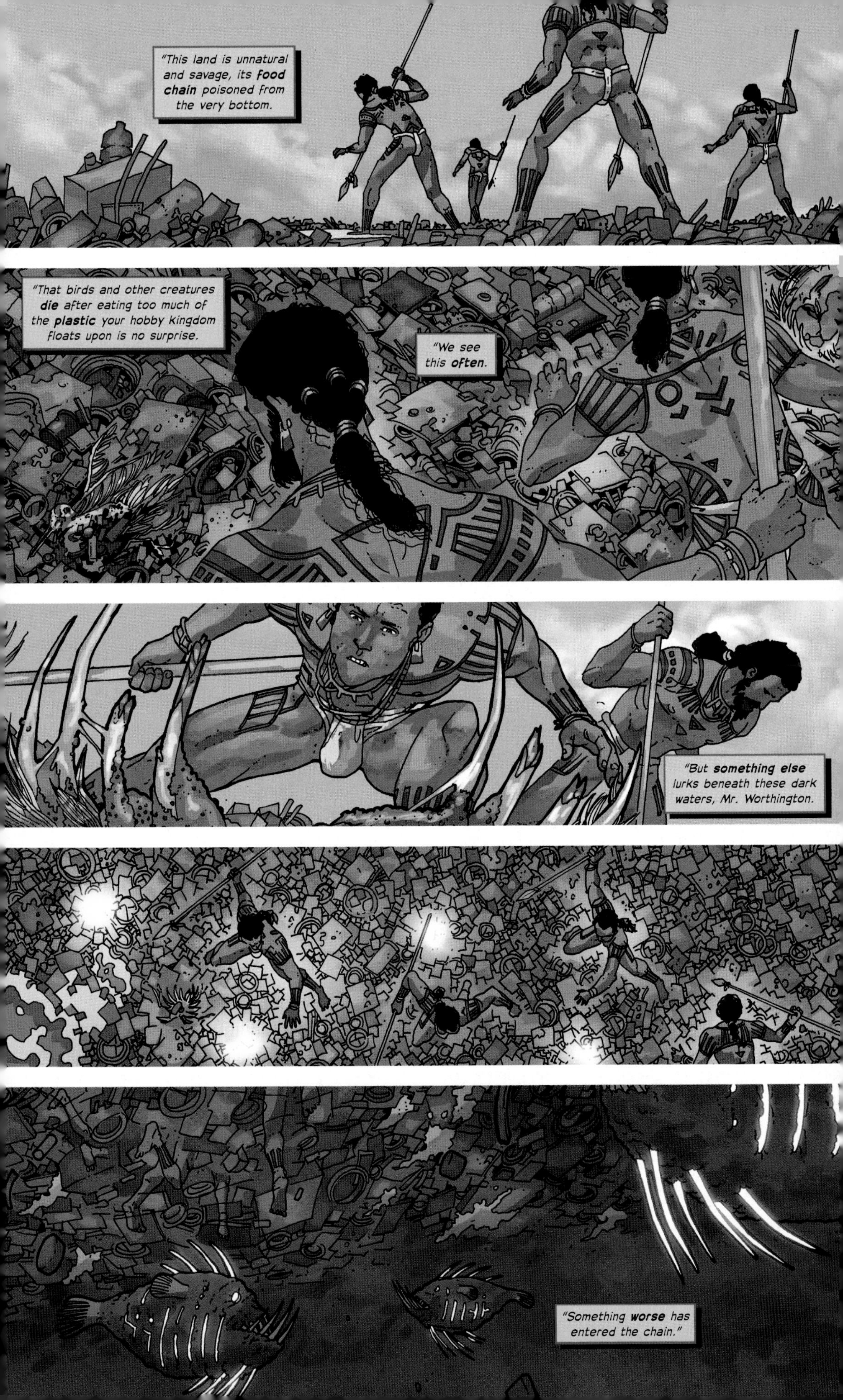
"This land is unnatural and savage, its **food chain** poisoned from the very bottom.
"That birds and other creatures **die** after eating too much of the **plastic** your hobby kingdom floats upon is no surprise.
"We see this **often**.
"But **something else** lurks beneath these dark waters, Mr. Worthington.
"Something **worse** has entered the chain."

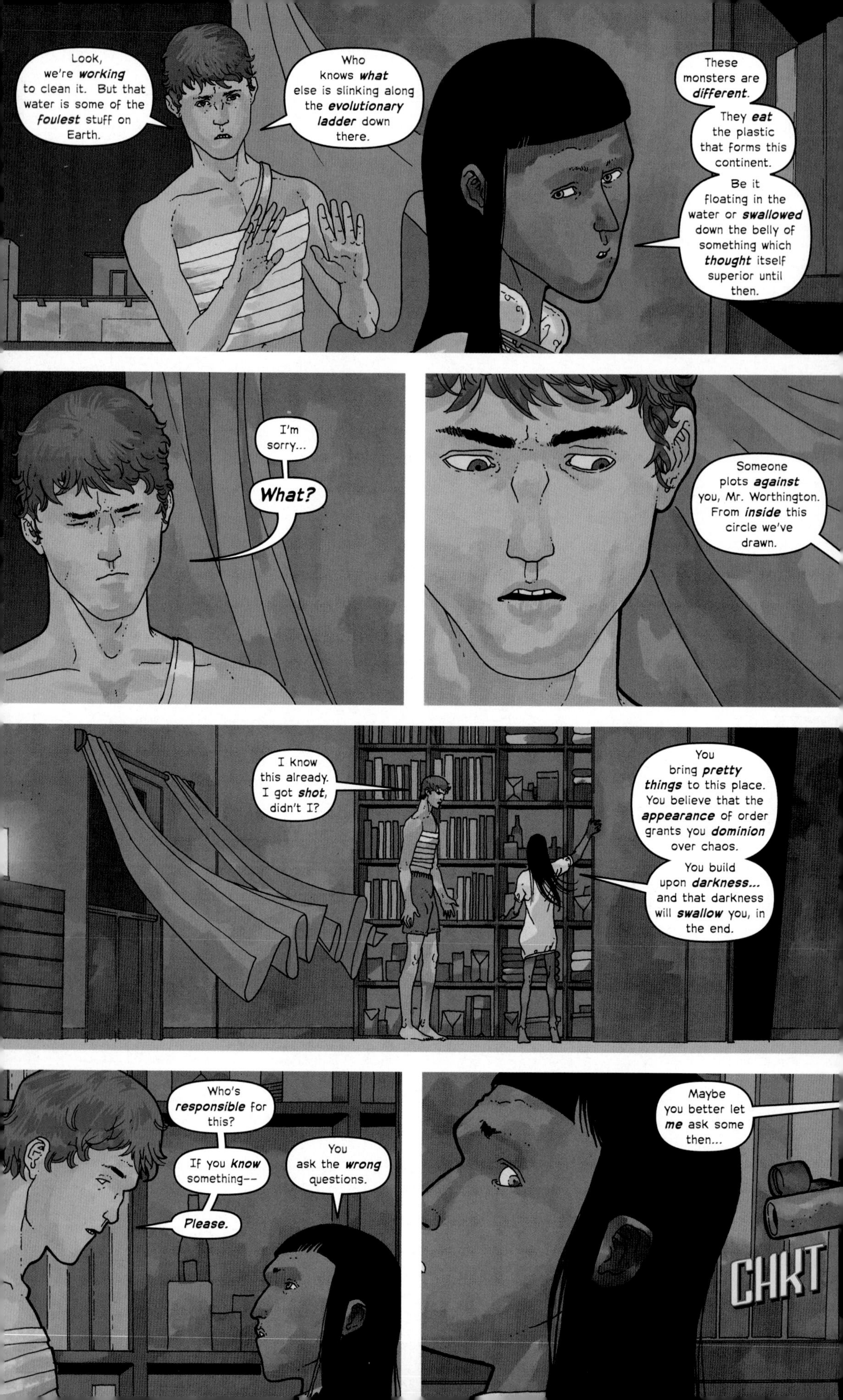

Look, we're *working* to clean it. But that water is some of the *foulest* stuff on Earth.
Who knows *what* else is slinking along the *evolutionary ladder* down there.
These monsters are *different*.
They *eat* the plastic that forms this continent.
Be it floating in the water or *swallowed* down the belly of something which *thought* itself superior until then.
I'm sorry...
What?
Someone plots *against* you, Mr. Worthington. From *inside* this circle we've drawn.
I know this already. I got *shot*, didn't I?
You bring *pretty things* to this place. You believe that the *appearance* of order grants you *dominion* over chaos.
You build upon *darkness...* and that darkness will *swallow* you, in the end.
Who's *responsible* for this?
If you *know* something--
Please.
You ask the *wrong* questions.
Maybe you better let *me* ask some then...
CHKT

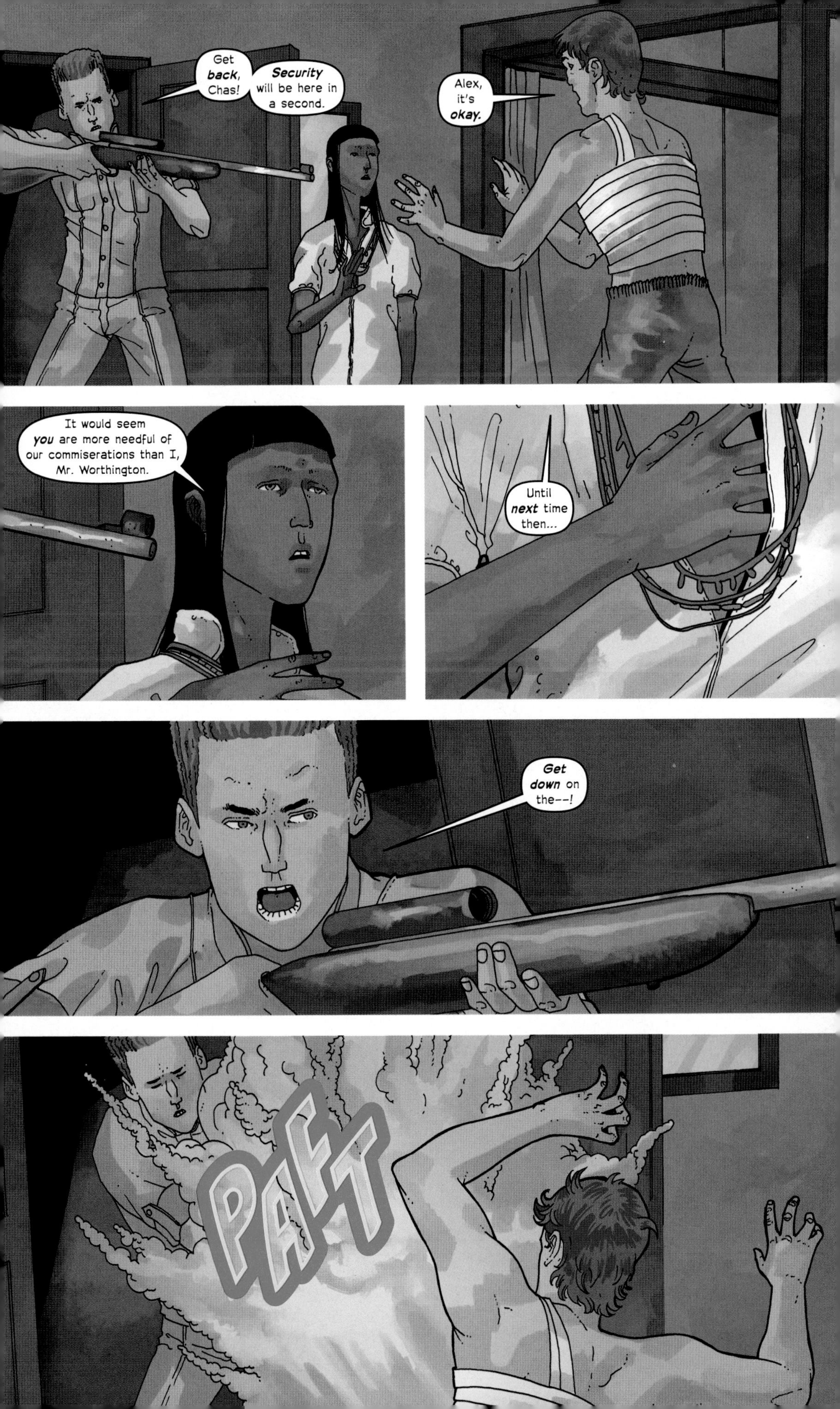
Get *back*, Chas!
Security will be here in a second.
Alex, it's *okay.*
It would seem *you* are more needful of our commiserations than I, Mr. Worthington.
Until *next* time then...
Get down on the--!
PAFT

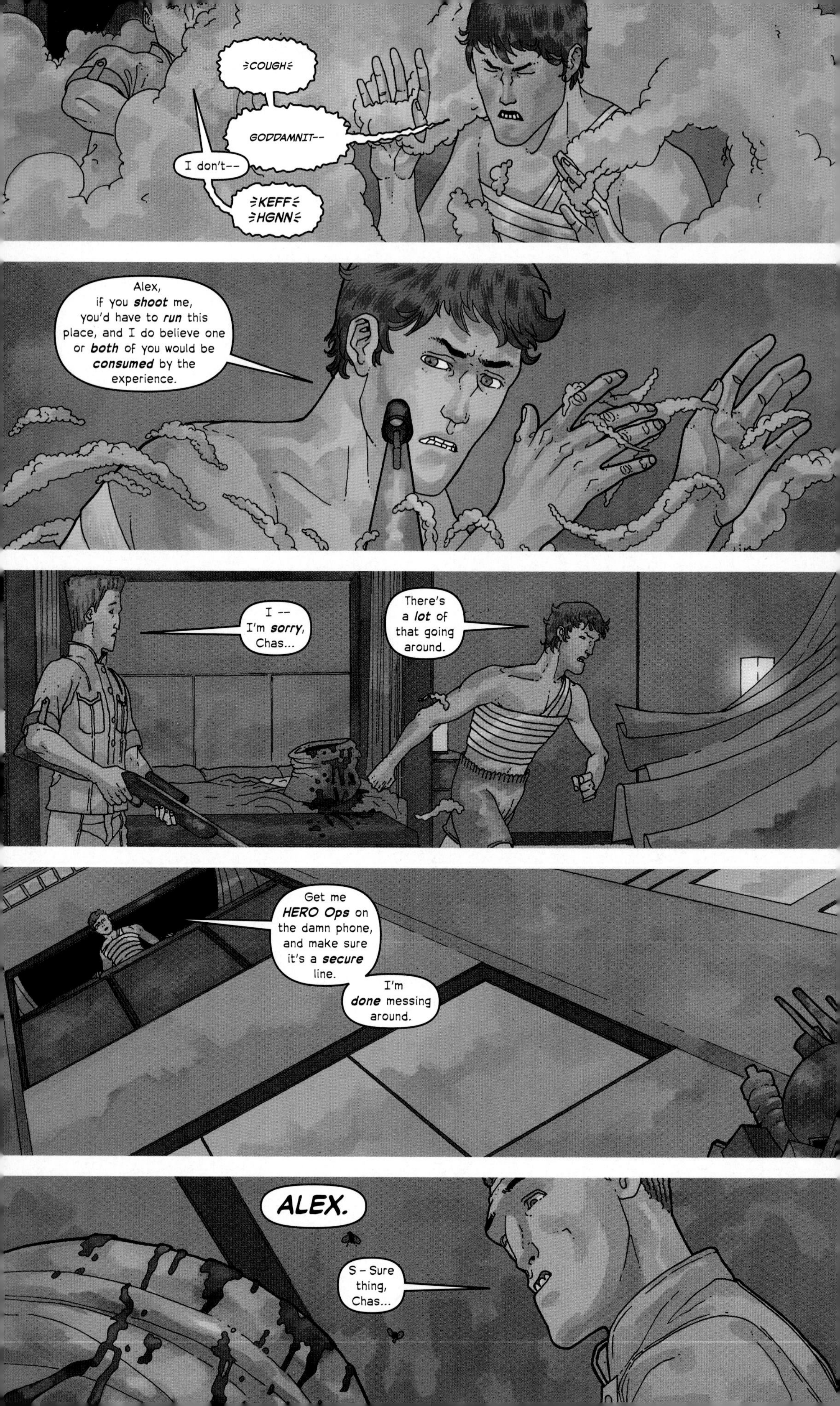

COUGH
GODDAMNIT--
I don't--
KEFF
HGNN
Alex, if you **shoot** me, you'd have to **run** this place, and I do believe one or **both** of you would be **consumed** by the experience.
I -- I'm **sorry**, Chas...
There's a **lot** of that going around.
Get me **HERO Ops** on the damn phone, and make sure it's a **secure** line.
I'm **done** messing around.
ALEX.
S – Sure thing, Chas...

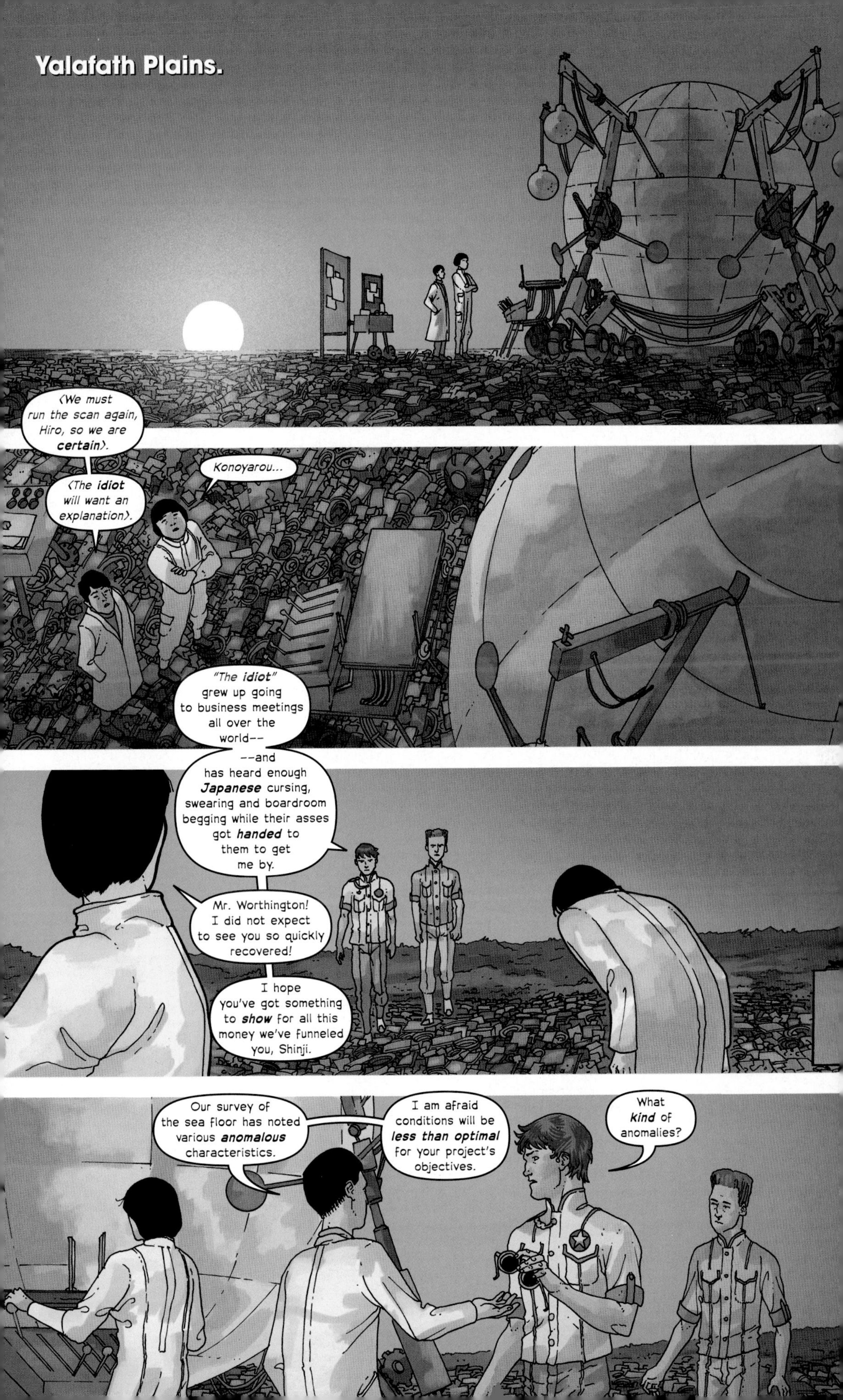
Yalafath Plains.
‹We must run the scan again, Hiro, so we are **certain**›.
‹The **idiot** will want an explanation›.
Konoyarou...
"The **idiot**" grew up going to business meetings all over the world--
--and has heard enough **Japanese** cursing, swearing and boardroom begging while their asses got **handed** to them to get me by.
Mr. Worthington! I did not expect to see you so quickly recovered!
I hope you've got something to **show** for all this money we've funneled you, Shinji.
Our survey of the sea floor has noted various **anomalous** characteristics.
I am afraid conditions will be **less than optimal** for your project's objectives.
What **kind** of anomalies?

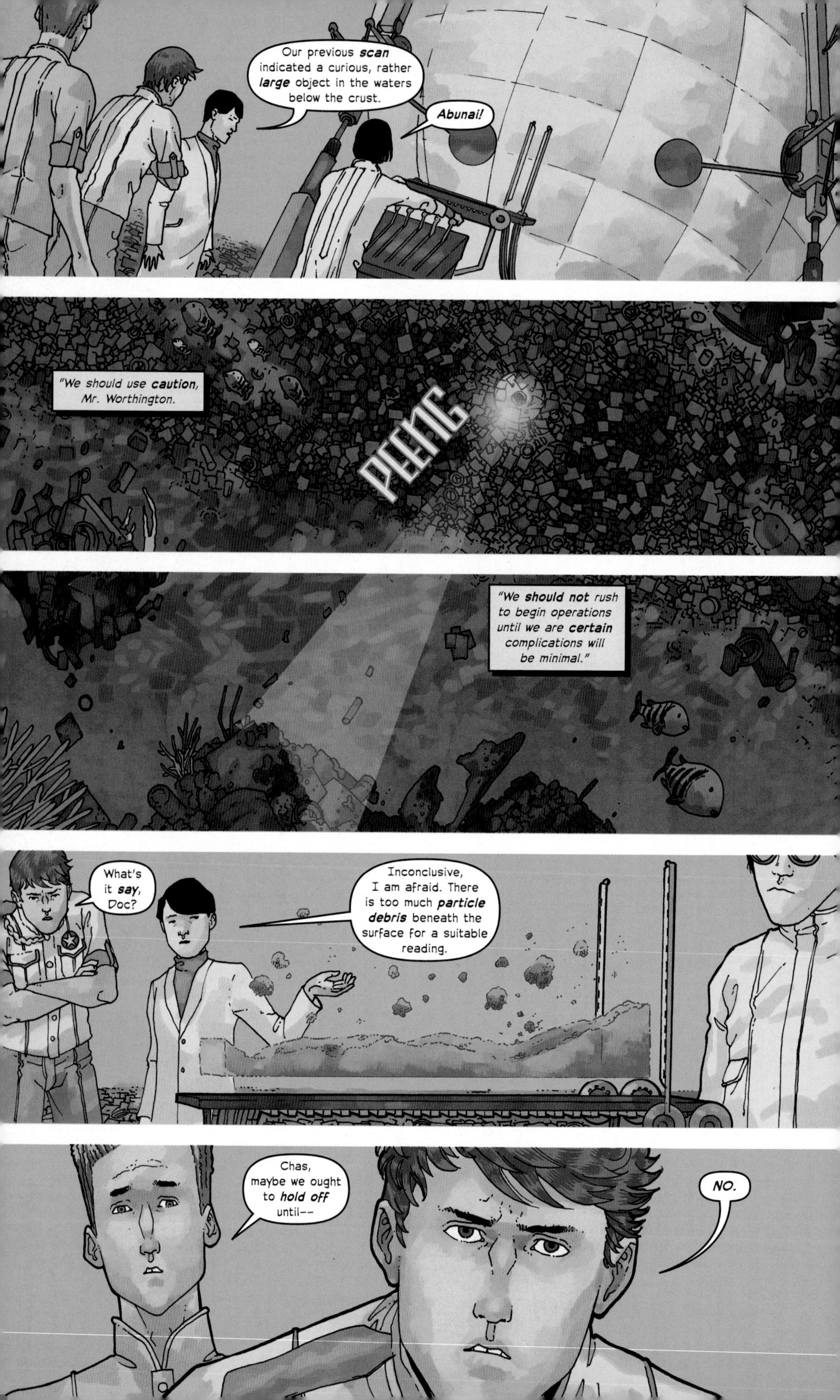

Our previous scan indicated a curious, rather large object in the waters below the crust.
Abunai!
"We should use caution, Mr. Worthington.
PEENG
"We should not rush to begin operations until we are certain complications will be minimal."
What's it say, Doc?
Inconclusive, I am afraid. There is too much particle debris beneath the surface for a suitable reading.
Chas, maybe we ought to hold off until--
NO.

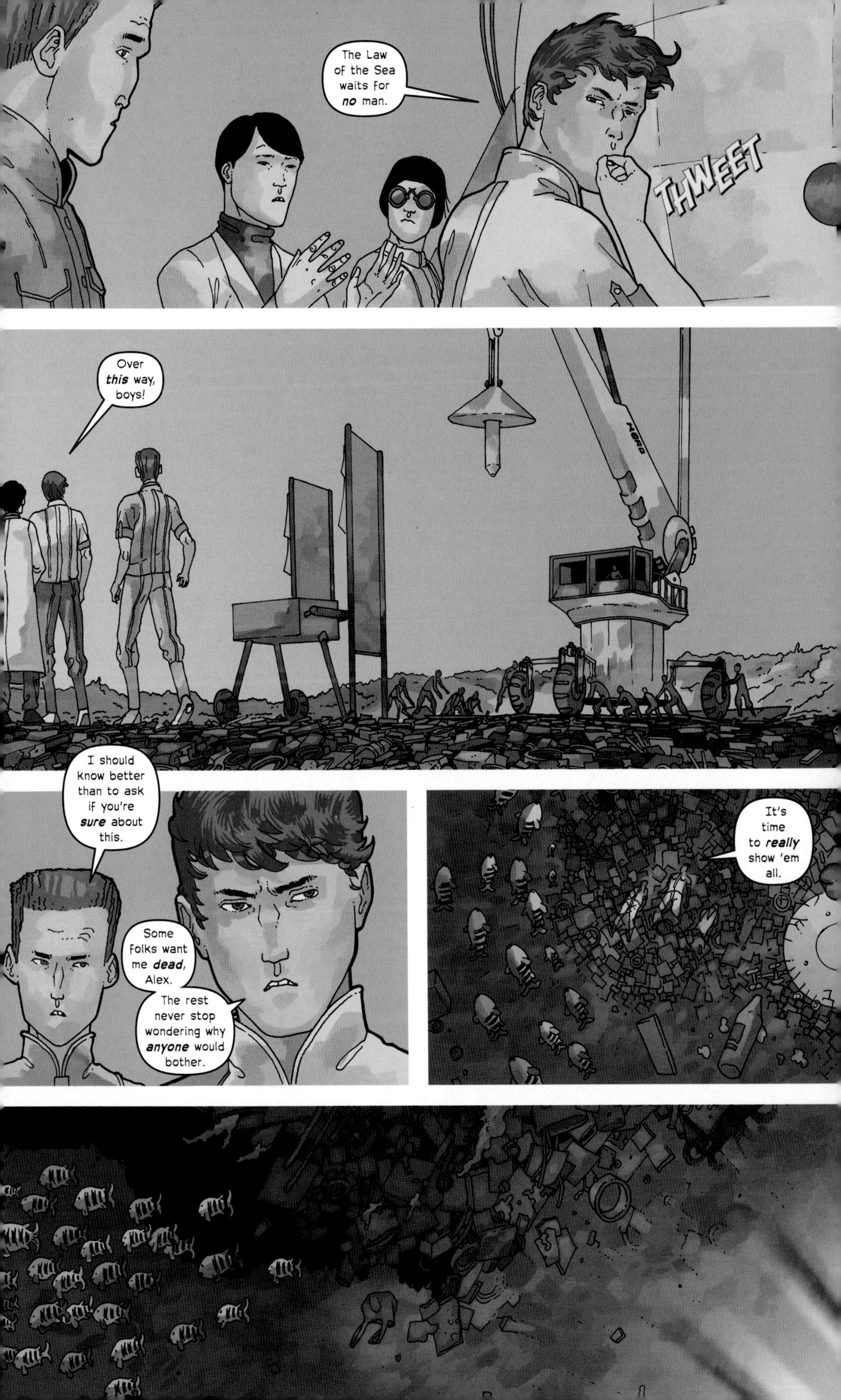
The Law of the Sea waits for **no** man.
THWEET
Over **this** way, boys!
I should know better than to ask if you're **sure** about this.
Some folks want me **dead**, Alex.
The rest never stop wondering why **anyone** would bother.
It's time to **really** show 'em all.

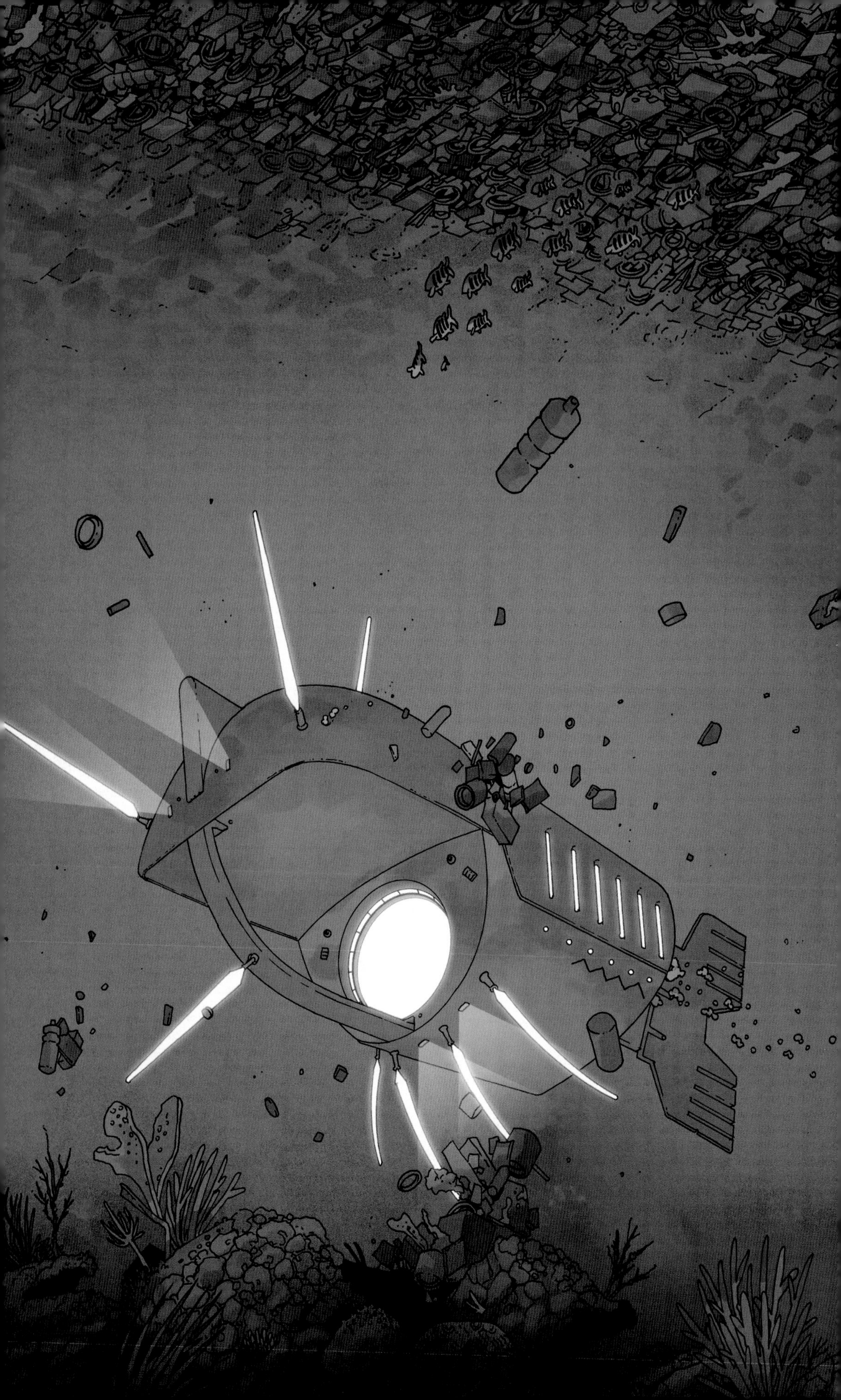

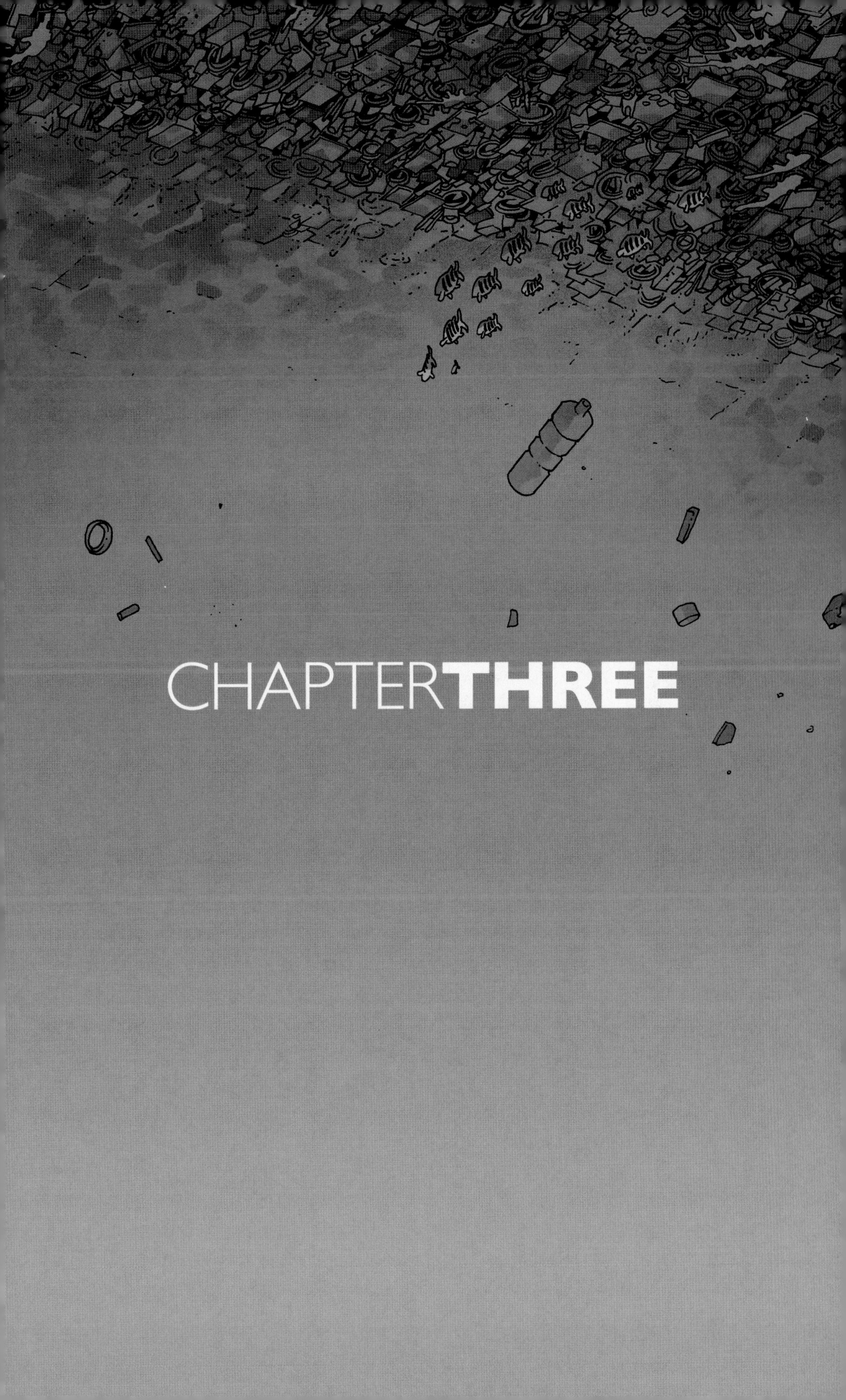

CHAPTER THREE

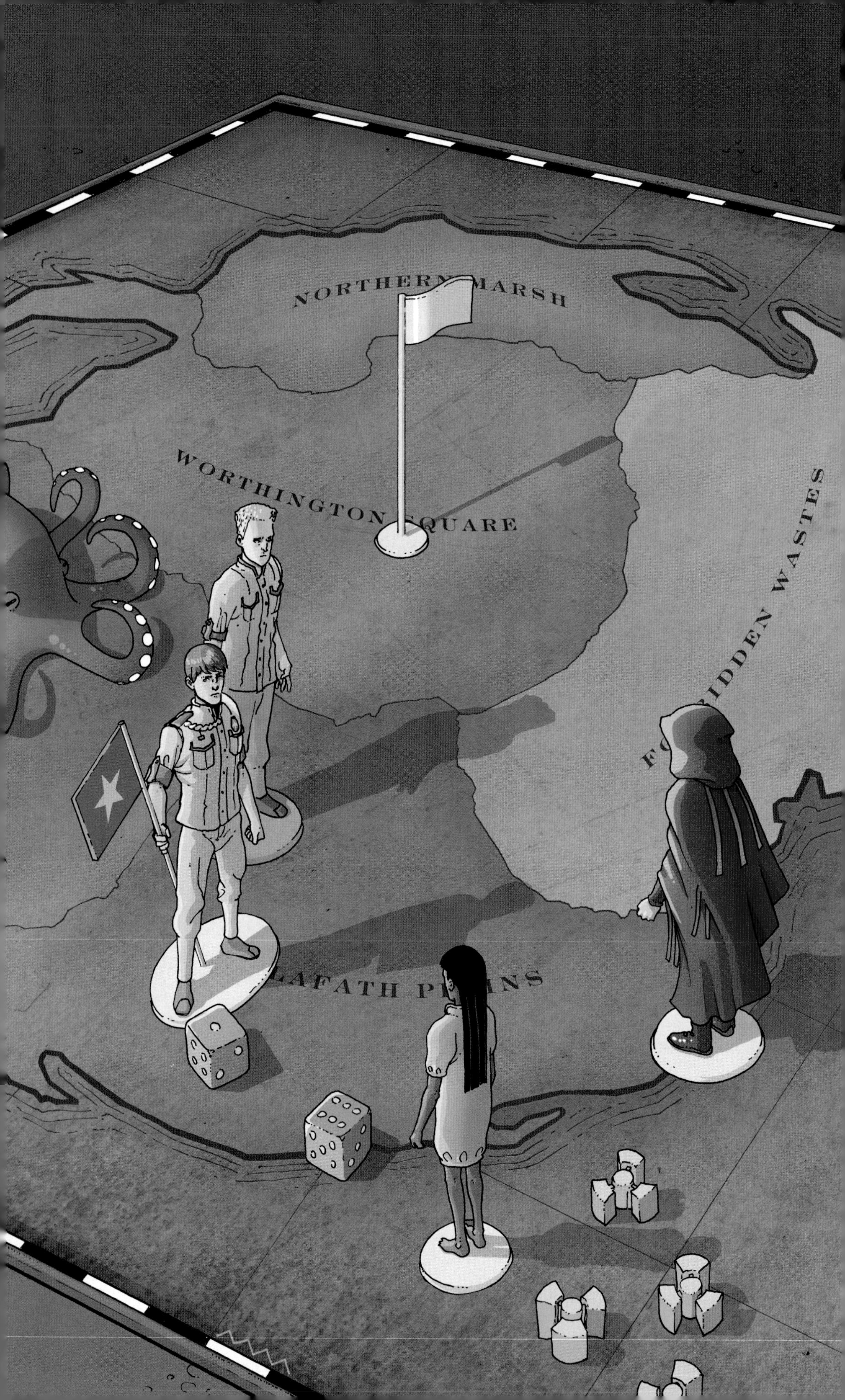
MARSH
WORTHINGTON
WASTES

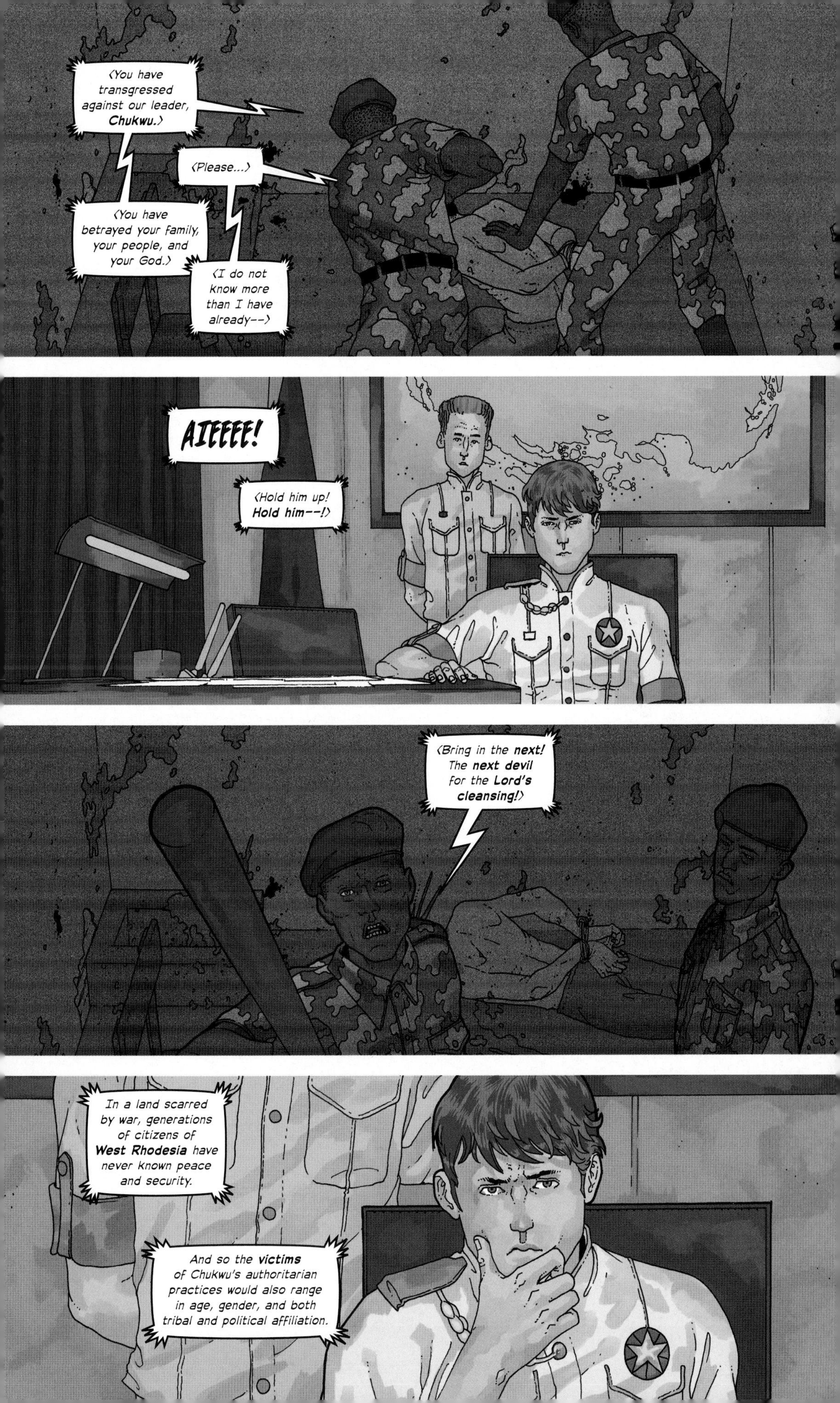

‹You have transgressed against our leader, **Chukwu.**›
‹Please...›
‹You have betrayed your family, your people, and your God.›
‹I do not know more than I have already--›
AIEEEE!
‹Hold him up! **Hold him--!**›
‹Bring in the **next!** The **next devil** for the **Lord's cleansing!**›
In a land scarred by war, generations of citizens of **West Rhodesia** have never known peace and security.
And so the **victims** of Chukwu's authoritarian practices would also range in age, gender, and both tribal and political affiliation.

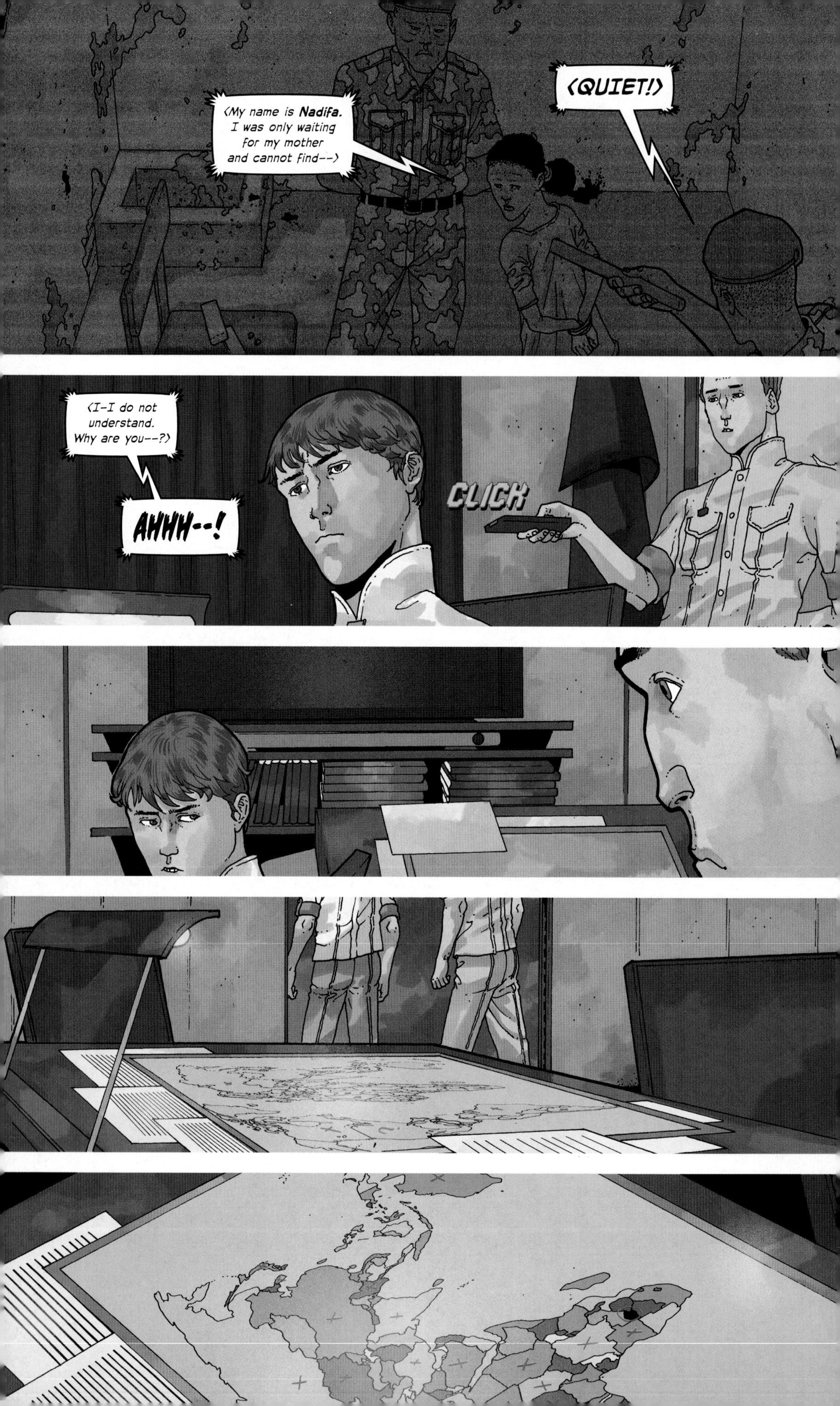

<My name is **Nadifa.** I was only waiting for my mother and cannot find-->
<QUIET!>
<I-I do not understand. Why are you--?>
AHHH--!
CLICK

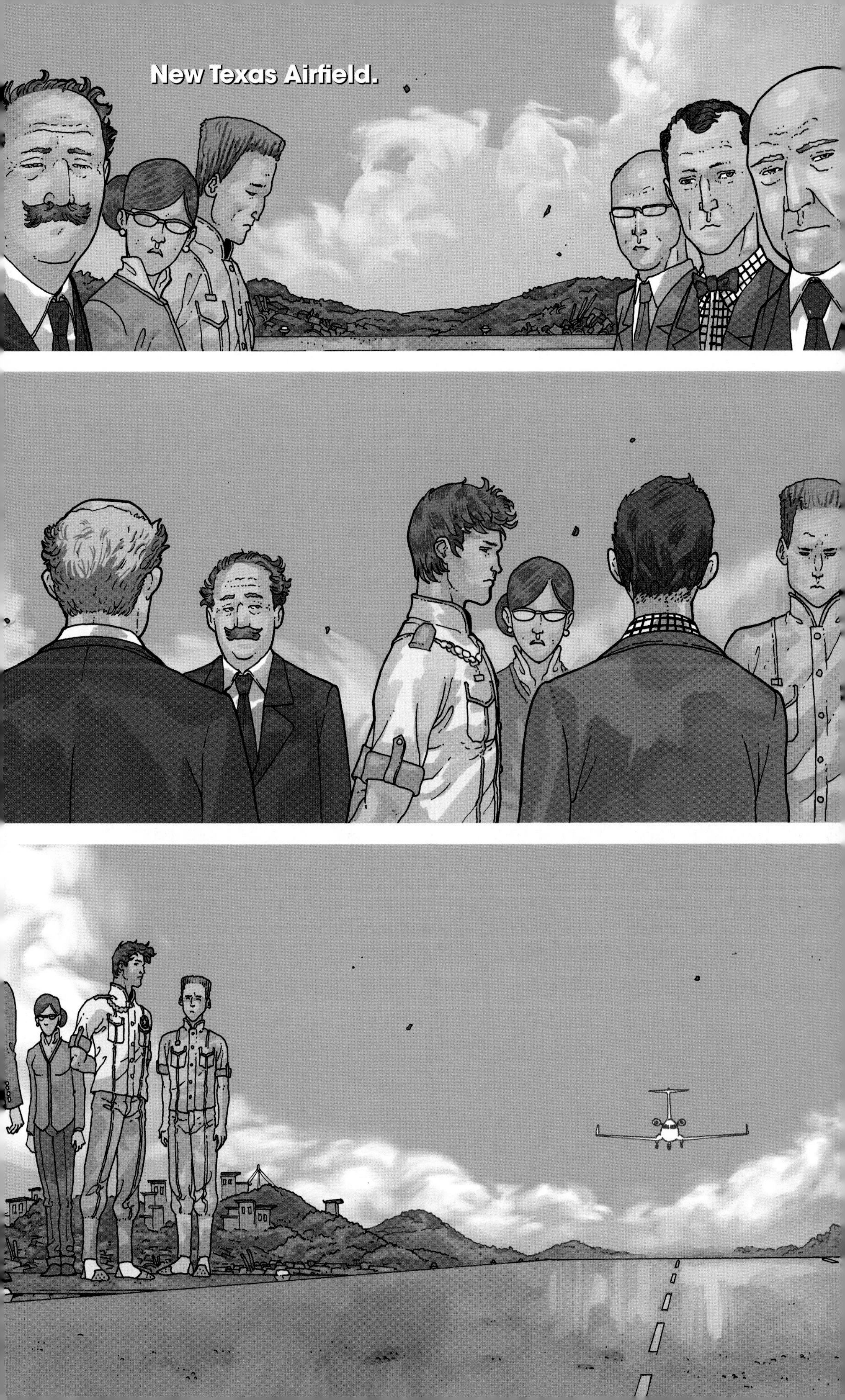
New Texas Airfield.

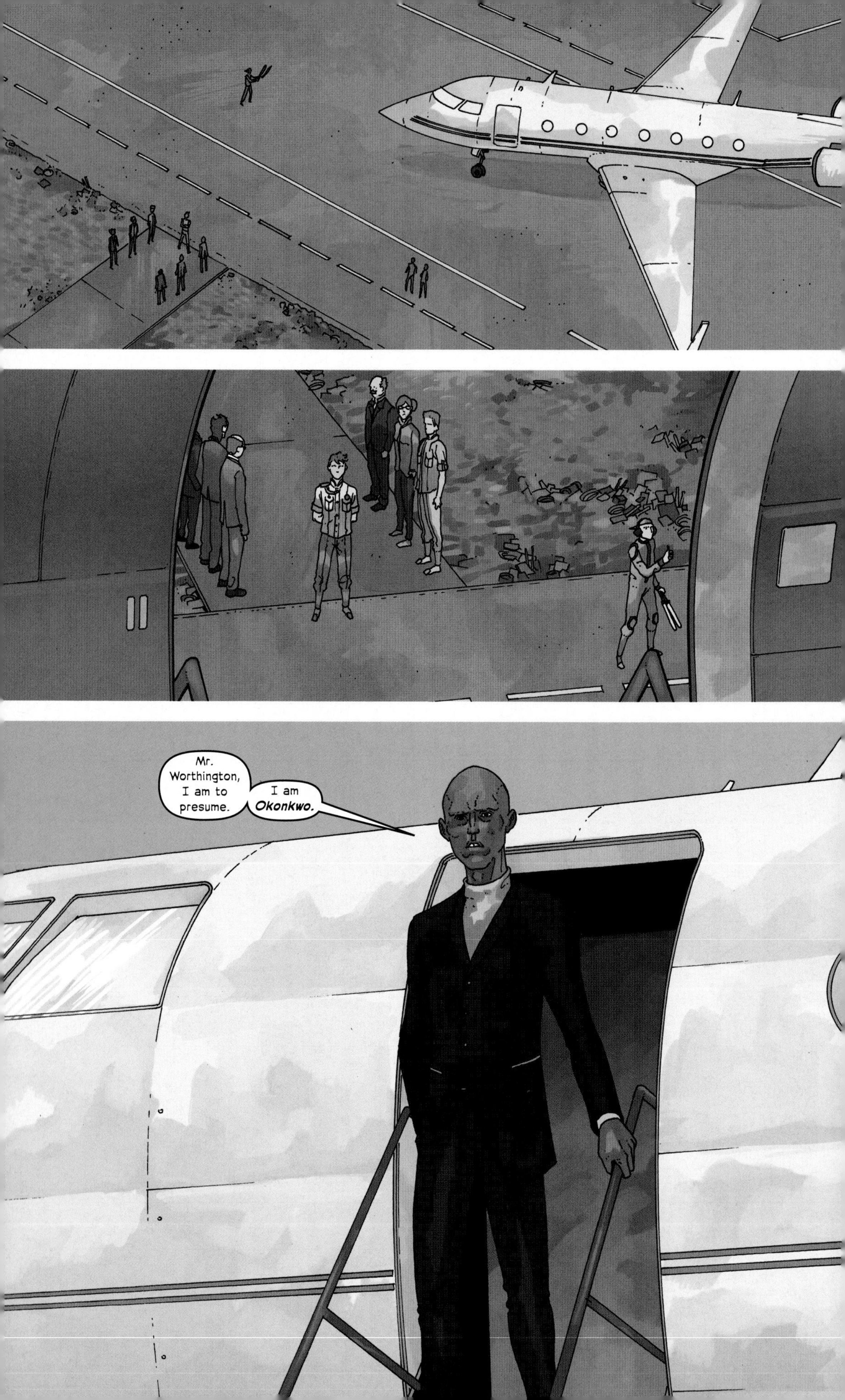
Mr. Worthington, I am to presume.
I am Okonkwo.

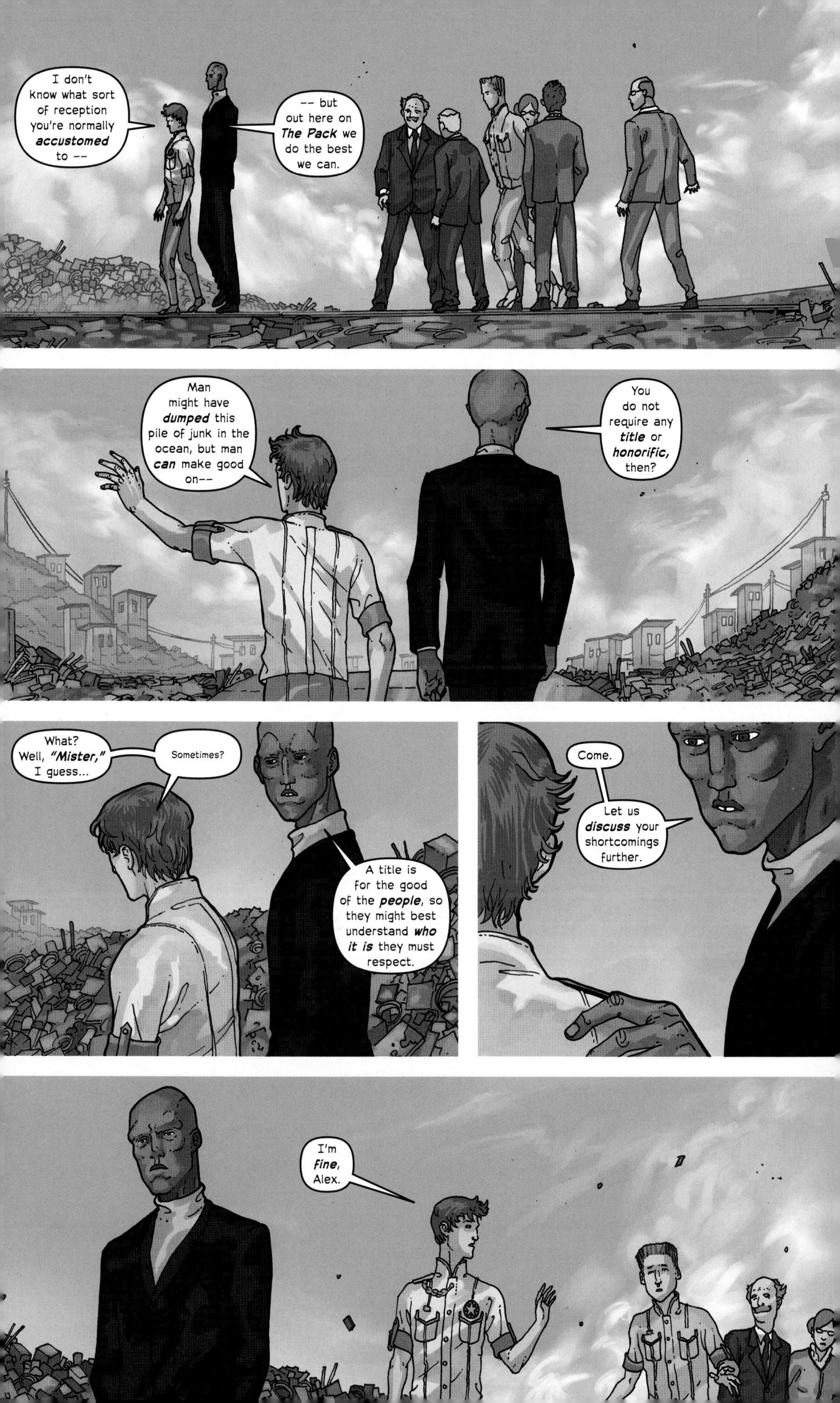
I don't know what sort of reception you're normally accustomed to --
-- but out here on The Pack we do the best we can.
Man might have dumped this pile of junk in the ocean, but man can make good on--
You do not require any title or honorific, then?
What? Well, "Mister," I guess...
Sometimes?
A title is for the good of the people, so they might best understand who it is they must respect.
Come.
Let us discuss your shortcomings further.
I'm fine, Alex.

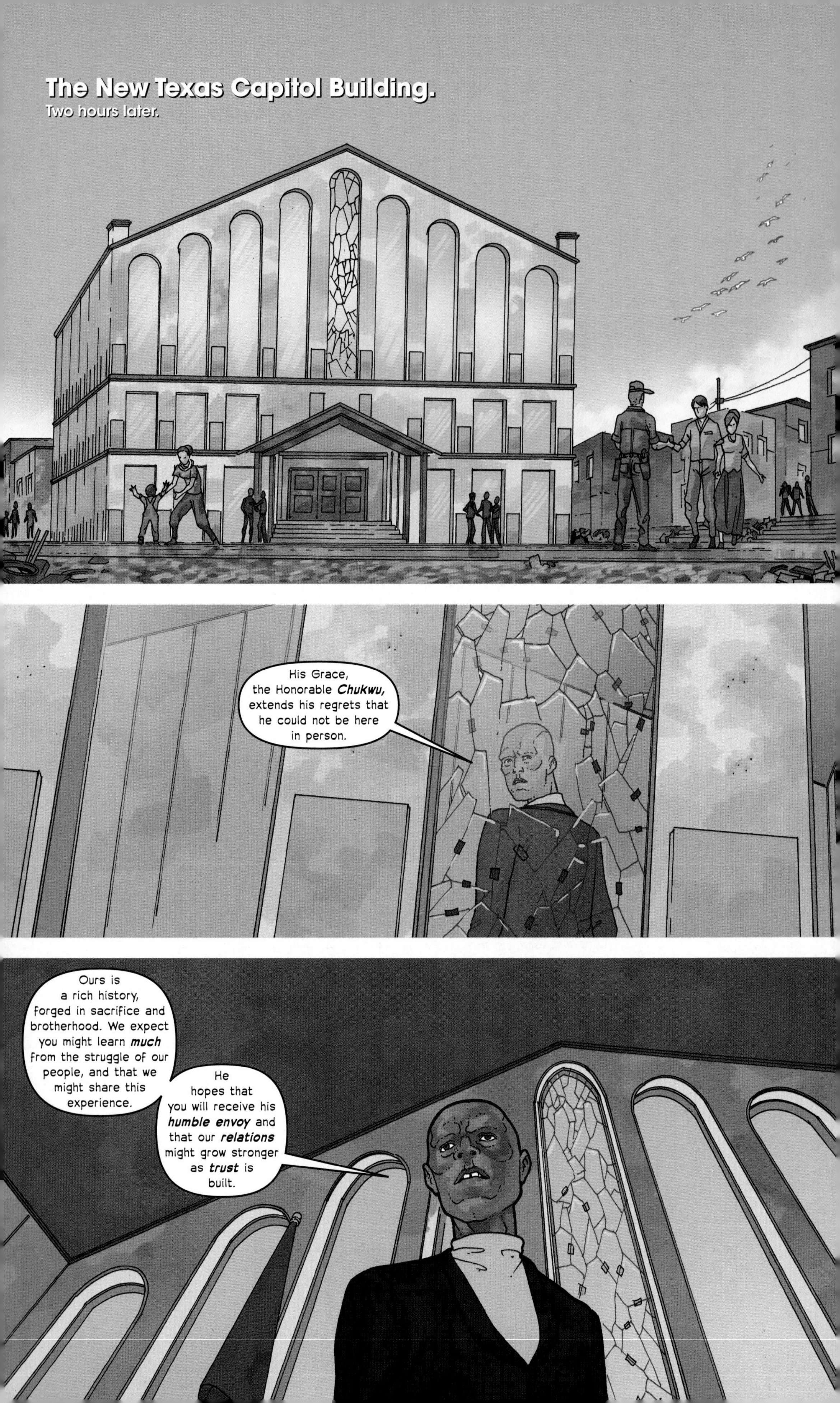
The New Texas Capitol Building.
Two hours later.
His Grace, the Honorable Chukwu, extends his regrets that he could not be here in person.
Ours is a rich history, forged in sacrifice and brotherhood. We expect you might learn much from the struggle of our people, and that we might share this experience.
He hopes that you will receive his humble envoy and that our relations might grow stronger as trust is built.

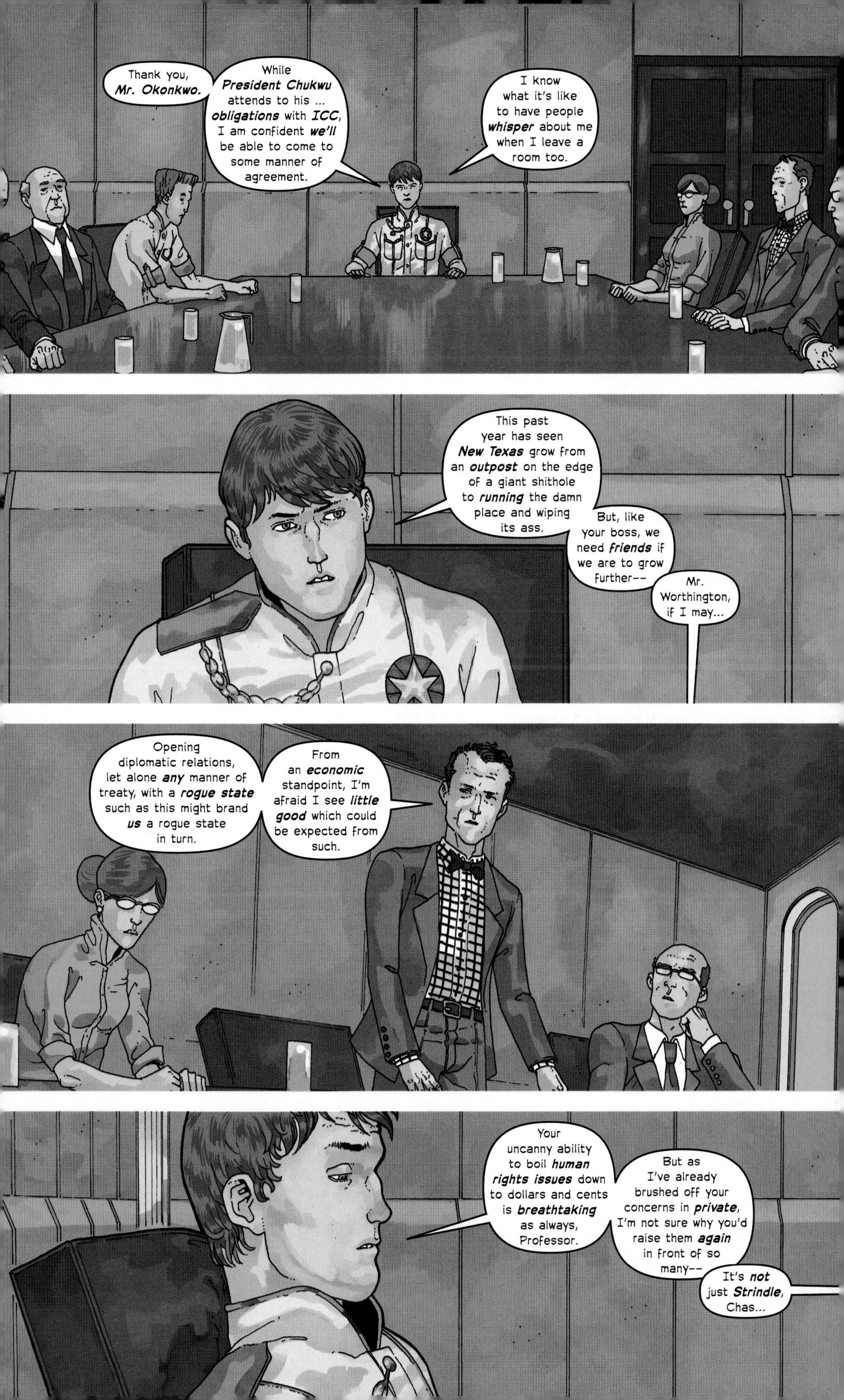
Thank you, Mr. Okonkwo.
While President Chukwu attends to his ... obligations with ICC, I am confident we'll be able to come to some manner of agreement.
I know what it's like to have people whisper about me when I leave a room too.
This past year has seen New Texas grow from an outpost on the edge of a giant shithole to running the damn place and wiping its ass.
But, like your boss, we need friends if we are to grow further--
Mr. Worthington, if I may...
Opening diplomatic relations, let alone any manner of treaty, with a rogue state such as this might brand us a rogue state in turn.
From an economic standpoint, I'm afraid I see little good which could be expected from such.
Your uncanny ability to boil human rights issues down to dollars and cents is breathtaking as always, Professor.
But as I've already brushed off your concerns in private, I'm not sure why you'd raise them again in front of so many--
It's not just Strindle, Chas...

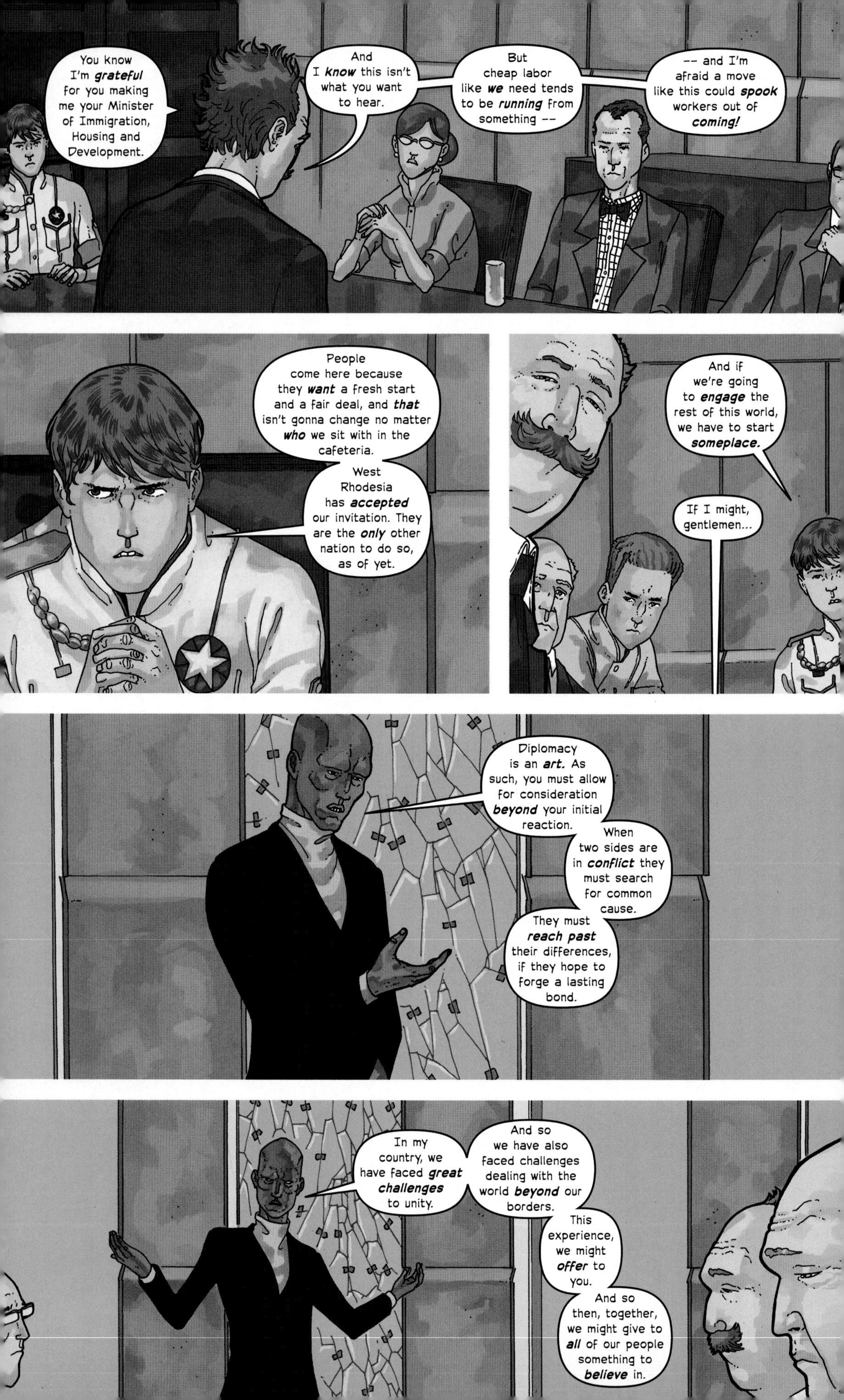

You know I'm ***grateful*** for you making me your Minister of Immigration, Housing and Development.
And I ***know*** this isn't what you want to hear.
But cheap labor like ***we*** need tends to be ***running*** from something --
-- and I'm afraid a move like this could ***spook*** workers out of ***coming!***
People come here because they ***want*** a fresh start and a fair deal, and ***that*** isn't gonna change no matter ***who*** we sit with in the cafeteria.
West Rhodesia has ***accepted*** our invitation. They are the ***only*** other nation to do so, as of yet.
And if we're going to ***engage*** the rest of this world, we have to start ***someplace.***
If I might, gentlemen...
Diplomacy is an ***art.*** As such, you must allow for consideration ***beyond*** your initial reaction.
When two sides are in ***conflict*** they must search for common cause.
They must ***reach past*** their differences, if they hope to forge a lasting bond.
In my country, we have faced ***great challenges*** to unity.
And so we have also faced challenges dealing with the world ***beyond*** our borders.
This experience, we might ***offer*** to you.
And so then, together, we might give to ***all*** of our people something to ***believe*** in.

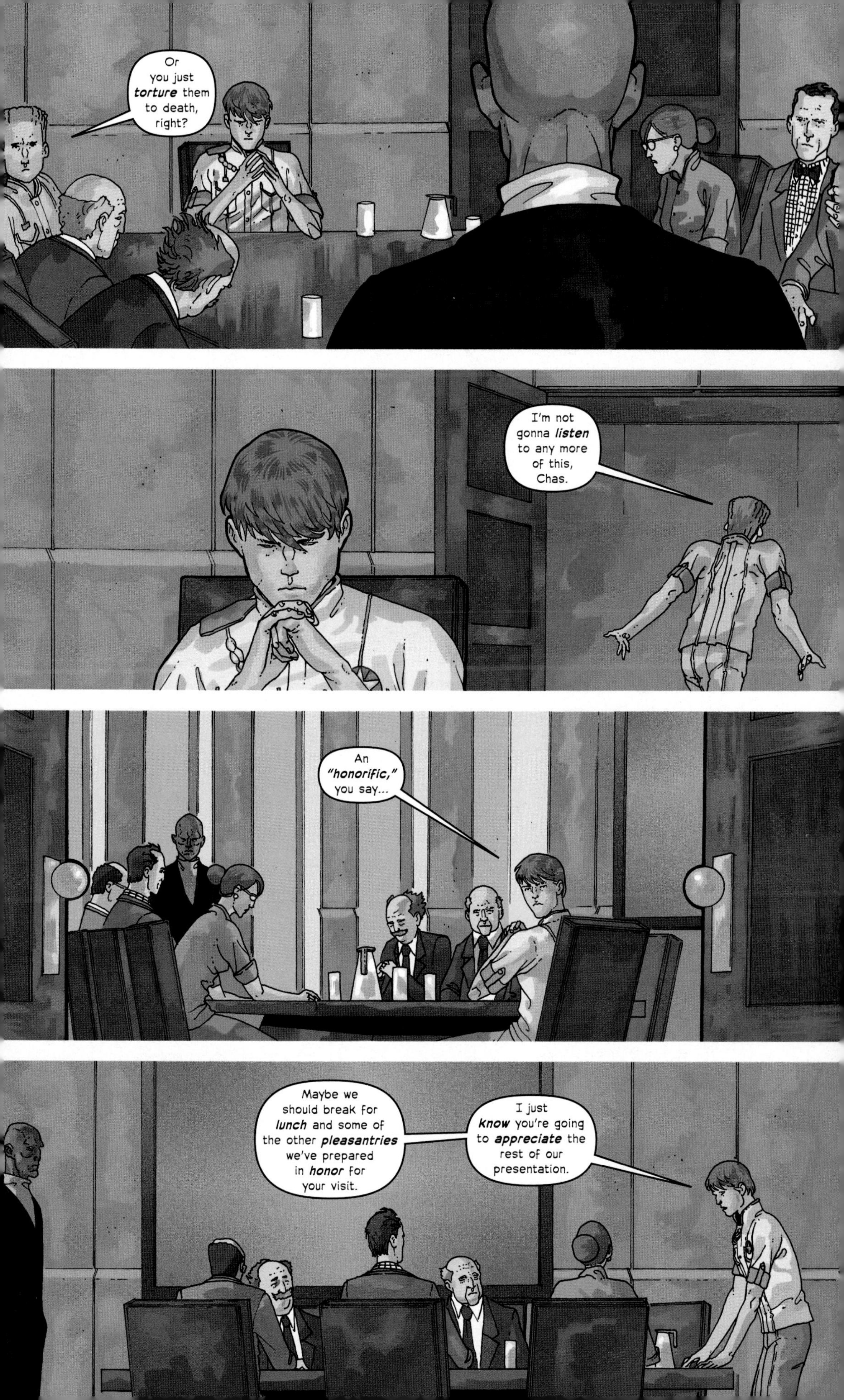

Or you just torture them to death, right?
I'm not gonna listen to any more of this, Chas.
An "honorific," you say...
Maybe we should break for lunch and some of the other pleasantries we've prepared in honor for your visit.
I just know you're going to appreciate the rest of our presentation.

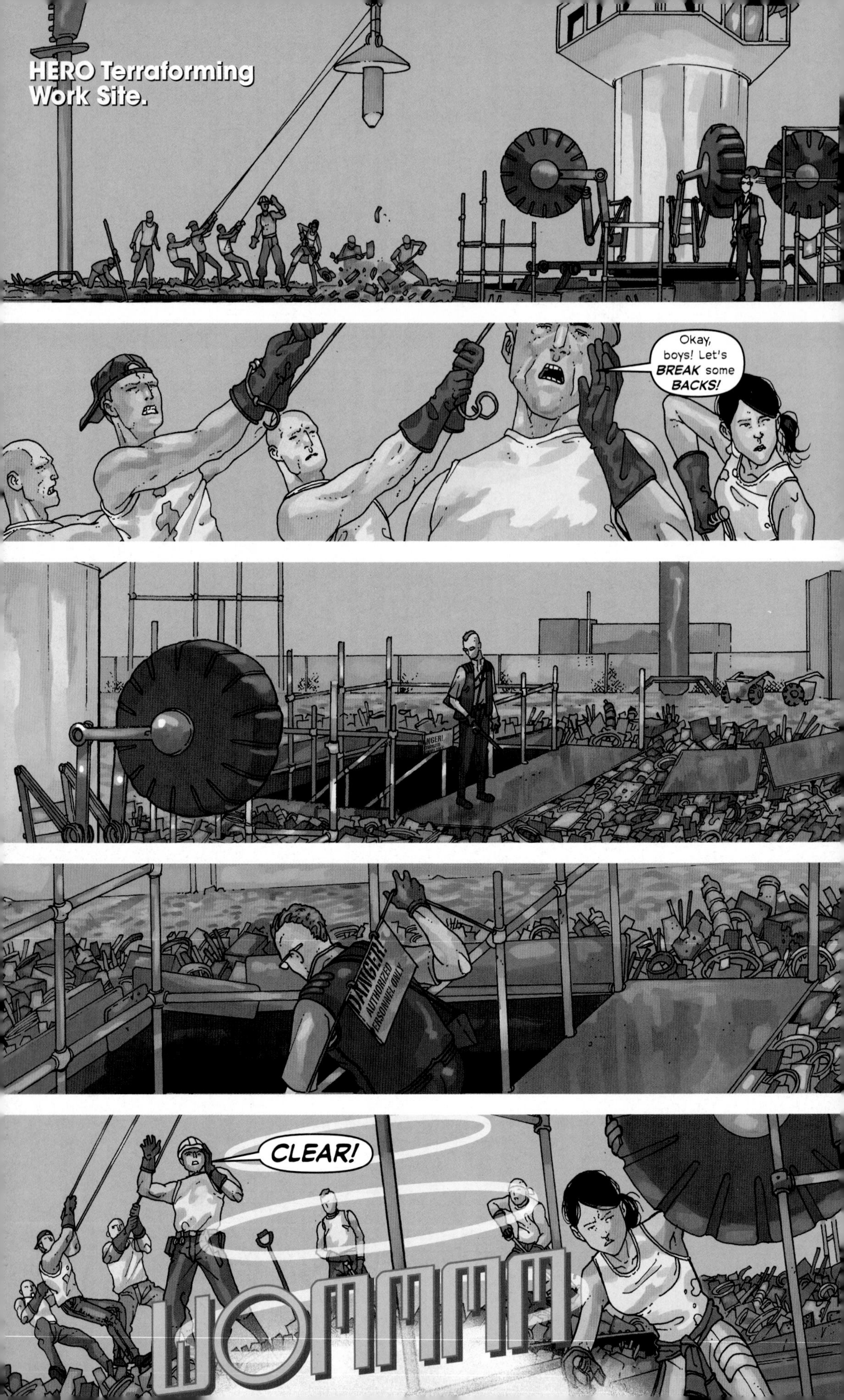
HERO Terraforming
Work Site.
Okay, boys! Let's BREAK some BACKS!
DANGER! AUTHORIZED PERSONNEL ONLY
CLEAR!
WOMMMM

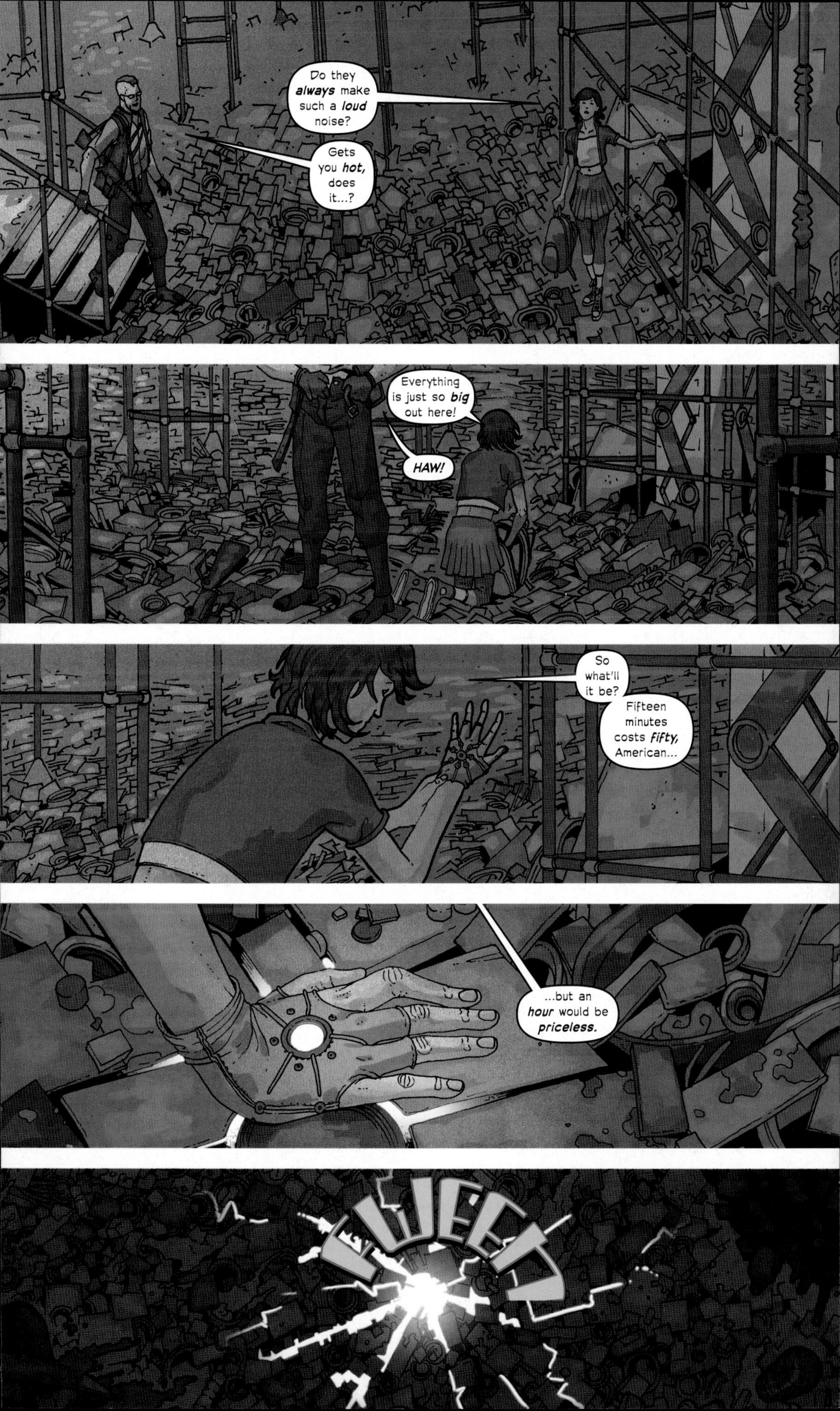
Do they *always* make such a *loud* noise?
Gets you *hot,* does it...?
Everything is just so *big* out here!
HAW!
So what'll it be?
Fifteen minutes costs *fifty,* American...
...but an *hour* would be *priceless.*
FWEEP

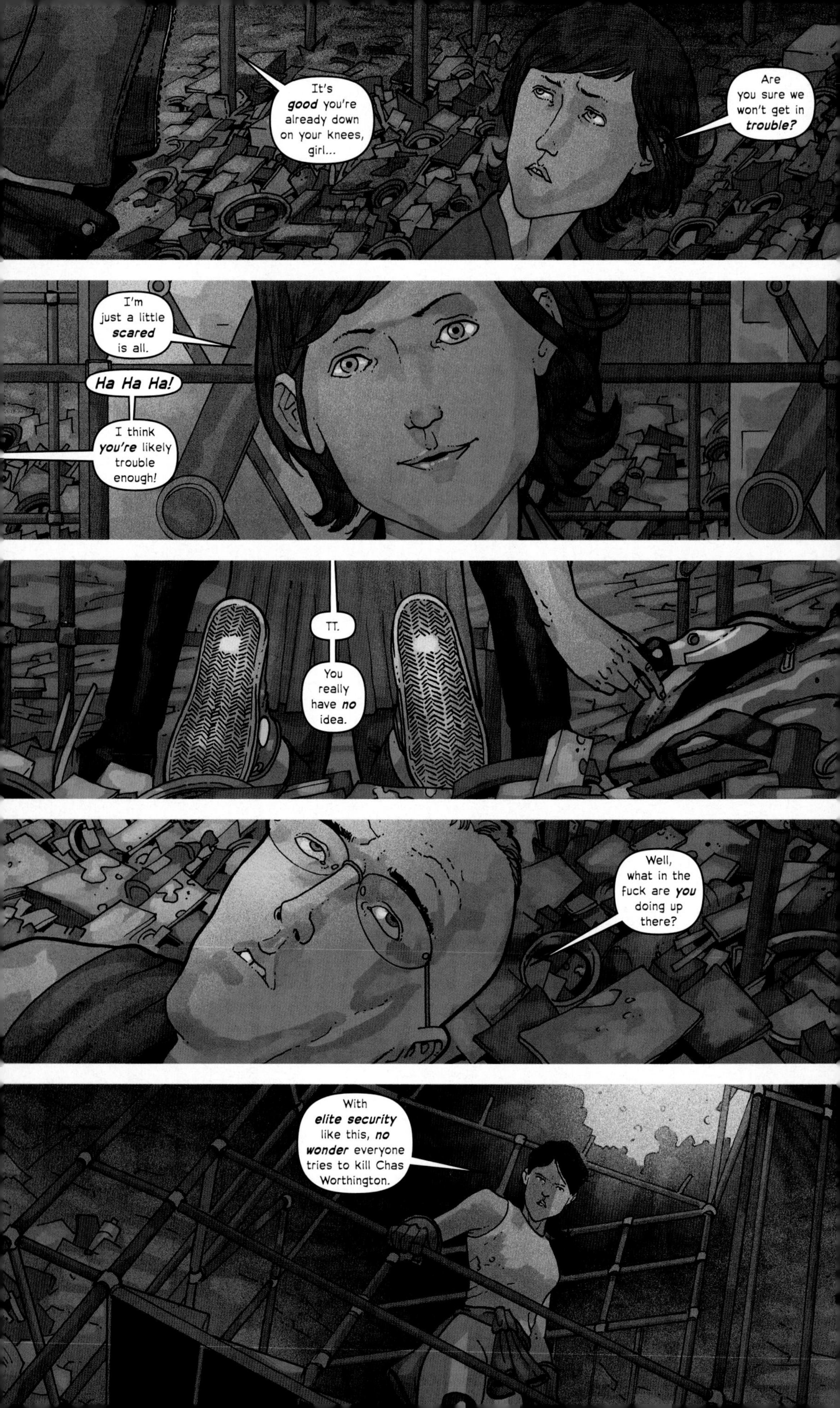

It's *good* you're already down on your knees, girl...
Are you sure we won't get in *trouble?*
I'm just a little *scared* is all.
Ha Ha Ha!
I think *you're* likely trouble enough!
TT.
You really have *no* idea.
Well, what in the fuck are *you* doing up there?
With *elite security* like this, *no wonder* everyone tries to kill Chas Worthington.

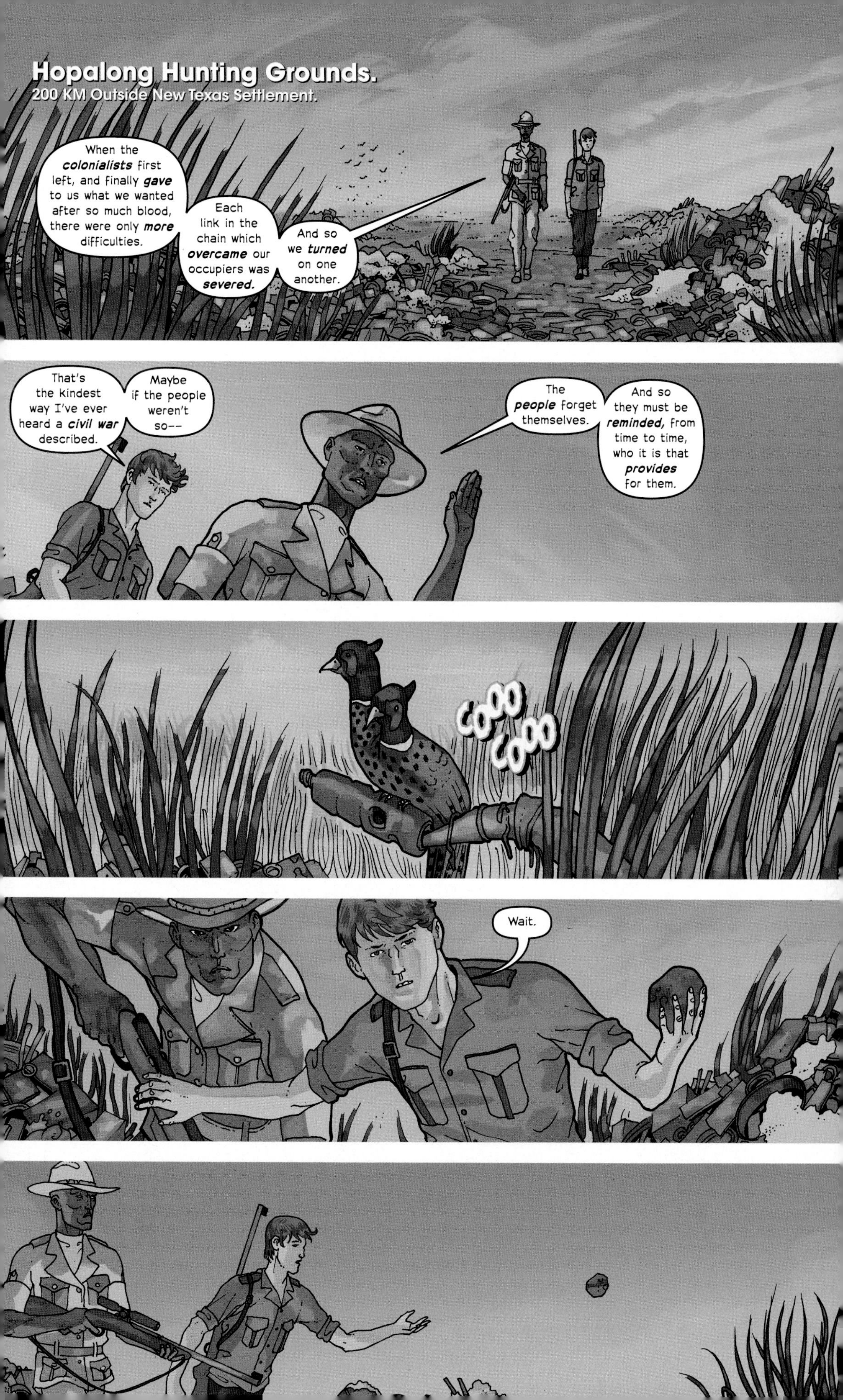
Hopalong Hunting Grounds.
200 KM Outside New Texas Settlement.
When the *colonialists* first left, and finally *gave* to us what we wanted after so much blood, there were only *more* difficulties.
Each link in the chain which *overcame* our occupiers was *severed.*
And so we *turned* on one another.
That's the kindest way I've ever heard a *civil war* described.
Maybe if the people weren't so--
The *people* forget themselves.
And so they must be *reminded,* from time to time, who it is that *provides* for them.
COOO
COOO
Wait.

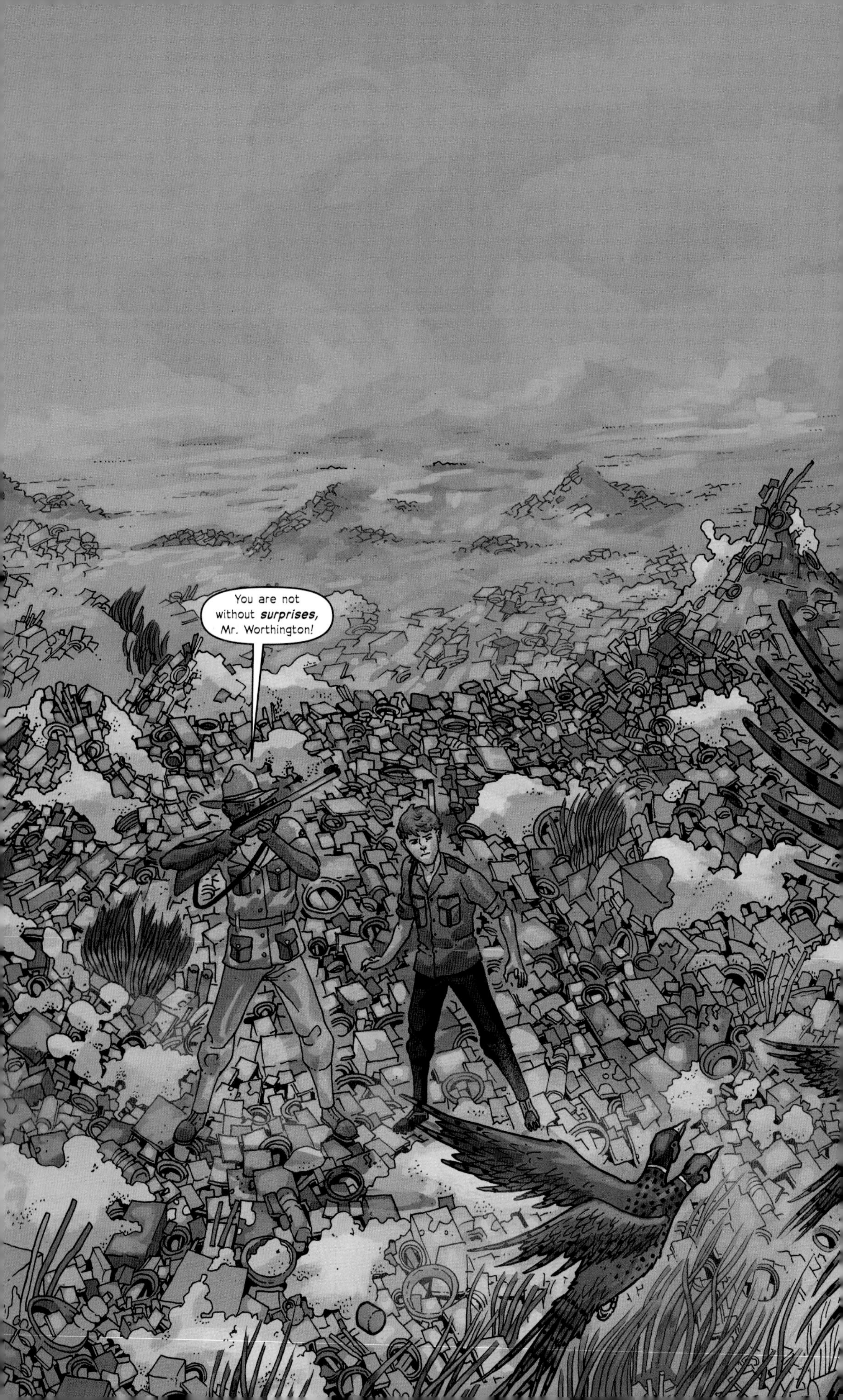
You are not without *surprises,* Mr. Worthington!

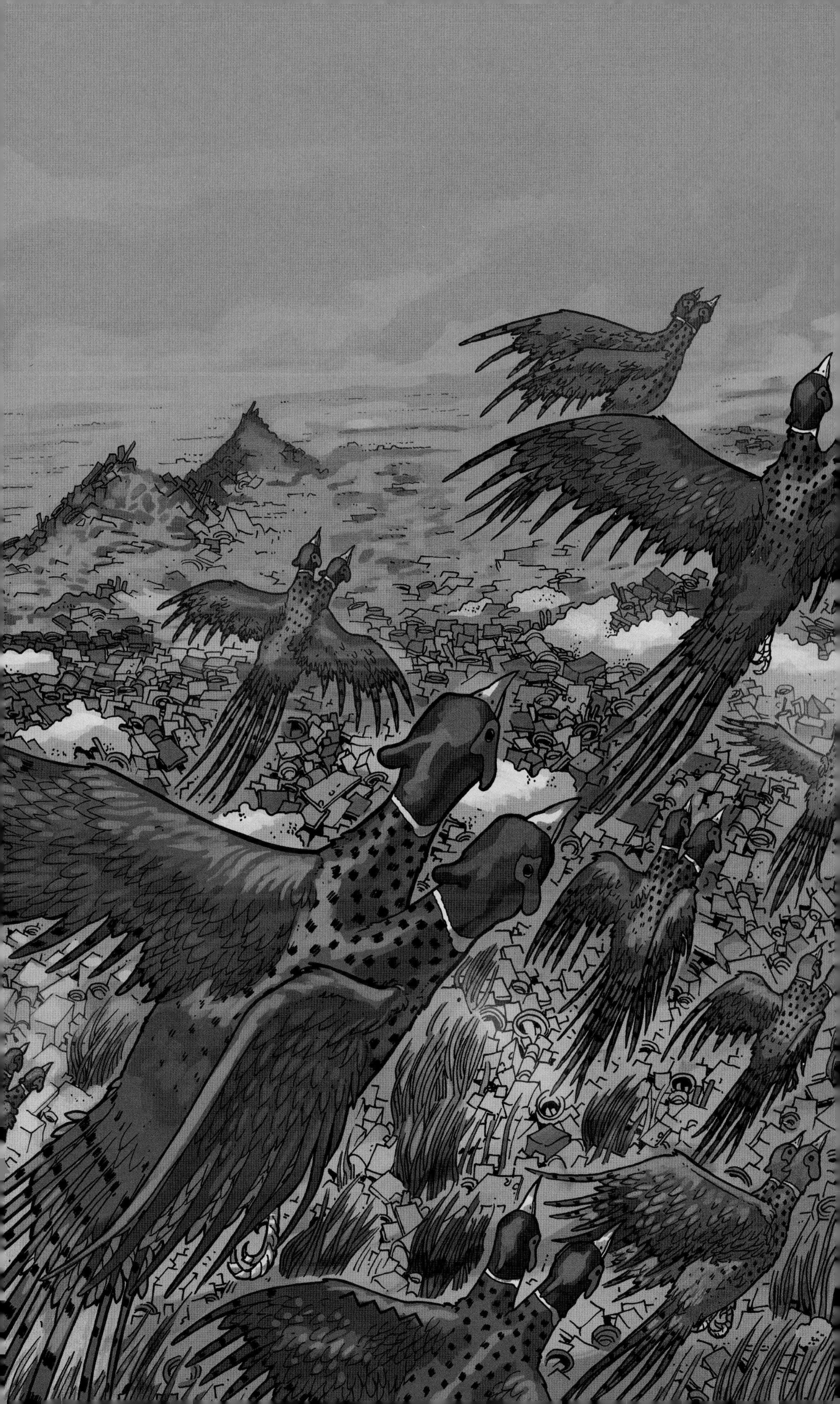

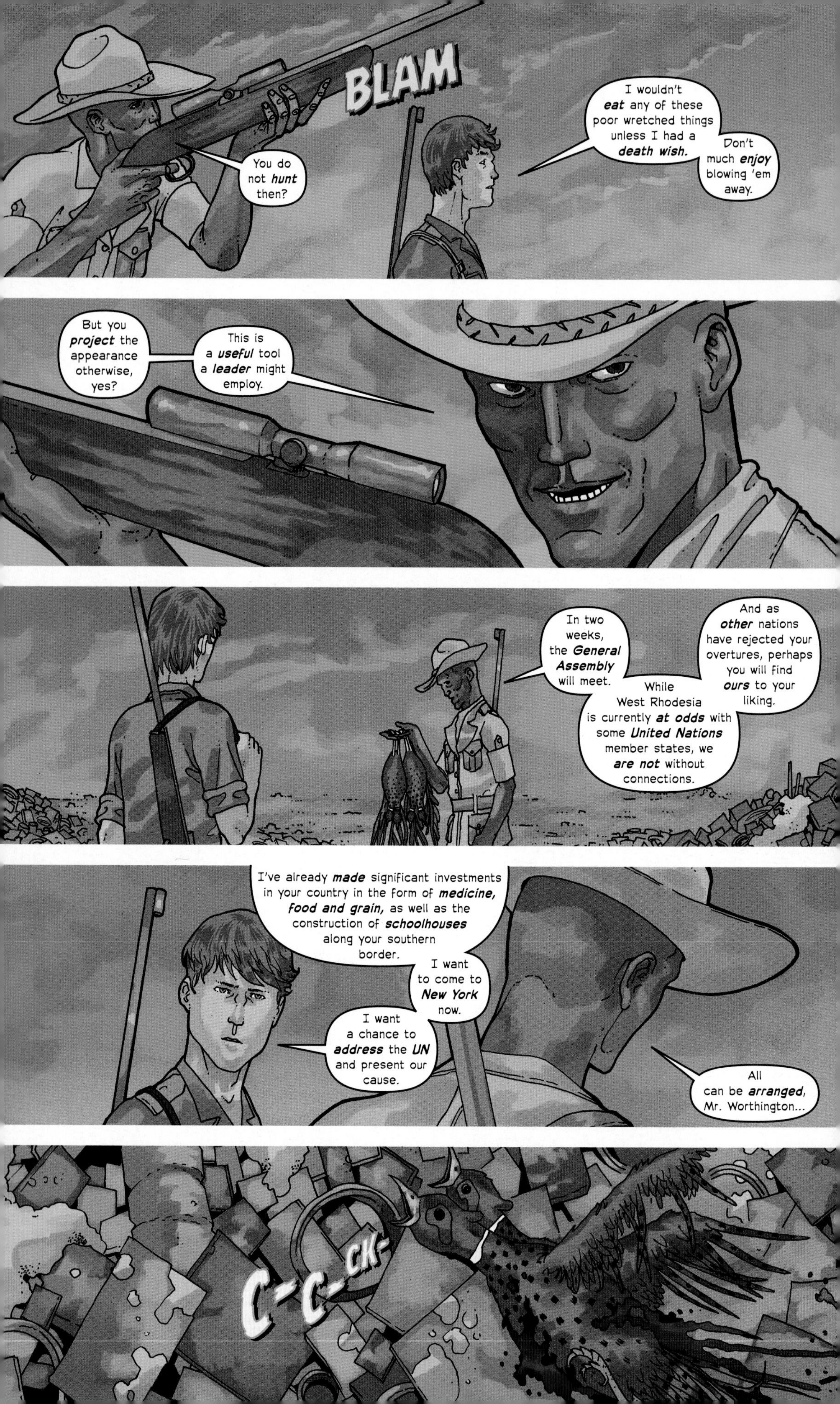
BLAM
You do not *hunt* then?
I wouldn't *eat* any of these poor wretched things unless I had a *death wish.*
Don't much *enjoy* blowing 'em away.
But you *project* the appearance otherwise, yes?
This is a *useful* tool a *leader* might employ.
In two weeks, the *General Assembly* will meet.
While West Rhodesia is currently *at odds* with some *United Nations* member states, we *are not* without connections.
And as *other* nations have rejected your overtures, perhaps you will find *ours* to your liking.
I've already *made* significant investments in your country in the form of *medicine, food and grain,* as well as the construction of *schoolhouses* along your southern border.
I want to come to *New York* now.
I want a chance to *address* the *UN* and present our cause.
All can be *arranged,* Mr. Worthington...
C-C-CK-

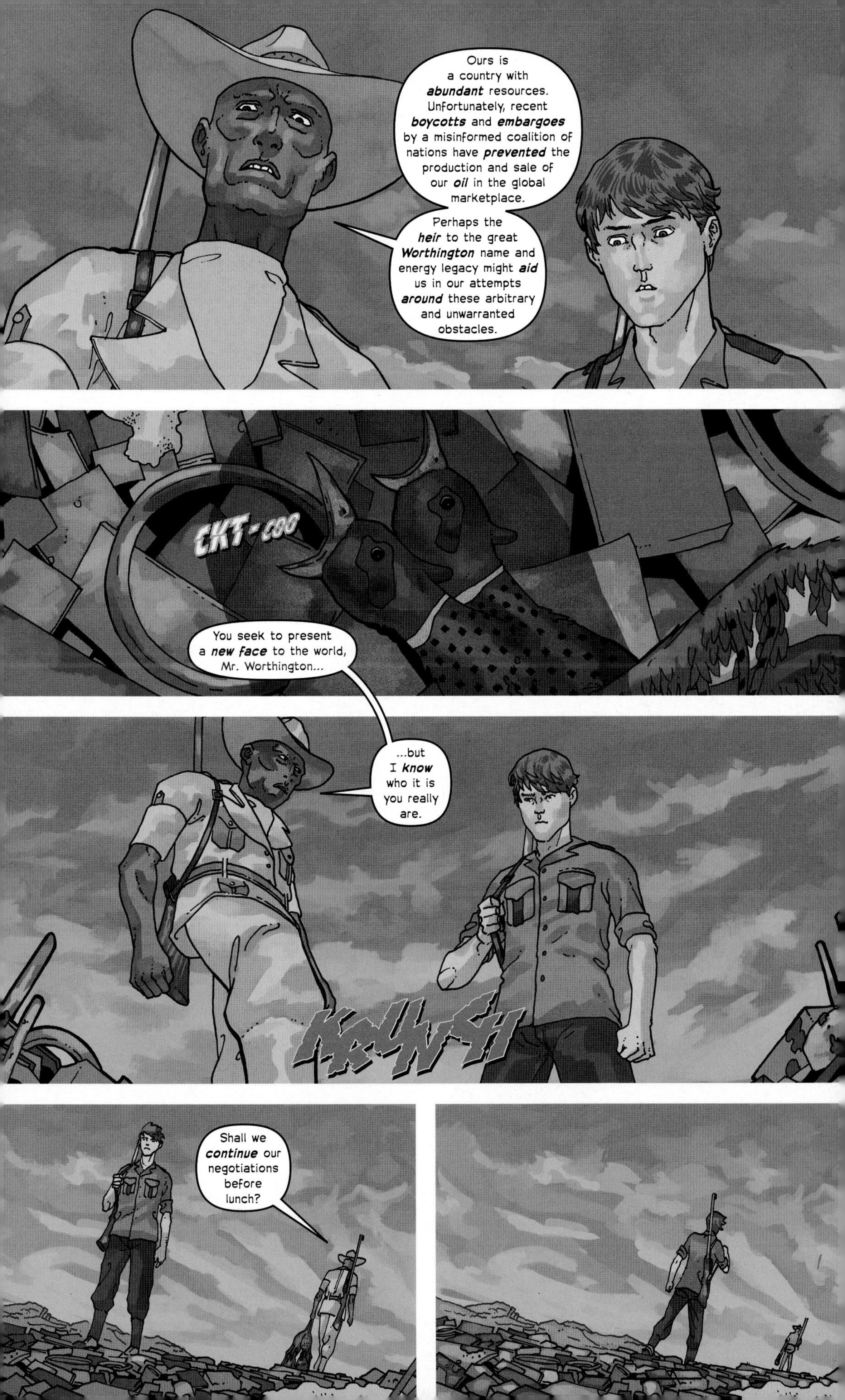
Ours is a country with abundant resources. Unfortunately, recent boycotts and embargoes by a misinformed coalition of nations have prevented the production and sale of our oil in the global marketplace.
Perhaps the heir to the great Worthington name and energy legacy might aid us in our attempts around these arbitrary and unwarranted obstacles.
CKT-COO
You seek to present a new face to the world, Mr. Worthington...
...but I know who it is you really are.
KRUNCH
Shall we continue our negotiations before lunch?

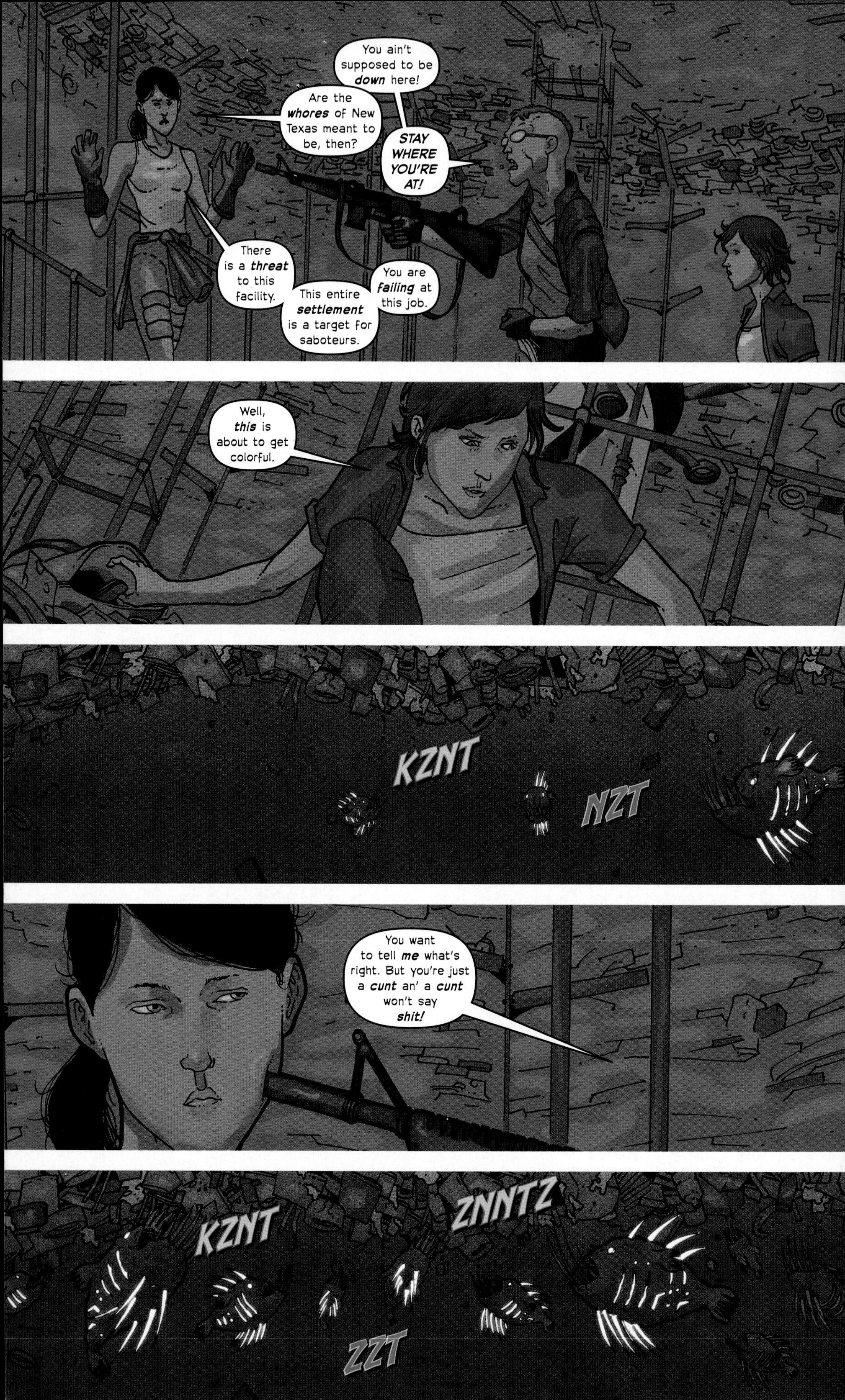
You ain't supposed to be down here!
Are the whores of New Texas meant to be, then?
STAY WHERE YOU'RE AT!
There is a threat to this facility.
This entire settlement is a target for saboteurs.
You are failing at this job.
Well, this is about to get colorful.
KZNT
NZT
You want to tell me what's right. But you're just a cunt an' a cunt won't say shit!
KZNT
ZNNTZ
ZZT

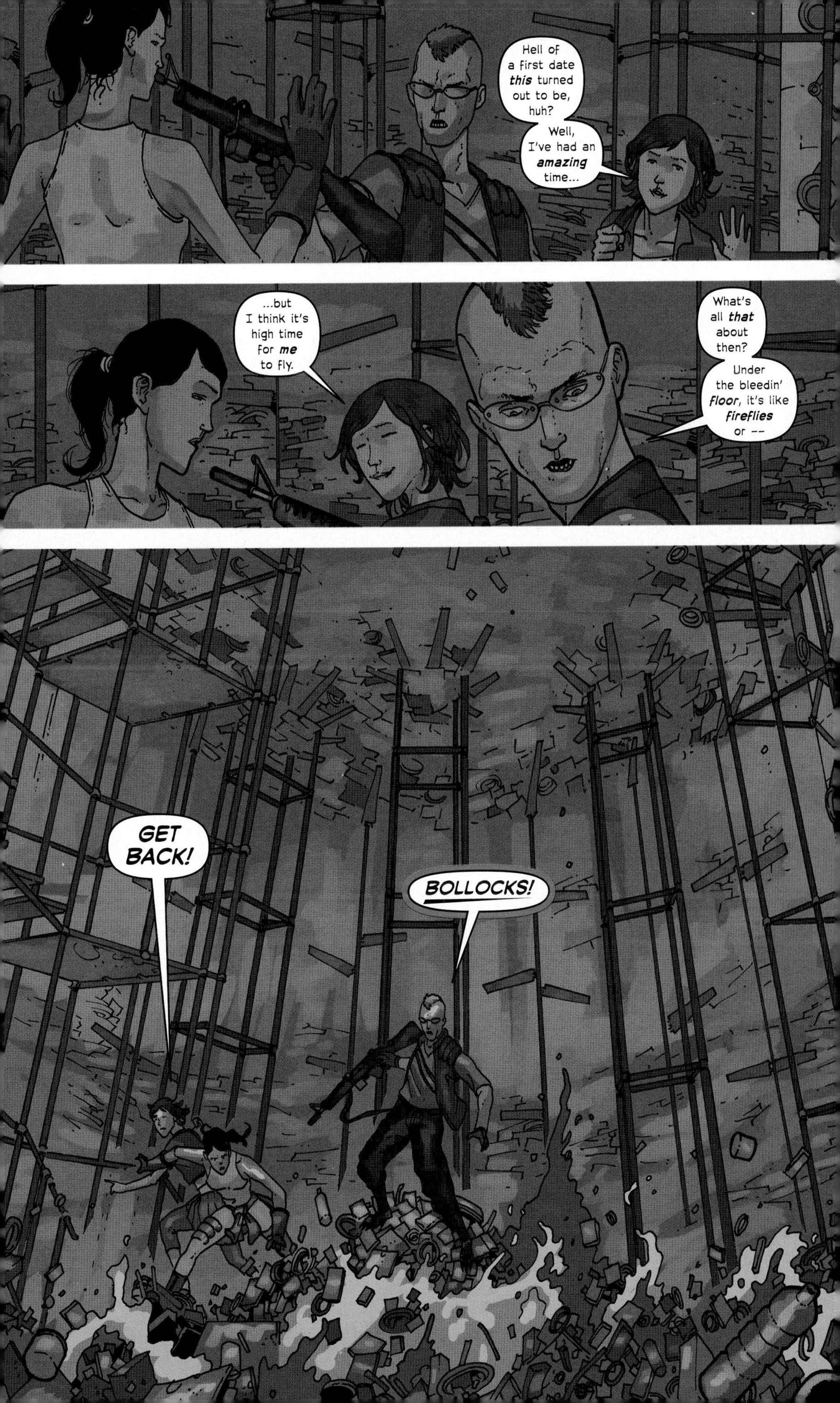
Hell of a first date **this** turned out to be, huh?
Well, I've had an **amazing** time...
...but I think it's high time for **me** to fly.
What's all **that** about then?
Under the bleedin' **floor**, it's like **fireflies** or --
GET BACK!
BOLLOCKS!

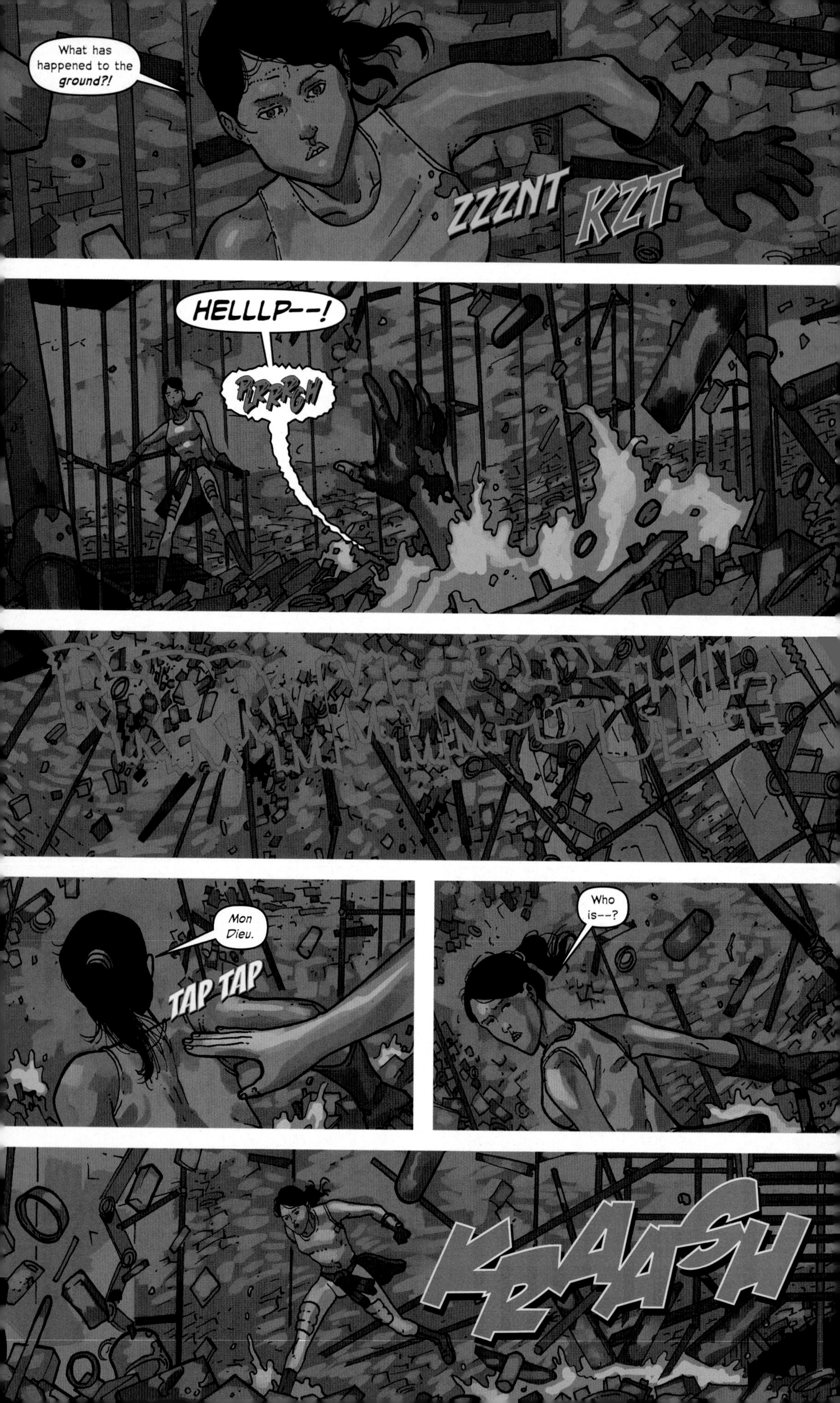
What has happened to the *ground?!*
ZZZNT
KZT
HELLLP--!
PLRRRGH
Mon Dieu.
TAP TAP
Who is--?
KRAATSH

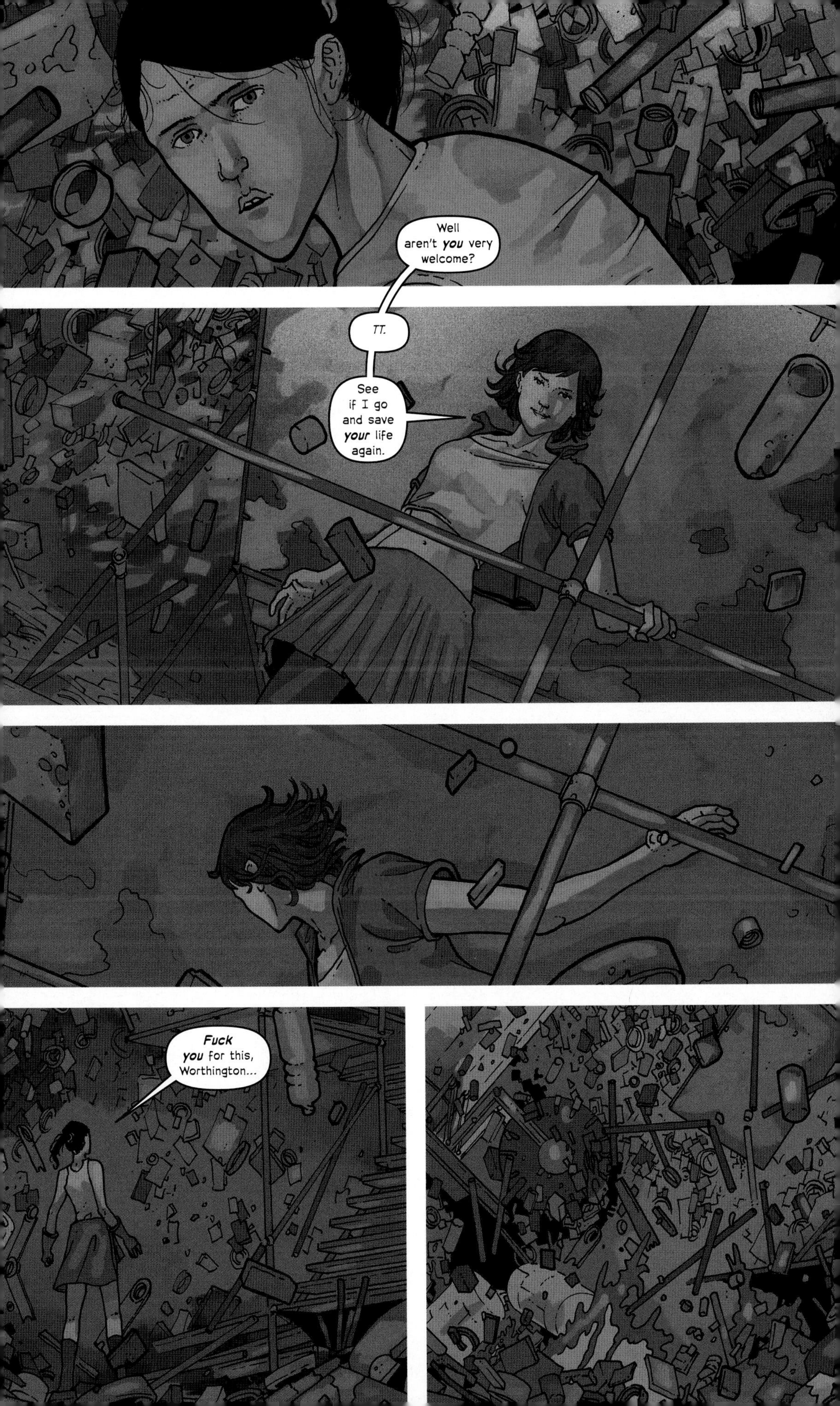
Well aren't *you* very welcome?
TT.
See if I go and save *your* life again.
Fuck you for this, Worthington...

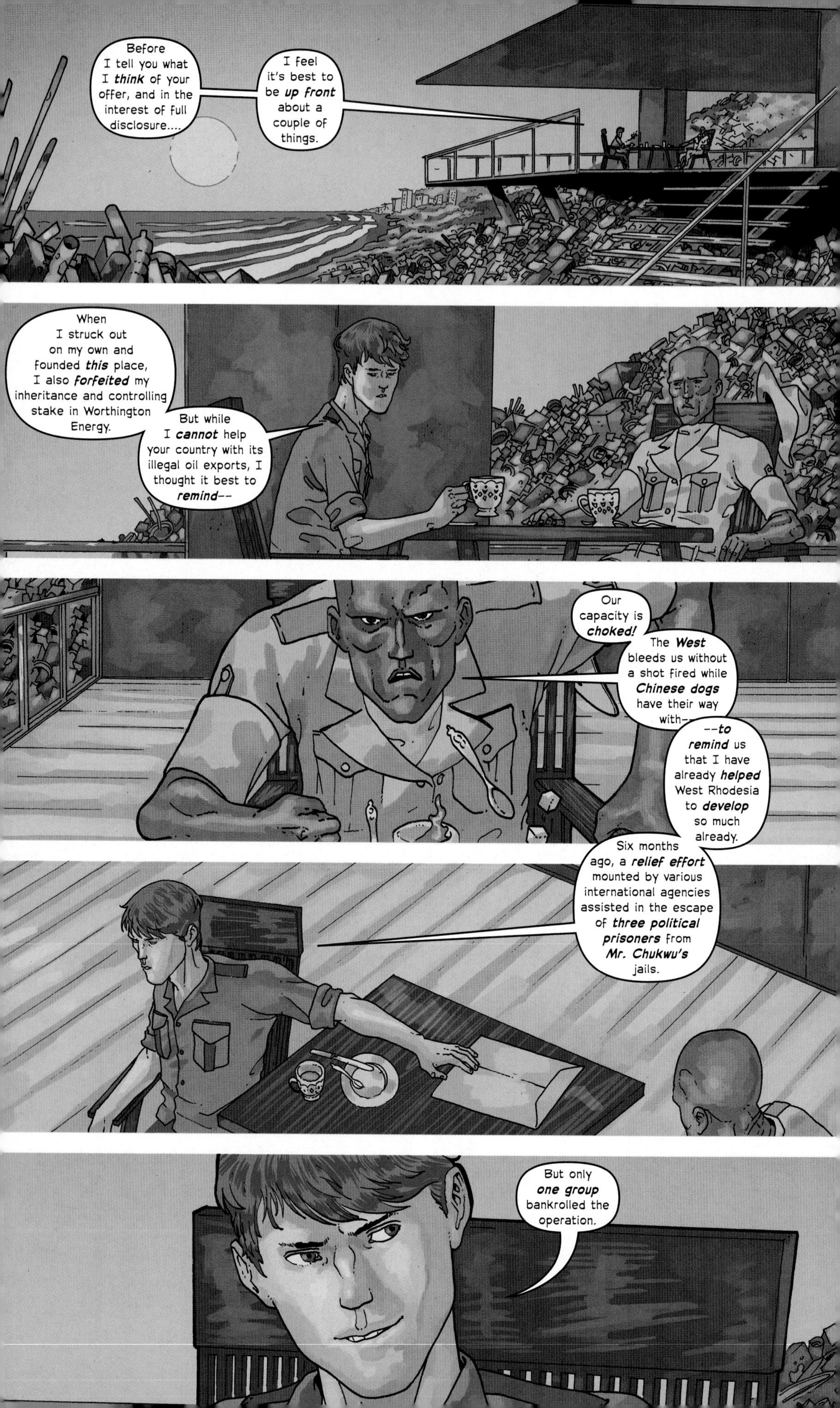

Before I tell you what I *think* of your offer, and in the interest of full disclosure....
I feel it's best to be *up front* about a couple of things.
When I struck out on my own and founded *this* place, I also *forfeited* my inheritance and controlling stake in Worthington Energy.
But while I *cannot* help your country with its illegal oil exports, I thought it best to *remind*--
Our capacity is *choked!*
The *West* bleeds us without a shot fired while *Chinese dogs* have their way with--
--*to remind* us that I have already *helped* West Rhodesia to *develop* so much already.
Six months ago, a *relief effort* mounted by various international agencies assisted in the escape of *three political prisoners* from *Mr. Chukwu's* jails.
But only *one group* bankrolled the operation.

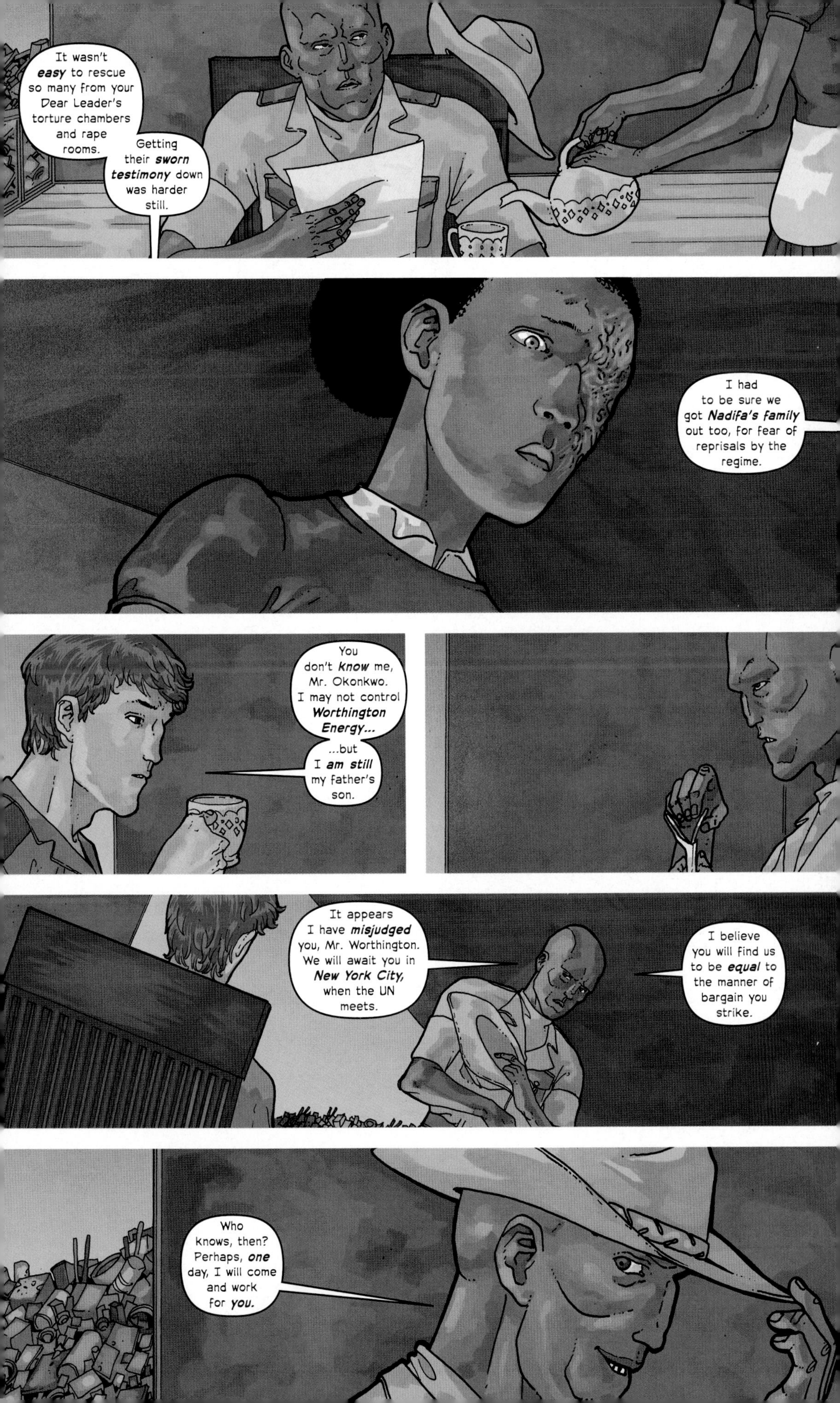
It wasn't easy to rescue so many from your Dear Leader's torture chambers and rape rooms.
Getting their sworn testimony down was harder still.
I had to be sure we got Nadifa's family out too, for fear of reprisals by the regime.
You don't know me, Mr. Okonkwo. I may not control Worthington Energy...
...but I am still my father's son.
It appears I have misjudged you, Mr. Worthington. We will await you in New York City, when the UN meets.
I believe you will find us to be equal to the manner of bargain you strike.
Who knows, then? Perhaps, one day, I will come and work for you.

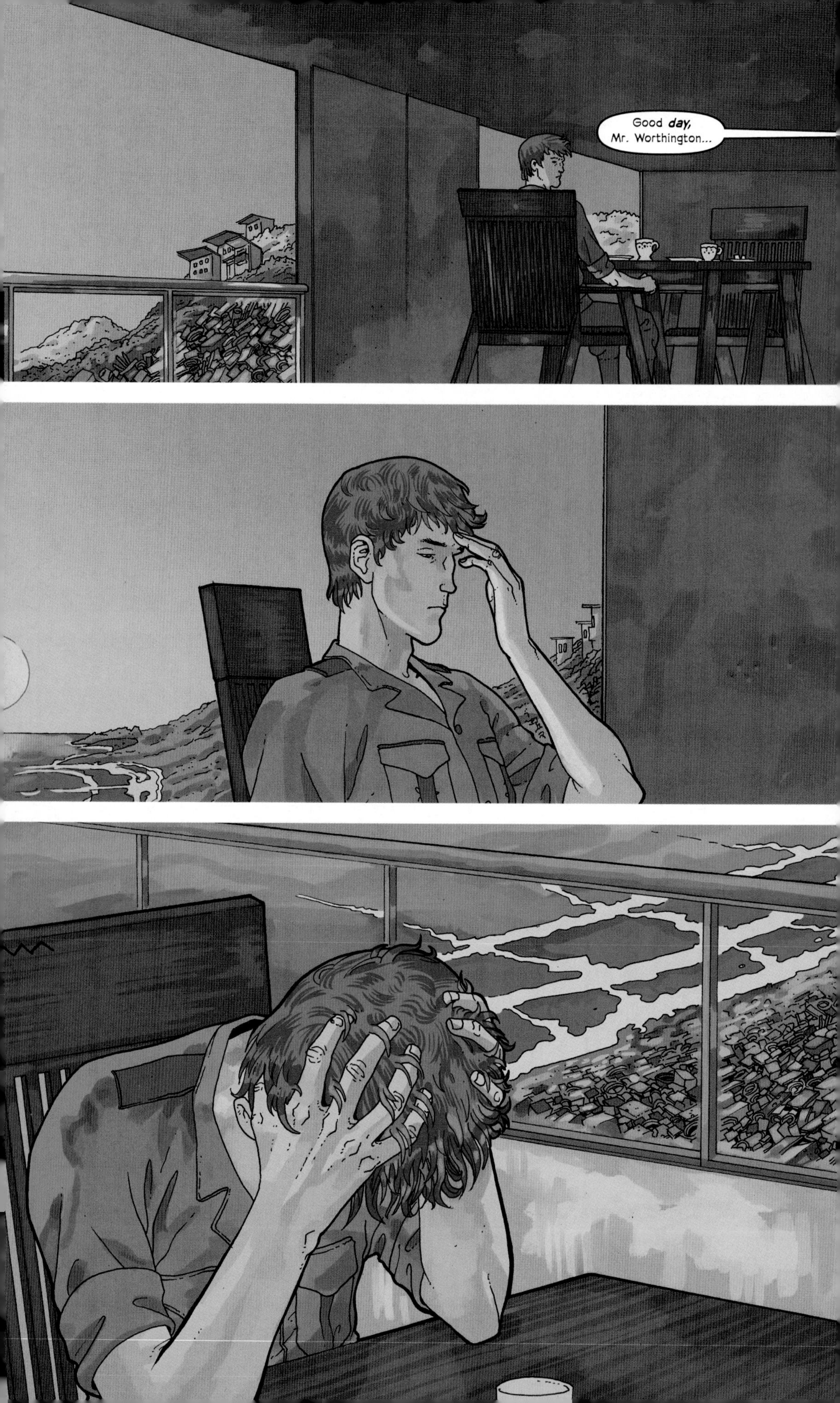
Good day, Mr. Worthington...

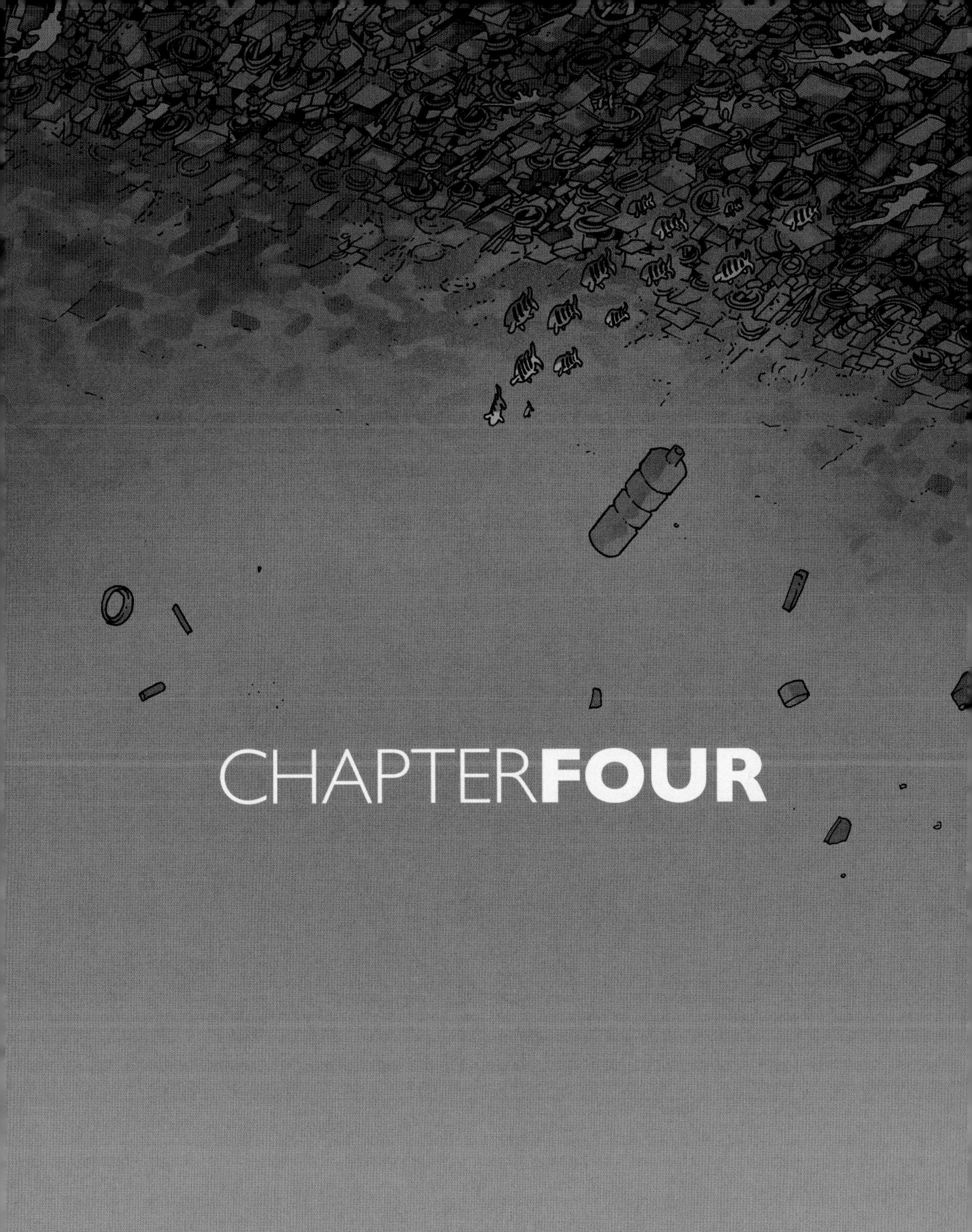

CHAPTER**FOUR**

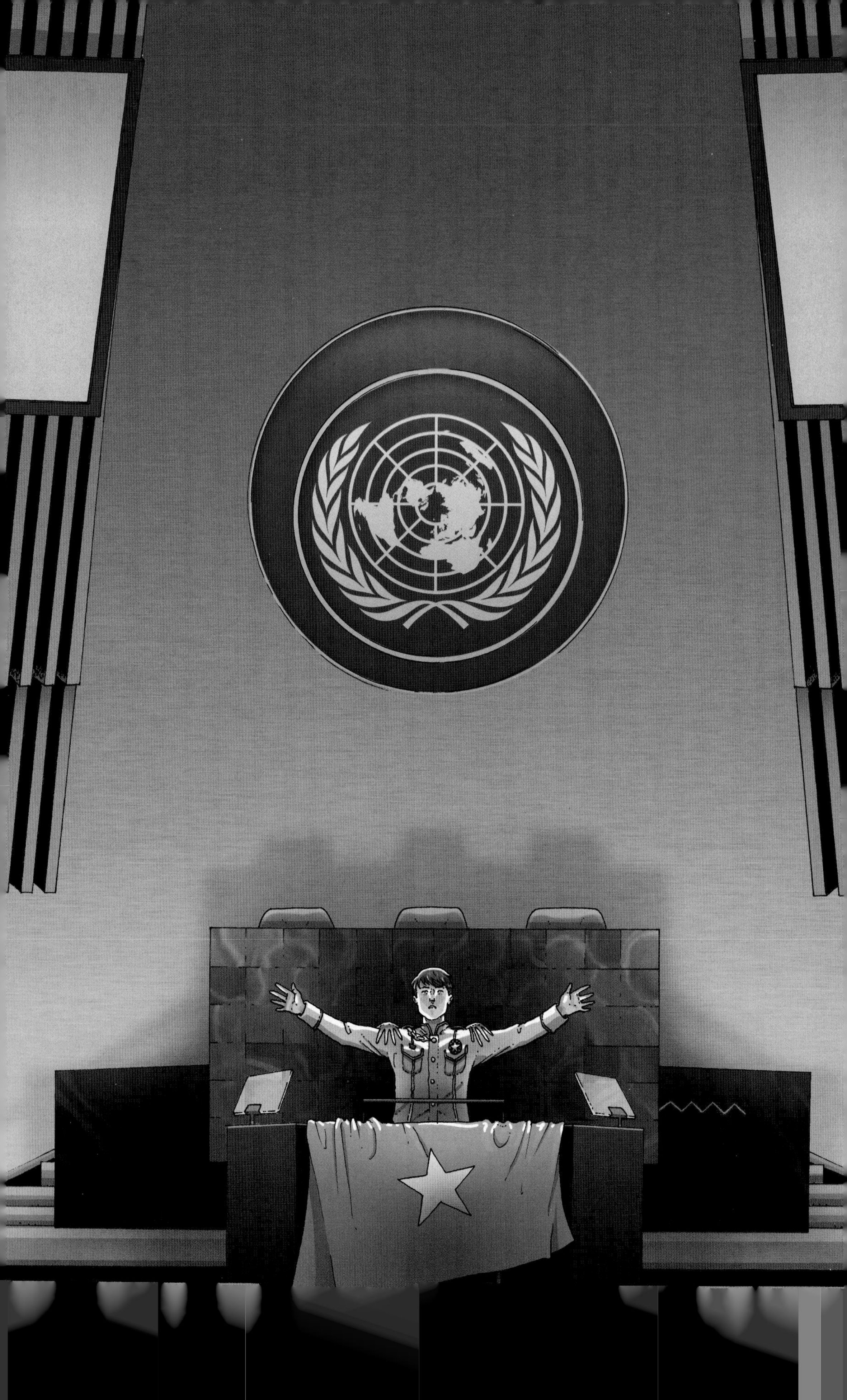

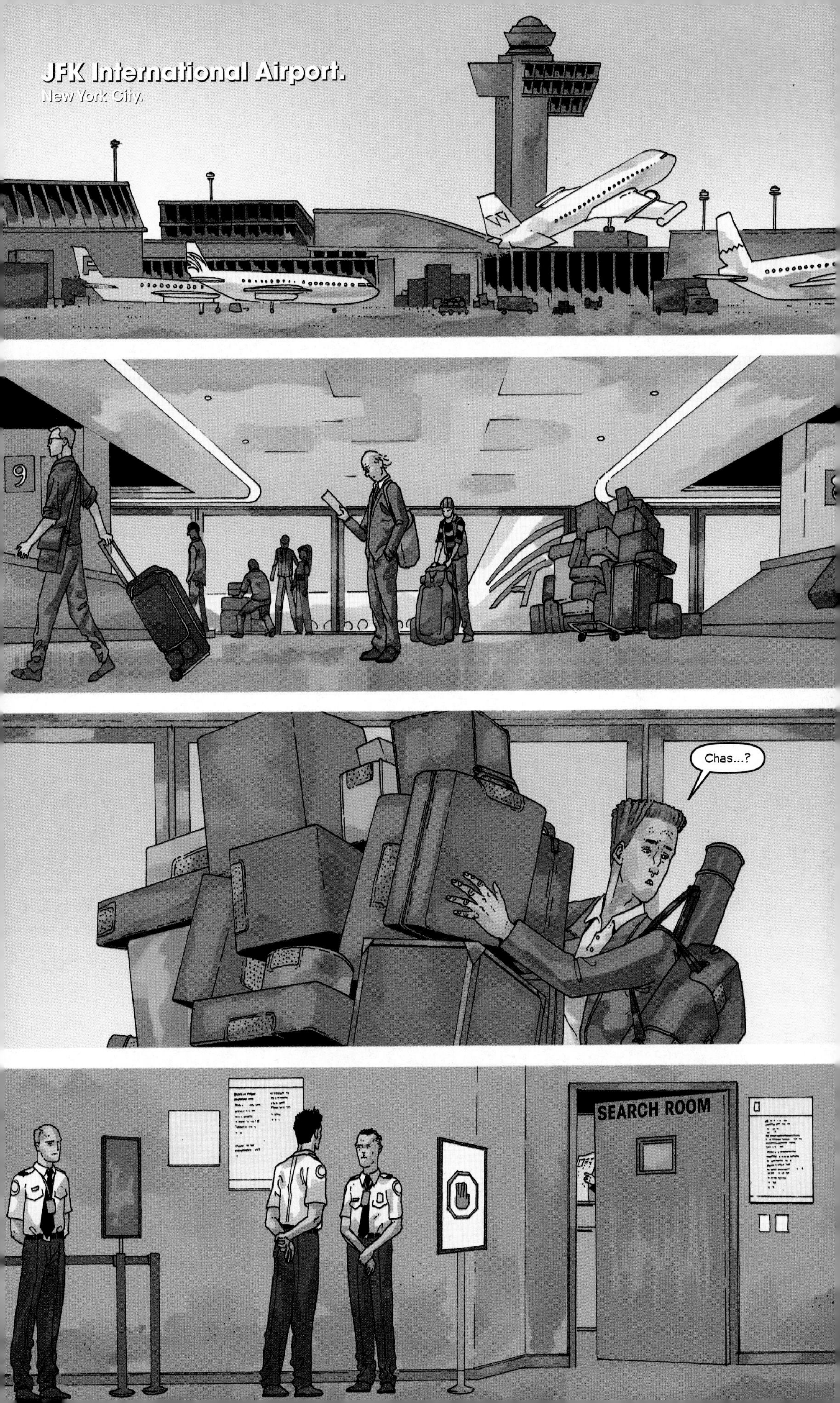

JFK International Airport.
New York City.
Chas...?
SEARCH ROOM

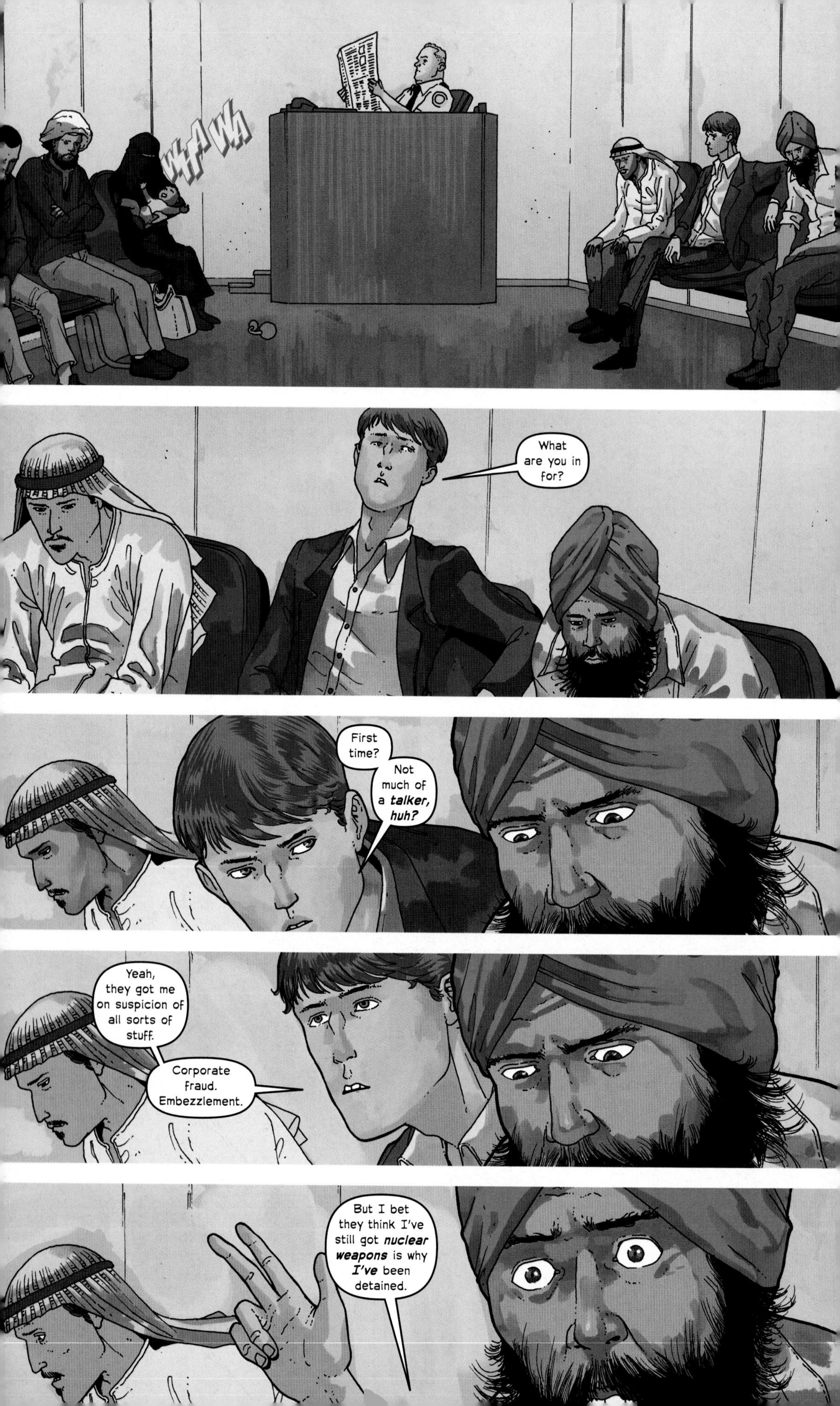
WHA WA
What are you in for?
First time?
Not much of a *talker, huh?*
Yeah, they got me on suspicion of all sorts of stuff.
Corporate fraud. Embezzlement.
But I bet they think I've still got ***nuclear weapons*** is why ***I've*** been detained.

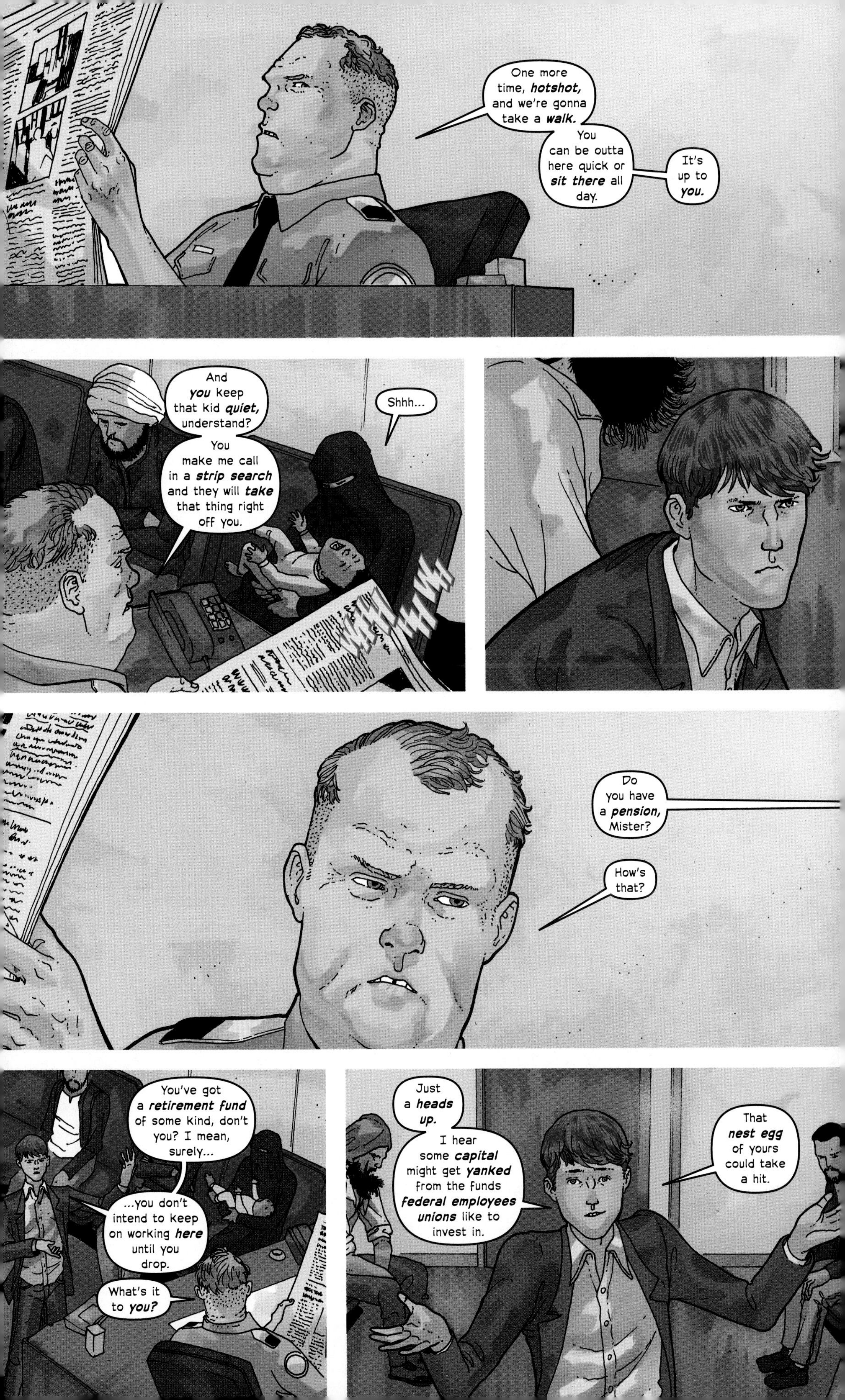
One more time, hotshot, and we're gonna take a walk.
You can be outta here quick or sit there all day.
It's up to you.
And you keep that kid quiet, understand?
You make me call in a strip search and they will take that thing right off you.
Shhh...
Do you have a pension, Mister?
How's that?
You've got a retirement fund of some kind, don't you? I mean, surely...
...you don't intend to keep on working here until you drop.
What's it to you?
Just a heads up.
I hear some capital might get yanked from the funds federal employees unions like to invest in.
That nest egg of yours could take a hit.

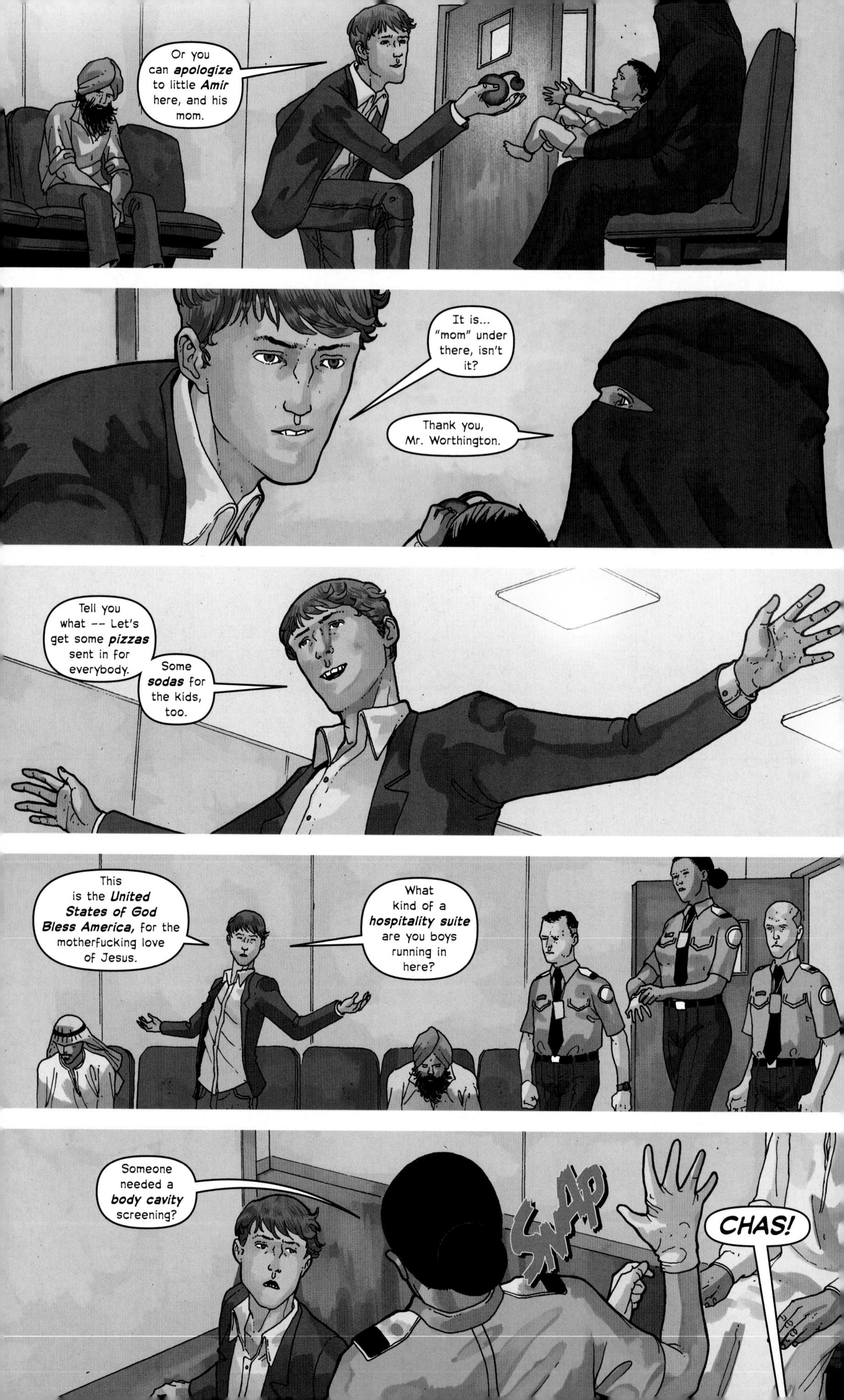

Or you can *apologize* to little *Amir* here, and his mom.
It is... "mom" under there, isn't it?
Thank you, Mr. Worthington.
Tell you what -- Let's get some *pizzas* sent in for everybody.
Some *sodas* for the kids, too.
This is the *United States of God Bless America,* for the motherfucking love of Jesus.
What kind of a *hospitality suite* are you boys running in here?
Someone needed a *body cavity* screening?
SNAP
CHAS!

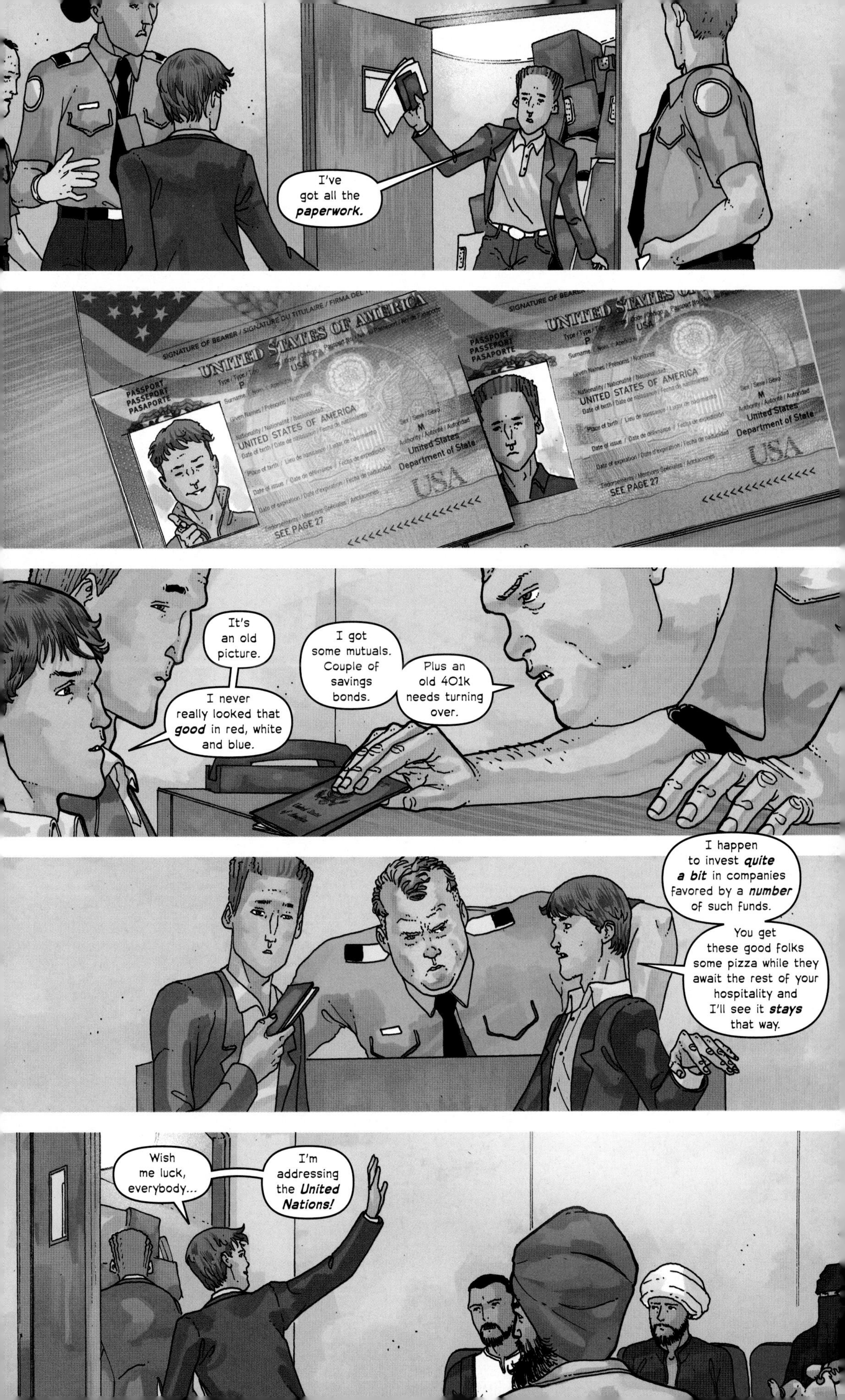
I've got all the *paperwork.*
PASSPORT PASSEPORT PASAPORTE
UNITED STATES OF AMERICA
United States Department of State
USA
SEE PAGE 27
It's an old picture.
I never really looked that *good* in red, white and blue.
I got some mutuals. Couple of savings bonds.
Plus an old 401k needs turning over.
I happen to invest *quite a bit* in companies favored by a *number* of such funds.
You get these good folks some pizza while they await the rest of your hospitality and I'll see it *stays* that way.
Wish me luck, everybody...
I'm addressing the *United Nations!*

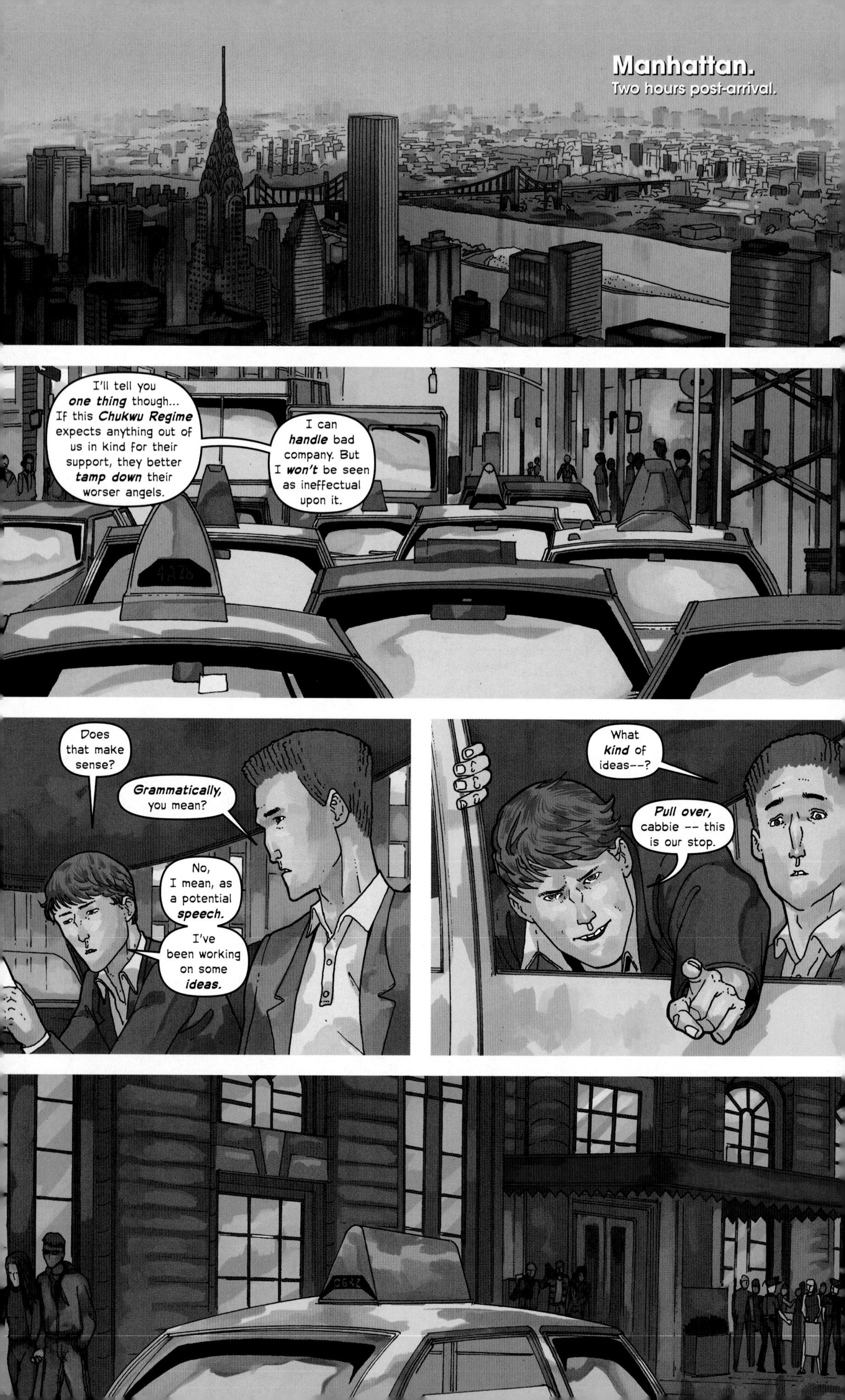

Manhattan.
Two hours post-arrival.
I'll tell you one thing though... If this Chukwu Regime expects anything out of us in kind for their support, they better tamp down their worser angels.
I can handle bad company. But I won't be seen as ineffectual upon it.
Does that make sense?
Grammatically, you mean?
No, I mean, as a potential speech.
I've been working on some ideas.
What kind of ideas--?
Pull over, cabbie -- this is our stop.

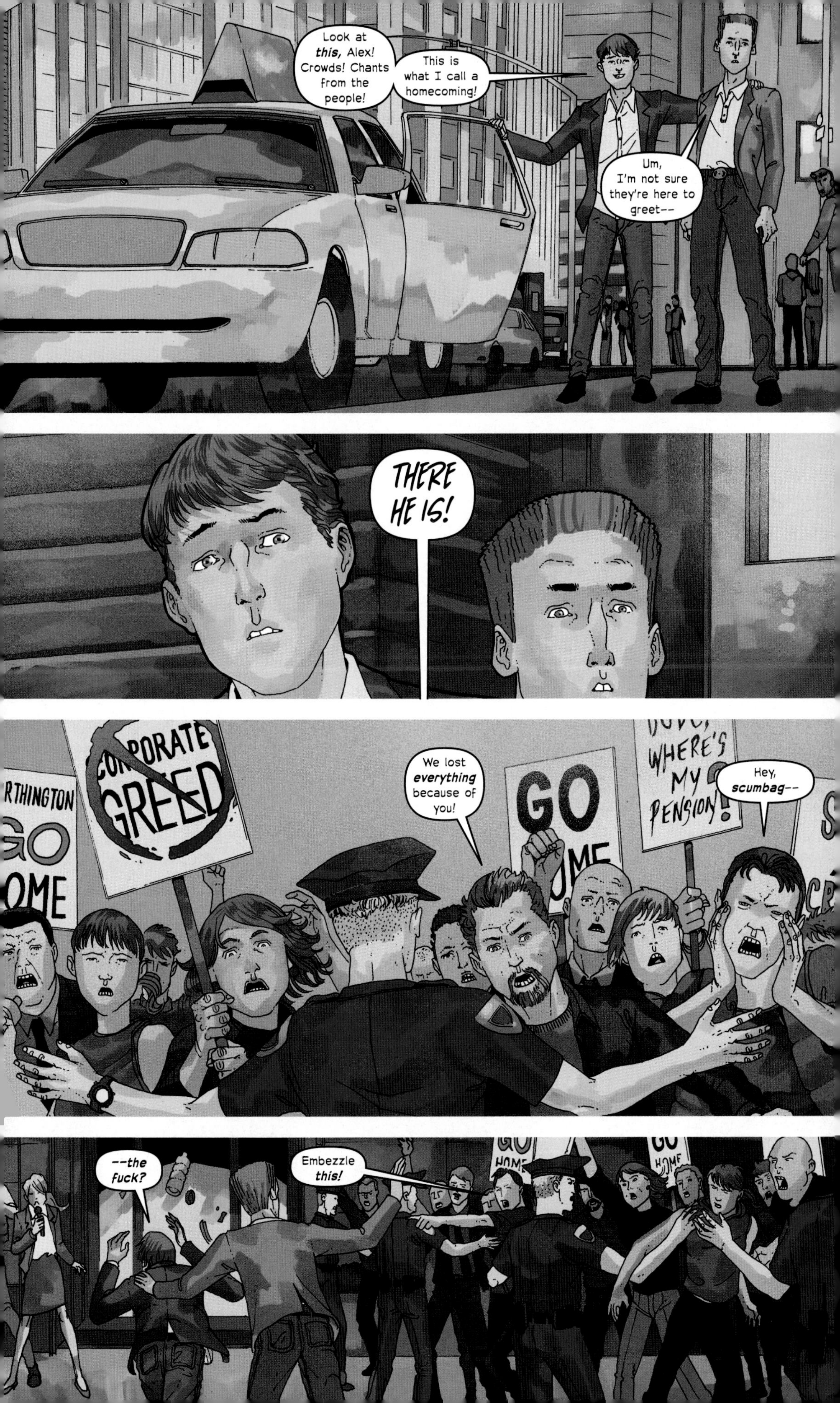
Look at *this,* Alex! Crowds! Chants from the people!
This is what I call a homecoming!
Um, I'm not sure they're here to greet--
THERE HE IS!
RTHINGTON GO OME
CORPORATE GREED
GO
WHERE'S MY PENSION!
We lost *everything* because of you!
Hey, *scumbag*--
--*the fuck?*
Embezzle *this!*
GO HOME
GO HOME

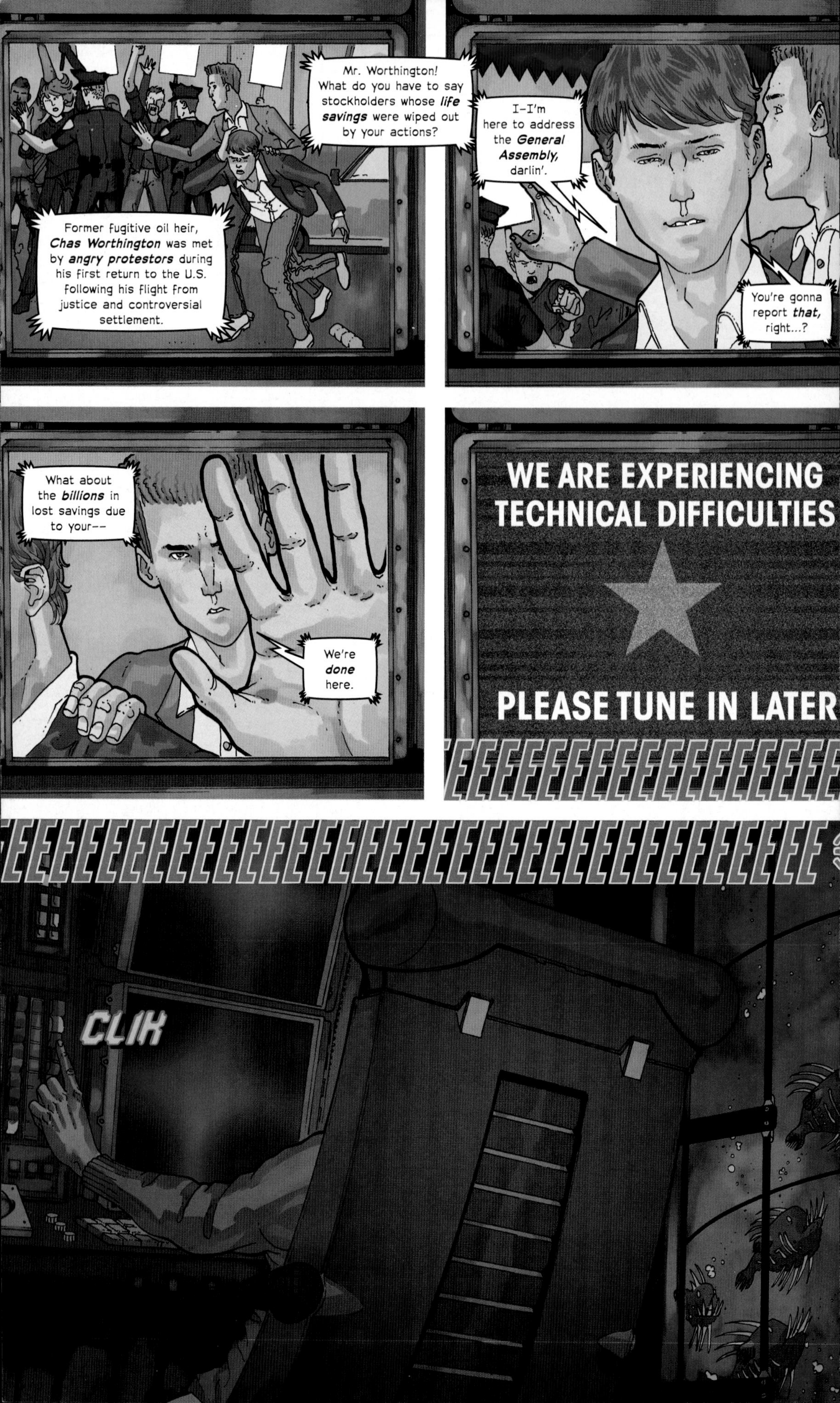
Former fugitive oil heir, **Chas Worthington** was met by **angry protestors** during his first return to the U.S. following his flight from justice and controversial settlement.
Mr. Worthington! What do you have to say stockholders whose **life savings** were wiped out by your actions?
I-I'm here to address the **General Assembly,** darlin'.
You're gonna report **that,** right...?
What about the **billions** in lost savings due to your--
We're **done** here.
WE ARE EXPERIENCING TECHNICAL DIFFICULTIES
PLEASE TUNE IN LATER
EEEEEEEEEEEEEEEEEE
EEEEEEEEEEEEEEEEEEEEEEEEEEEEEEEEEEEE
CLIK

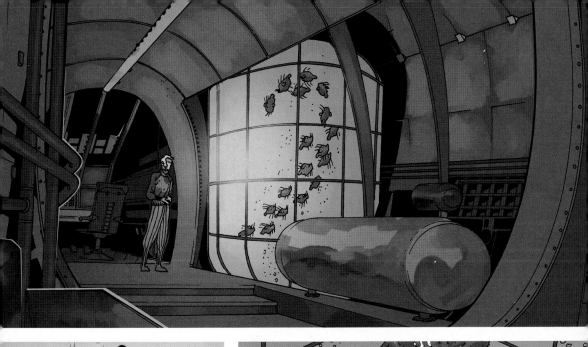

FWEE

KNZT KZT

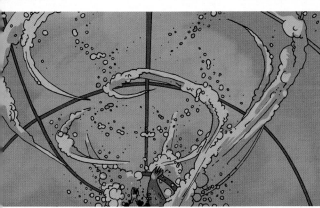

Safe travels, Mr. Worthington.

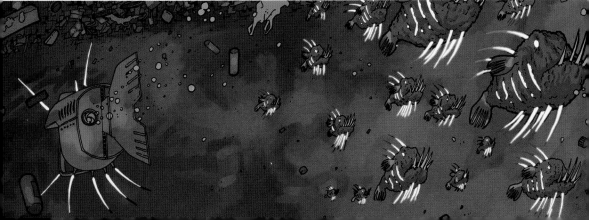

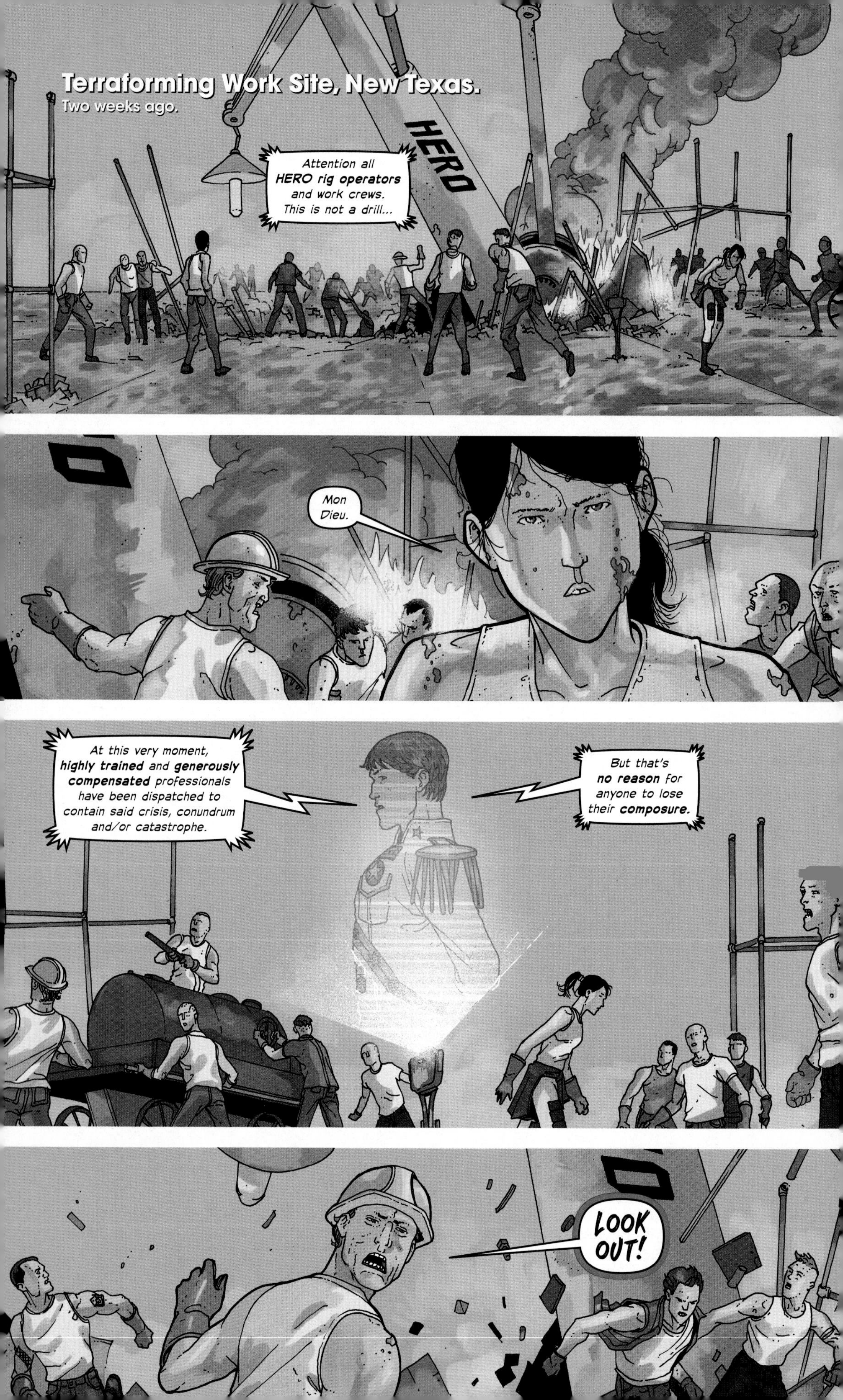
Terraforming Work Site, New Texas.
Two weeks ago.
HERO
Attention all HERO rig operators and work crews. This is not a drill...
Mon Dieu.
At this very moment, highly trained and generously compensated professionals have been dispatched to contain said crisis, conundrum and/or catastrophe.
But that's no reason for anyone to lose their composure.
LOOK OUT!

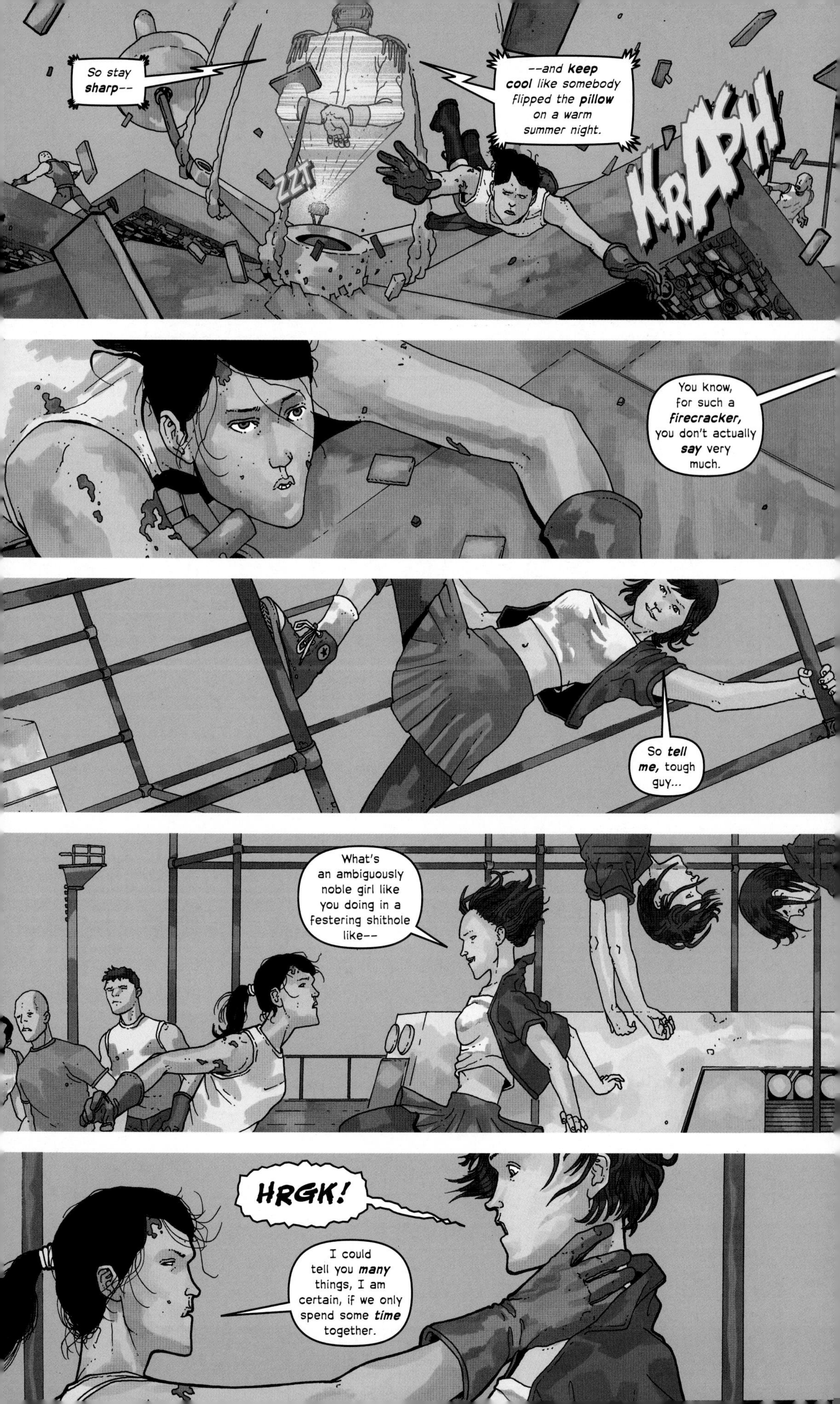
So stay sharp--
--and keep cool like somebody flipped the pillow on a warm summer night.
ZZT
KRASH
You know, for such a firecracker, you don't actually say very much.
So tell me, tough guy...
What's an ambiguously noble girl like you doing in a festering shithole like--
HRGK!
I could tell you many things, I am certain, if we only spend some time together.

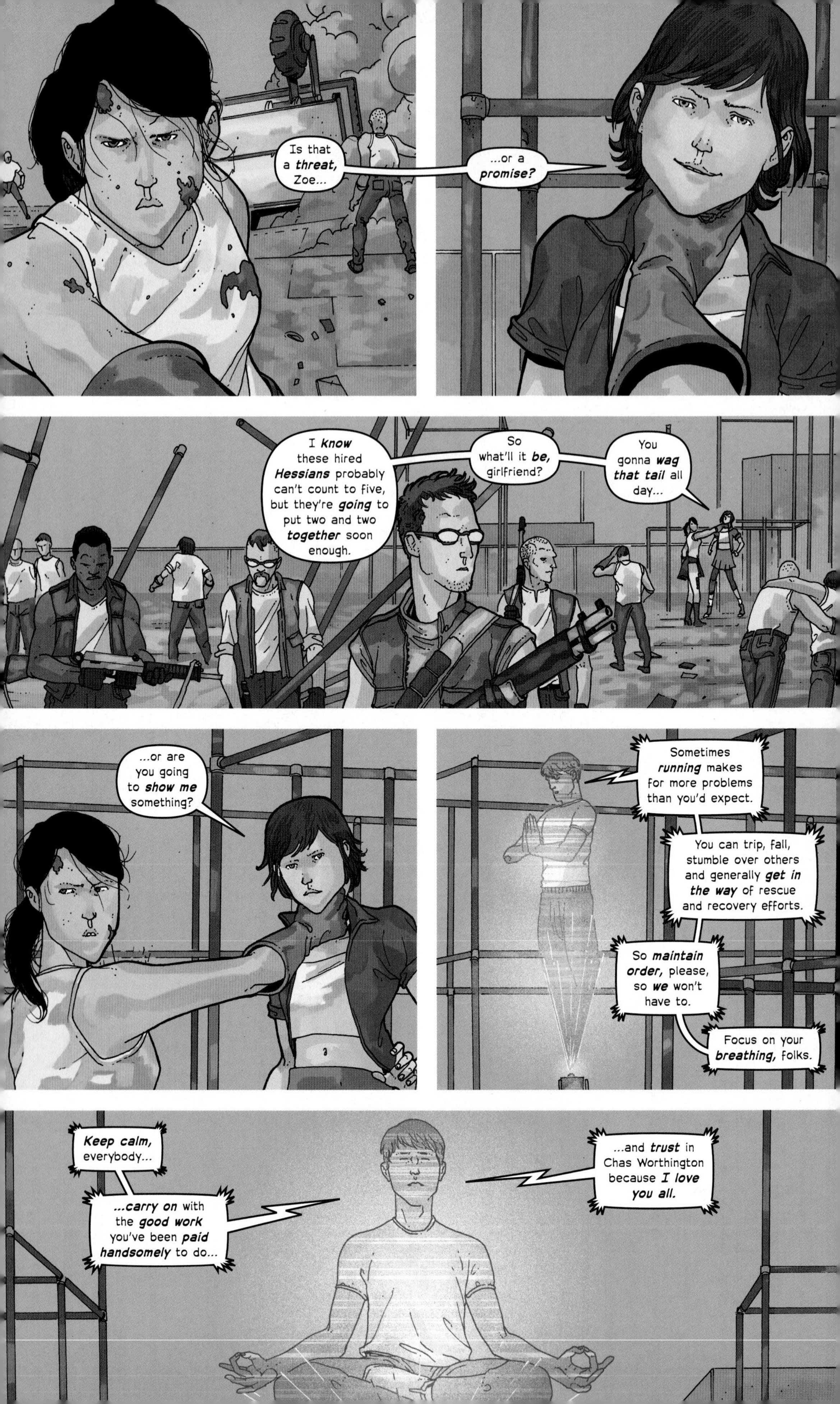

Is that a threat, Zoe...
...or a promise?
I know these hired Hessians probably can't count to five, but they're going to put two and two together soon enough.
So what'll it be, girlfriend?
You gonna wag that tail all day...
...or are you going to show me something?
Sometimes running makes for more problems than you'd expect.
You can trip, fall, stumble over others and generally get in the way of rescue and recovery efforts.
So maintain order, please, so we won't have to.
Focus on your breathing, folks.
Keep calm, everybody...
...carry on with the good work you've been paid handsomely to do...
...and trust in Chas Worthington because I love you all.

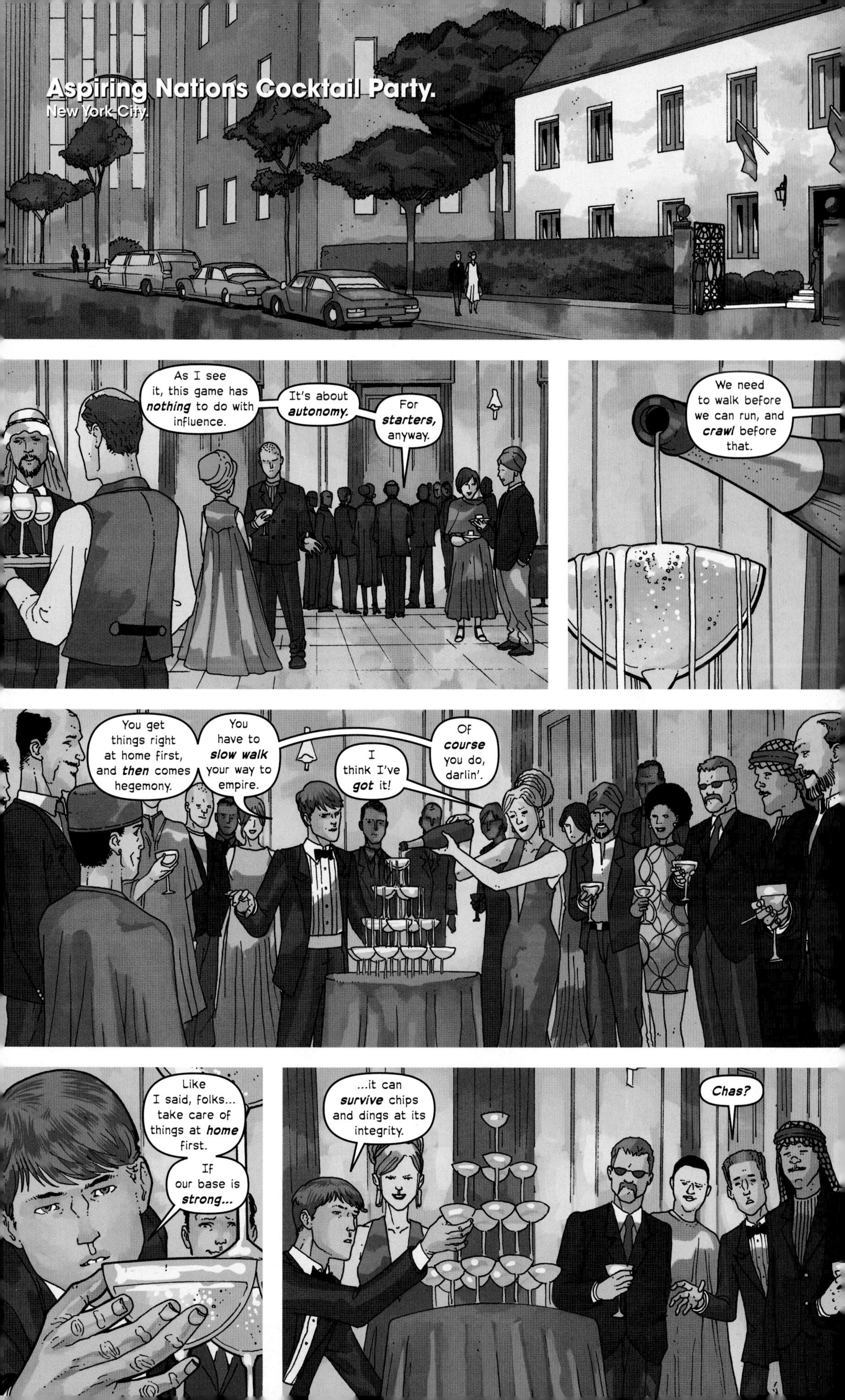

Aspiring Nations Cocktail Party.
New York City.
As I see it, this game has nothing to do with influence.
It's about autonomy.
For starters, anyway.
We need to walk before we can run, and crawl before that.
You get things right at home first, and then comes hegemony.
You have to slow walk your way to empire.
I think I've got it!
Of course you do, darlin'.
Like I said, folks... take care of things at home first.
If our base is strong...
...it can survive chips and dings at its integrity.
Chas?

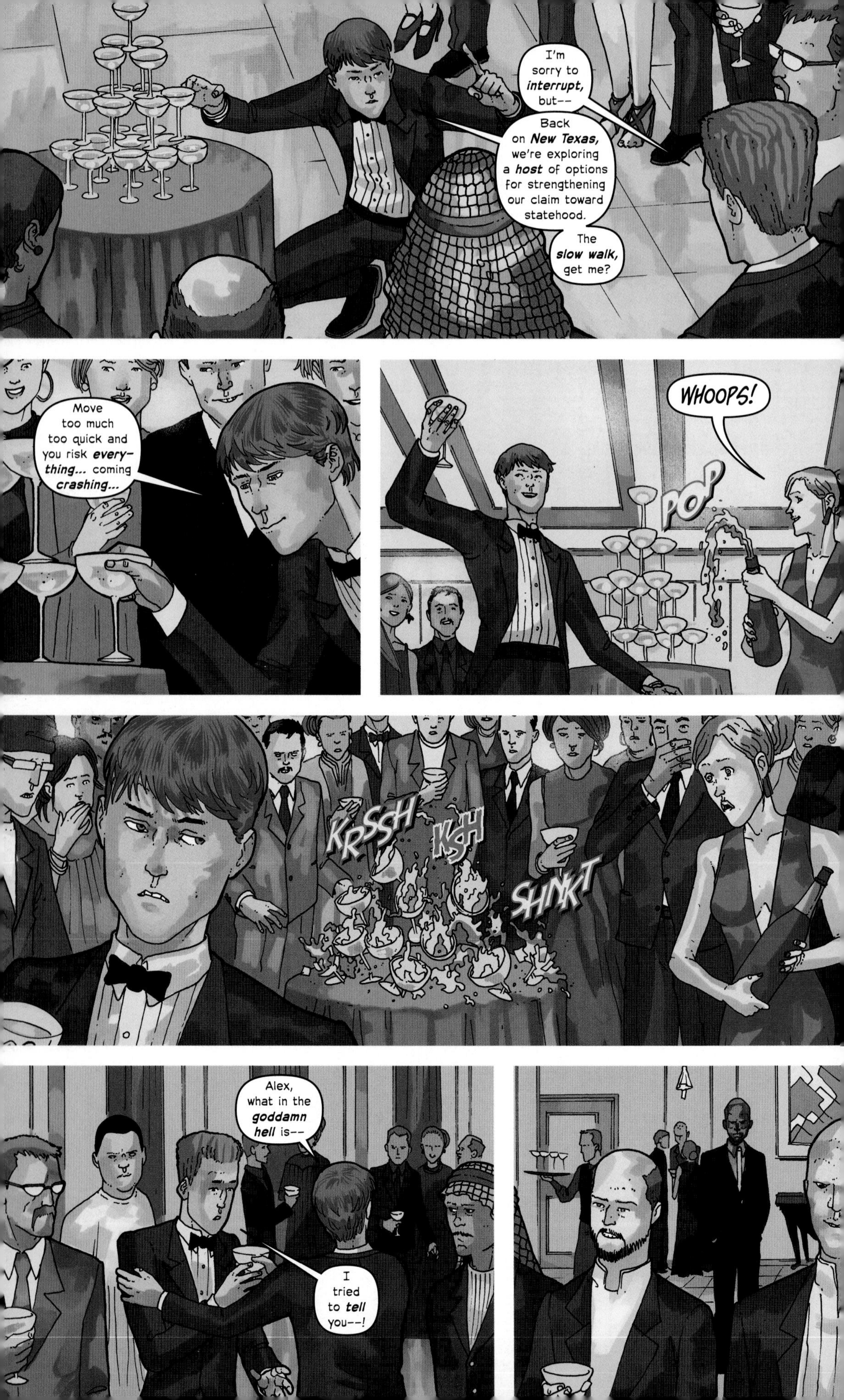
I'm sorry to interrupt, but--
Back on New Texas, we're exploring a host of options for strengthening our claim toward statehood.
The slow walk, get me?
Move too much too quick and you risk every-thing... coming crashing...
WHOOPS!
POP
KRSSH
KSH
SHNKT
Alex, what in the goddamn hell is--
I tried to tell you--!

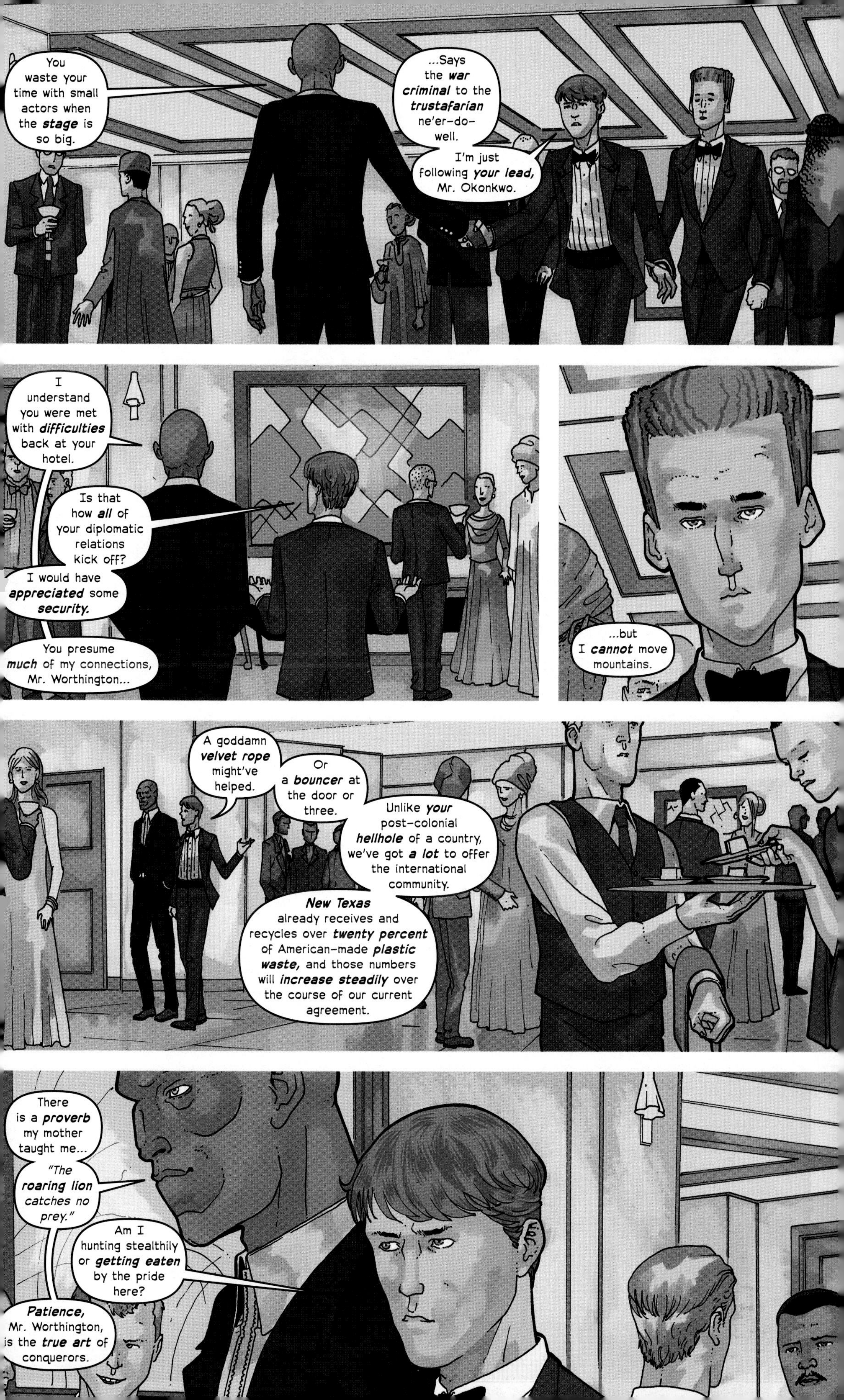
You waste your time with small actors when the *stage* is so big.
...Says the *war criminal* to the *trustafarian* ne'er-do-well.
I'm just following *your lead,* Mr. Okonkwo.
I understand you were met with *difficulties* back at your hotel.
Is that how *all* of your diplomatic relations kick off?
I would have *appreciated* some *security.*
You presume *much* of my connections, Mr. Worthington...
...but I *cannot* move mountains.
A goddamn *velvet rope* might've helped.
Or a *bouncer* at the door or three.
Unlike *your* post-colonial *hellhole* of a country, we've got *a lot* to offer the international community.
New Texas already receives and recycles over *twenty percent* of American-made *plastic waste,* and those numbers will *increase steadily* over the course of our current agreement.
There is a *proverb* my mother taught me...
"The roaring lion catches no prey."
Am I hunting stealthily or *getting eaten* by the pride here?
Patience, Mr. Worthington, is the *true art* of conquerors.

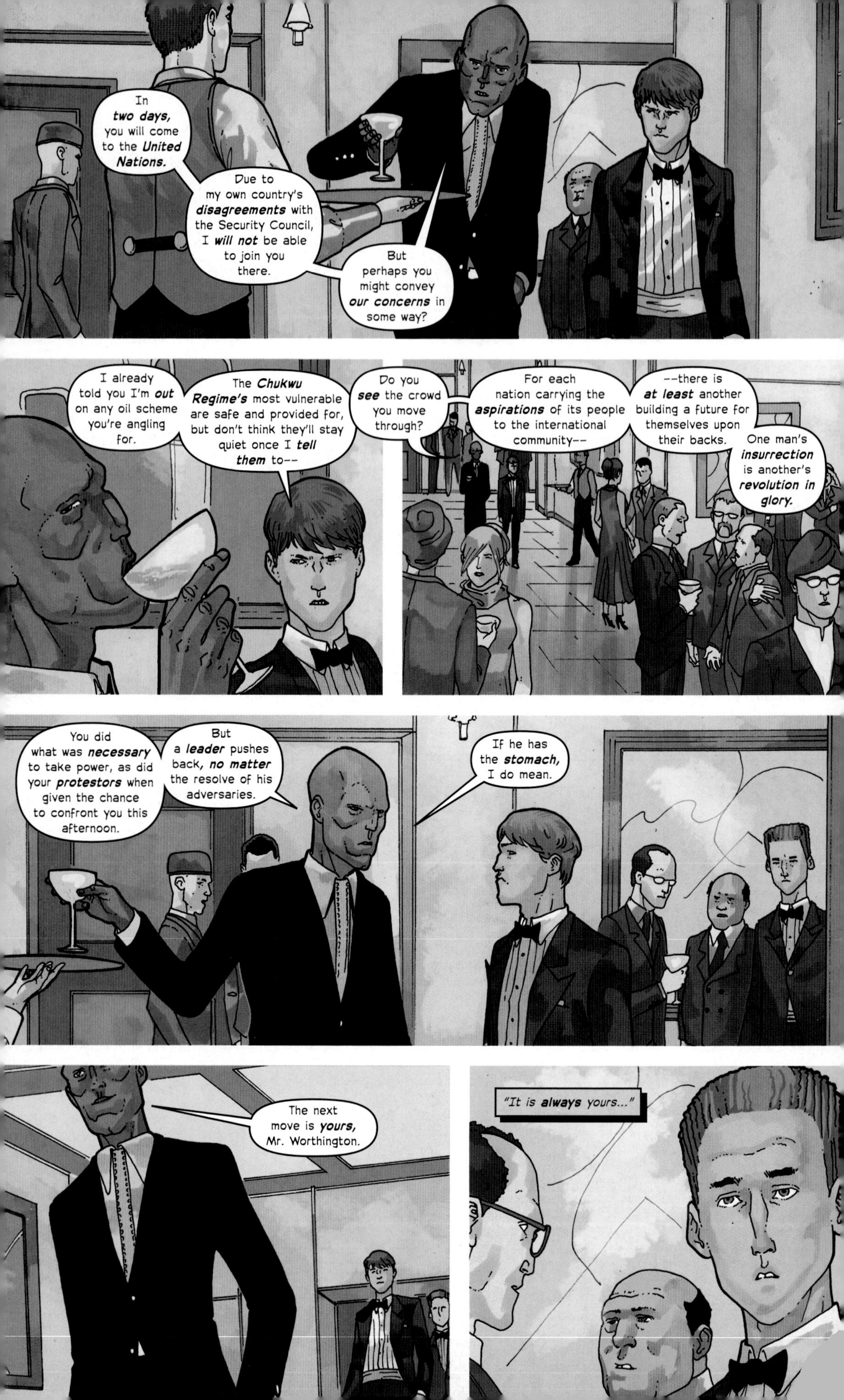
In two days, you will come to the United Nations.
Due to my own country's disagreements with the Security Council, I will not be able to join you there.
But perhaps you might convey our concerns in some way?
I already told you I'm out on any oil scheme you're angling for.
The Chukwu Regime's most vulnerable are safe and provided for, but don't think they'll stay quiet once I tell them to--
Do you see the crowd you move through?
For each nation carrying the aspirations of its people to the international community--
--there is at least another building a future for themselves upon their backs.
One man's insurrection is another's revolution in glory.
You did what was necessary to take power, as did your protestors when given the chance to confront you this afternoon.
But a leader pushes back, no matter the resolve of his adversaries.
If he has the stomach, I do mean.
The next move is yours, Mr. Worthington.
"It is always yours..."

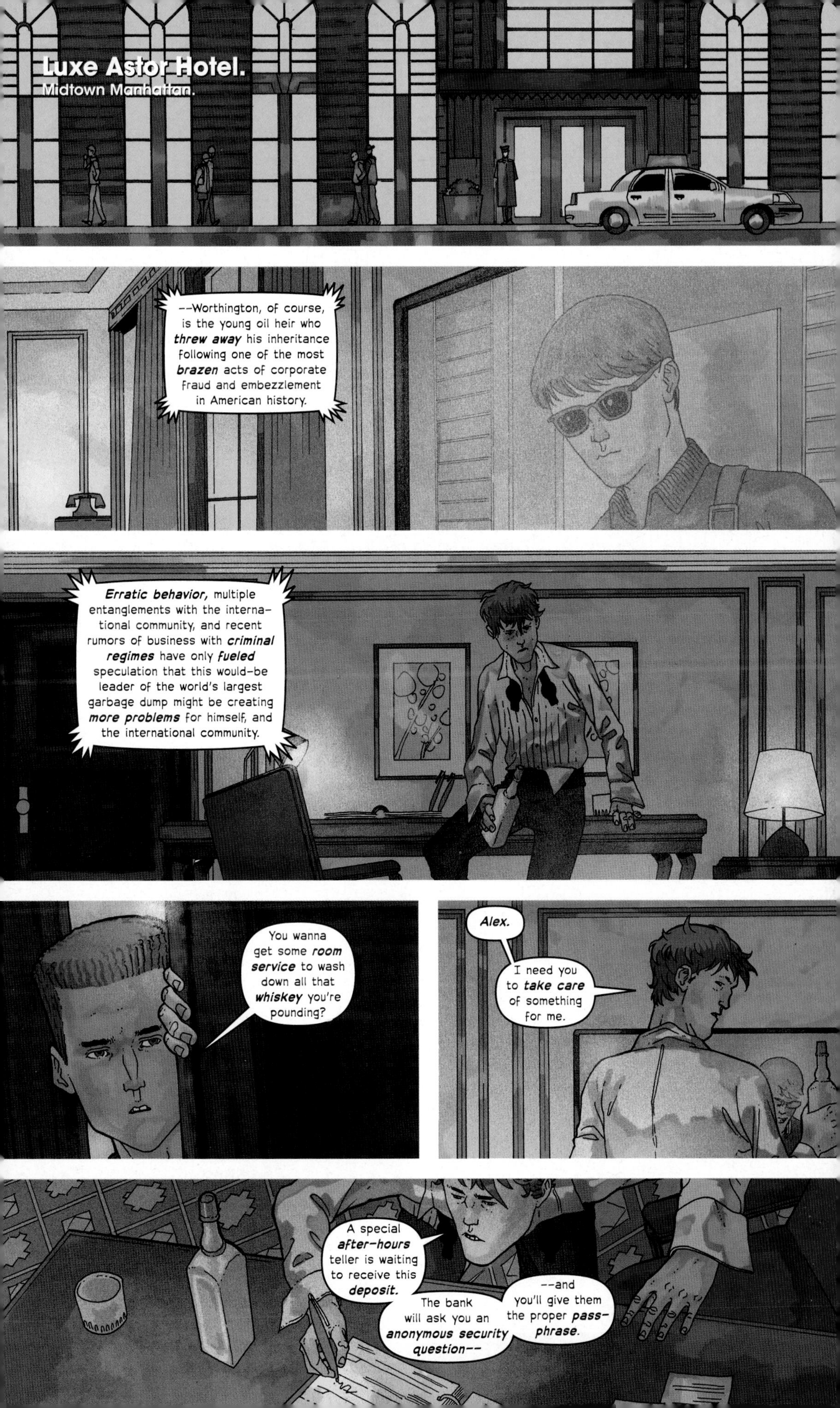

Luxe Astor Hotel.
Midtown Manhattan.
--Worthington, of course, is the young oil heir who threw away his inheritance following one of the most brazen acts of corporate fraud and embezzlement in American history.
Erratic behavior, multiple entanglements with the interna-tional community, and recent rumors of business with criminal regimes have only fueled speculation that this would-be leader of the world's largest garbage dump might be creating more problems for himself, and the international community.
You wanna get some room service to wash down all that whiskey you're pounding?
Alex.
I need you to take care of something for me.
A special after-hours teller is waiting to receive this deposit.
The bank will ask you an anonymous security question--
--and you'll give them the proper pass-phrase.

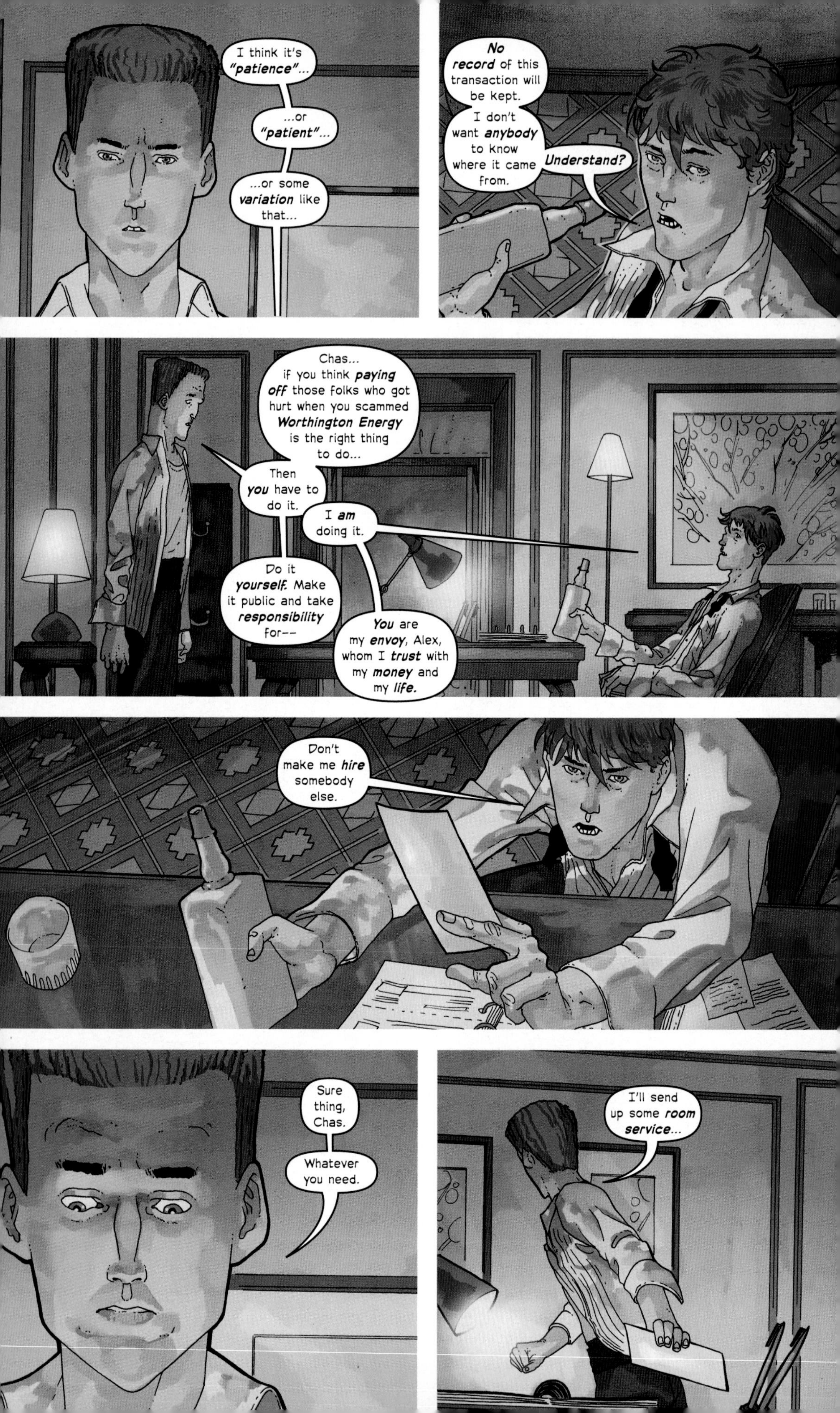
I think it's "patience"...
...or "patient"...
...or some variation like that...
No record of this transaction will be kept.
I don't want anybody to know where it came from.
Understand?
Chas... if you think paying off those folks who got hurt when you scammed Worthington Energy is the right thing to do...
Then you have to do it.
I am doing it.
Do it yourself. Make it public and take responsibility for--
You are my envoy, Alex, whom I trust with my money and my life.
Don't make me hire somebody else.
Sure thing, Chas.
Whatever you need.
I'll send up some room service...

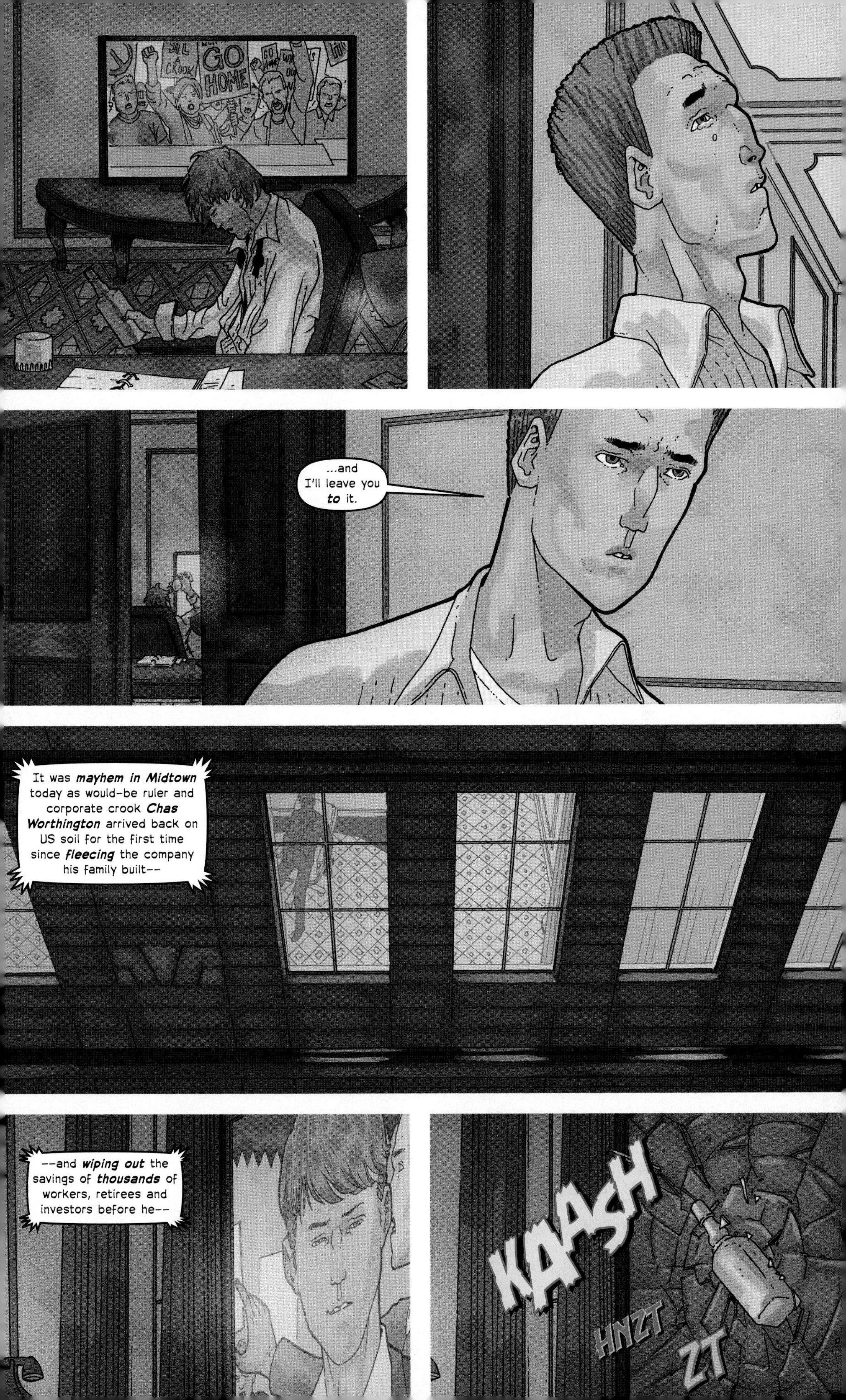
GO HOME
...and I'll leave you *to* it.
It was *mayhem in Midtown* today as would-be ruler and corporate crook *Chas Worthington* arrived back on US soil for the first time since *fleecing* the company his family built--
--and *wiping out* the savings of *thousands* of workers, retirees and investors before he--
KAASH
HNZT
ZT

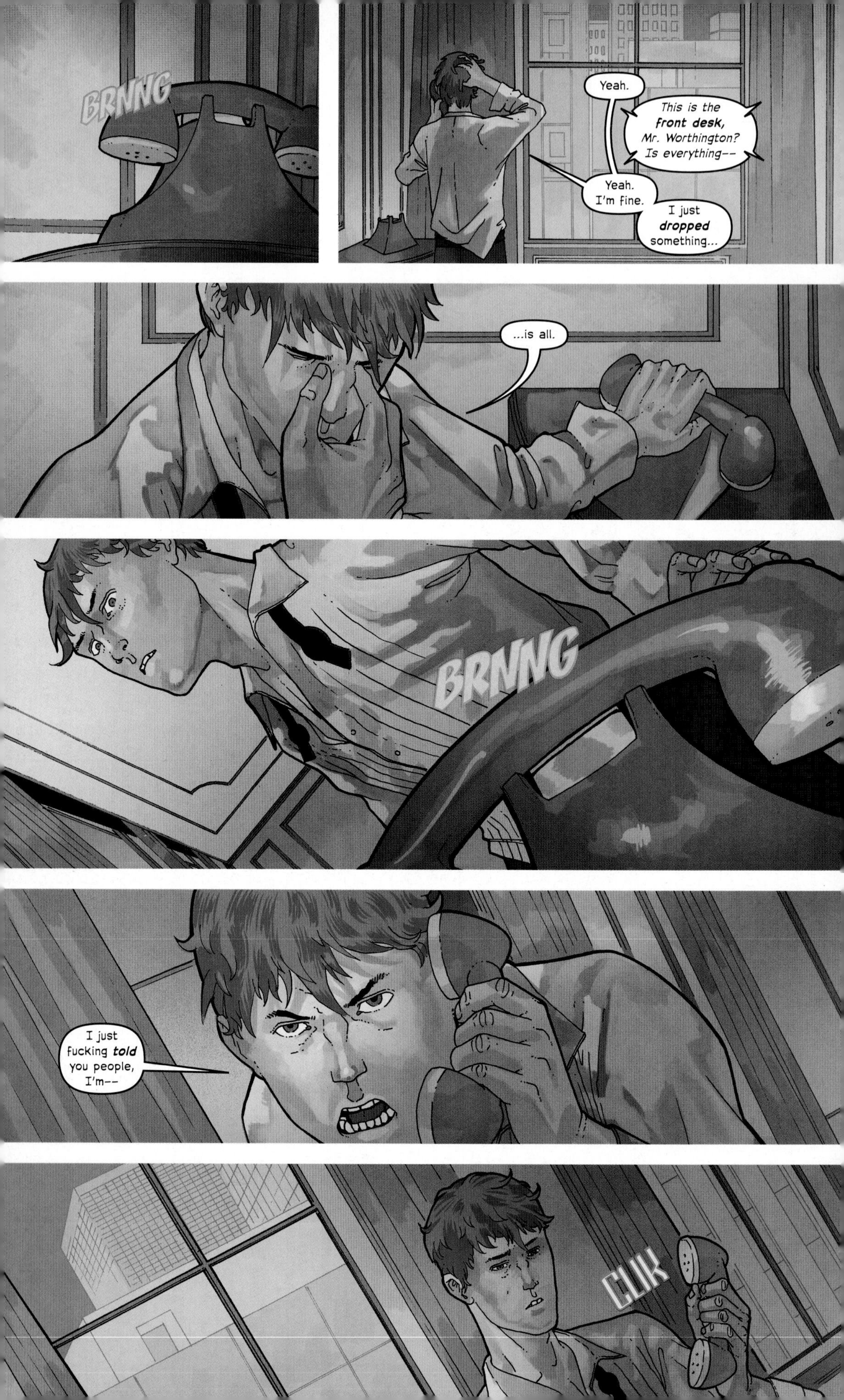
BRNNG
Yeah.
This is the **front desk,** Mr. Worthington? Is everything--
Yeah. I'm fine.
I just **dropped** something...
...is all.
BRNNG
I just fucking ***told*** you people, I'm--
CLIK

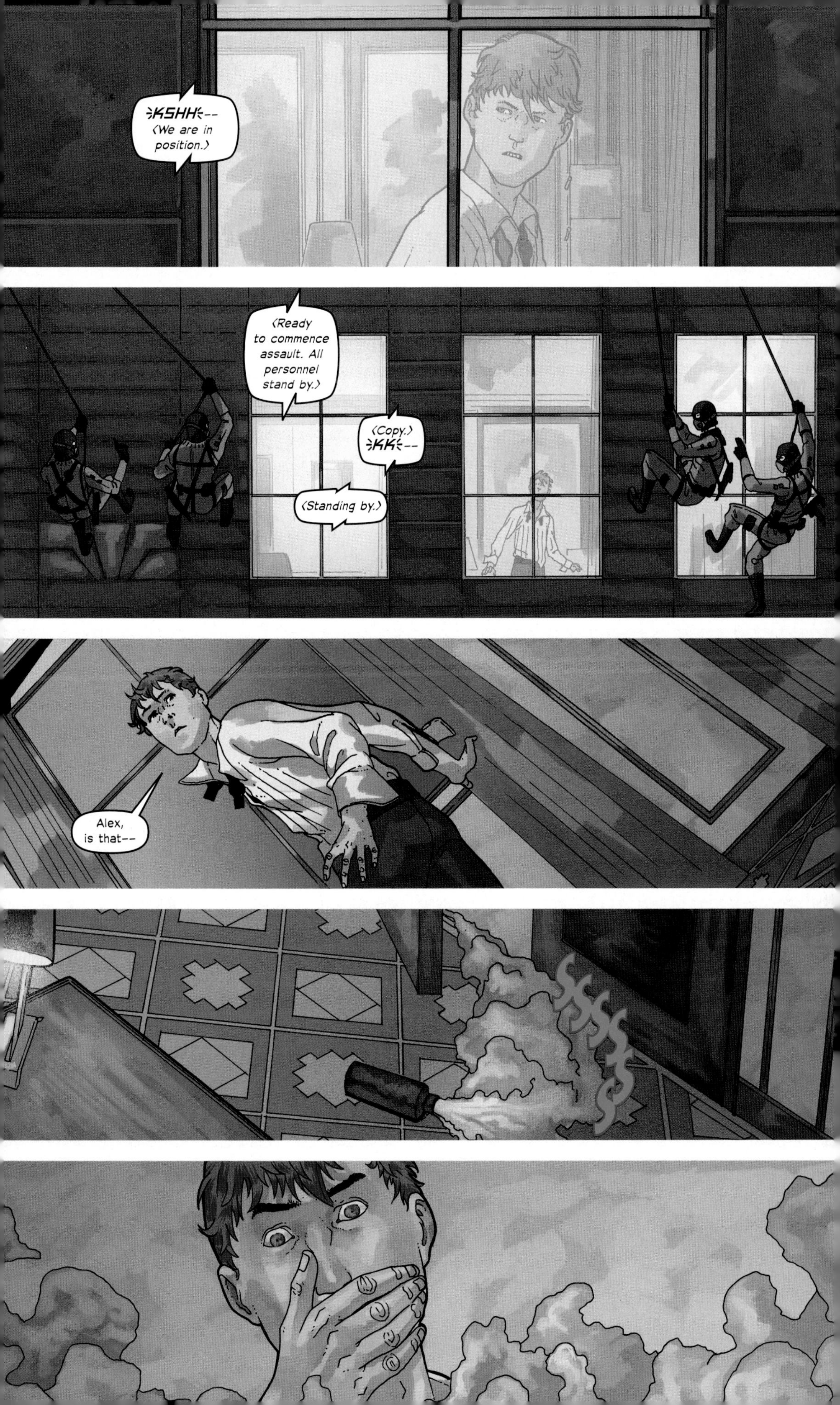

KSHH--
⟨We are in position.⟩
⟨Ready to commence assault. All personnel stand by.⟩
⟨Copy.⟩ KK--
⟨Standing by.⟩
Alex, is that--
SSSSS

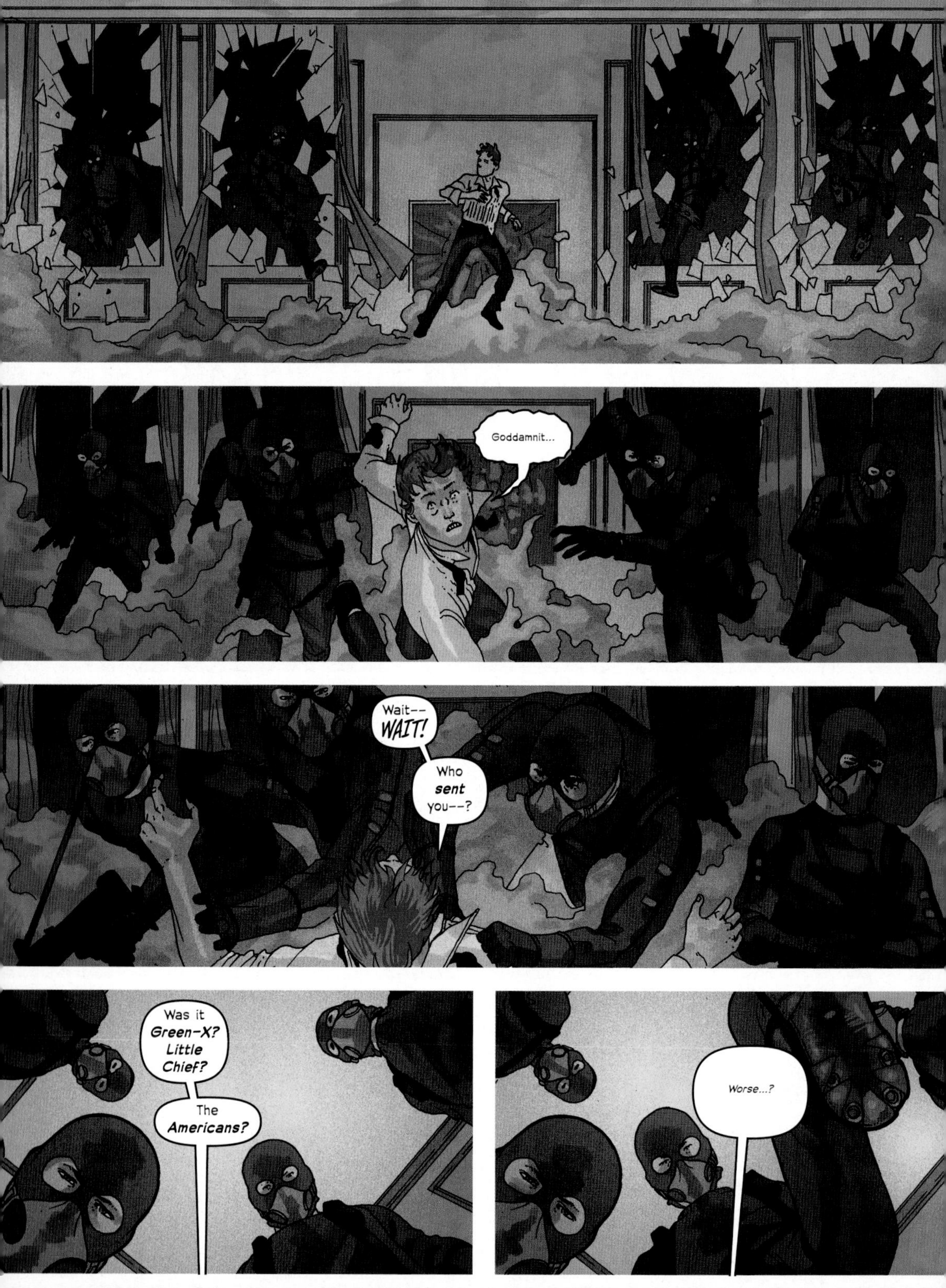
Goddamnit...
Wait-- WAIT!
Who sent you--?
Was it Green-X? Little Chief?
The Americans?
Worse...?

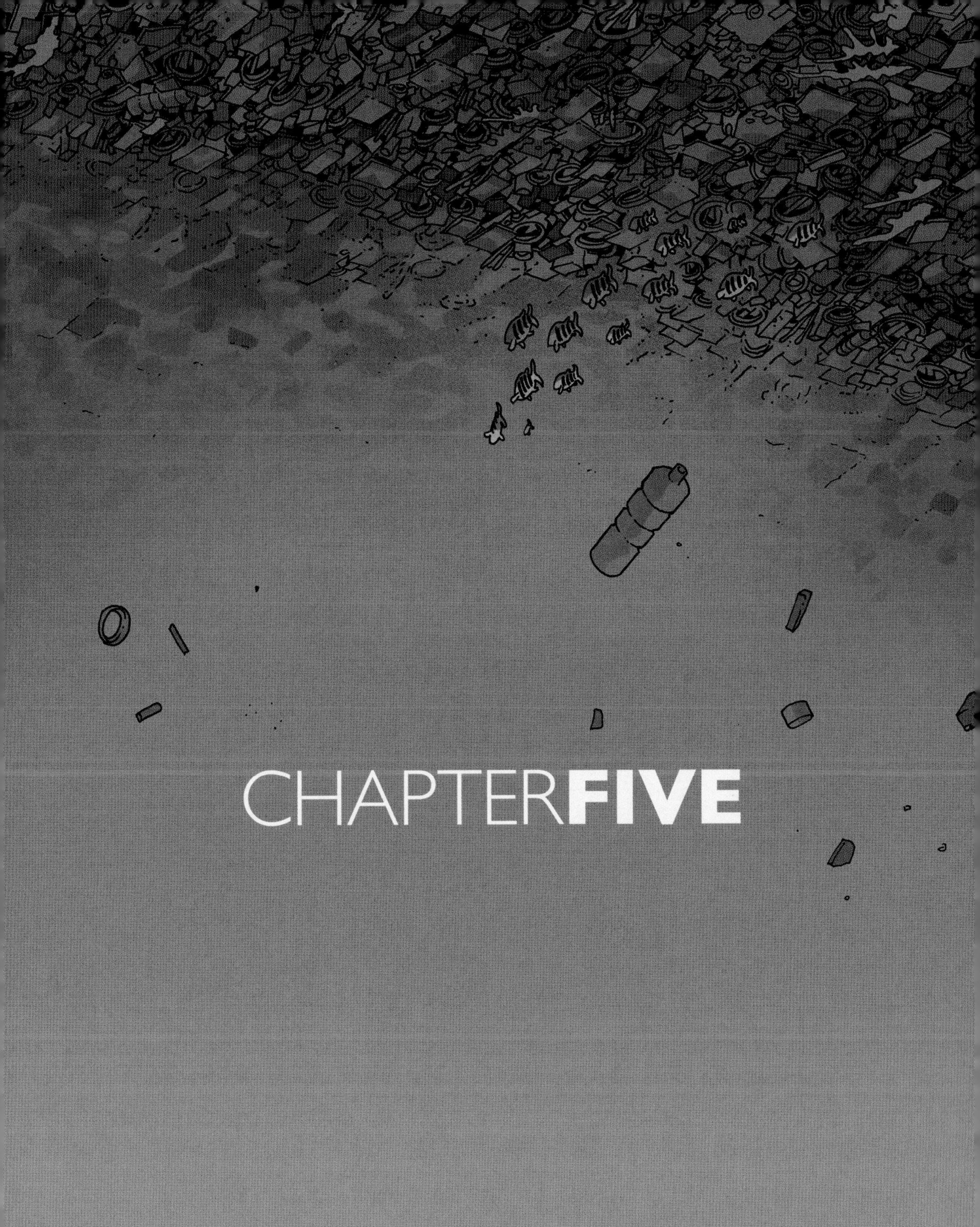

CHAPTER FIVE

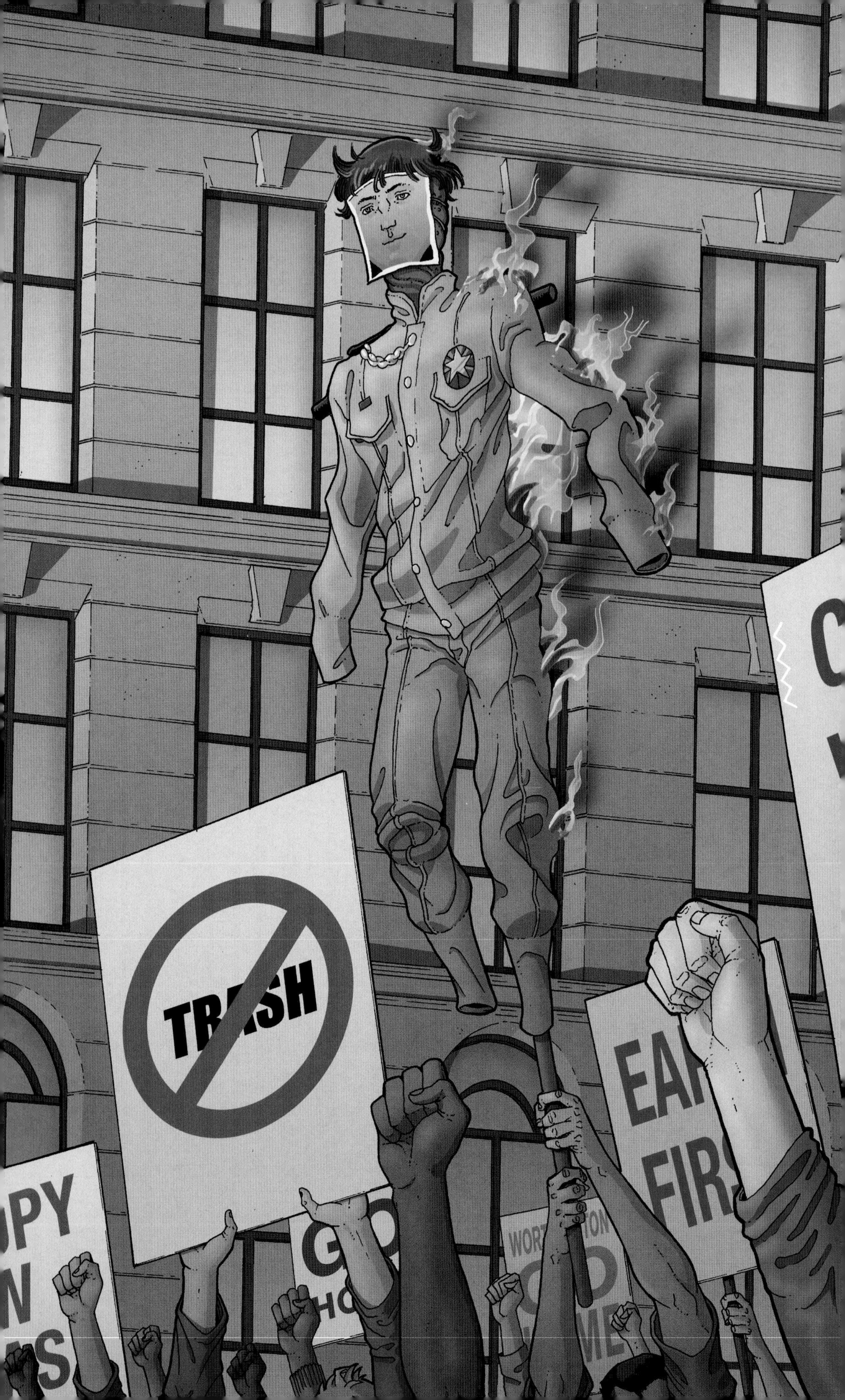
TRASH

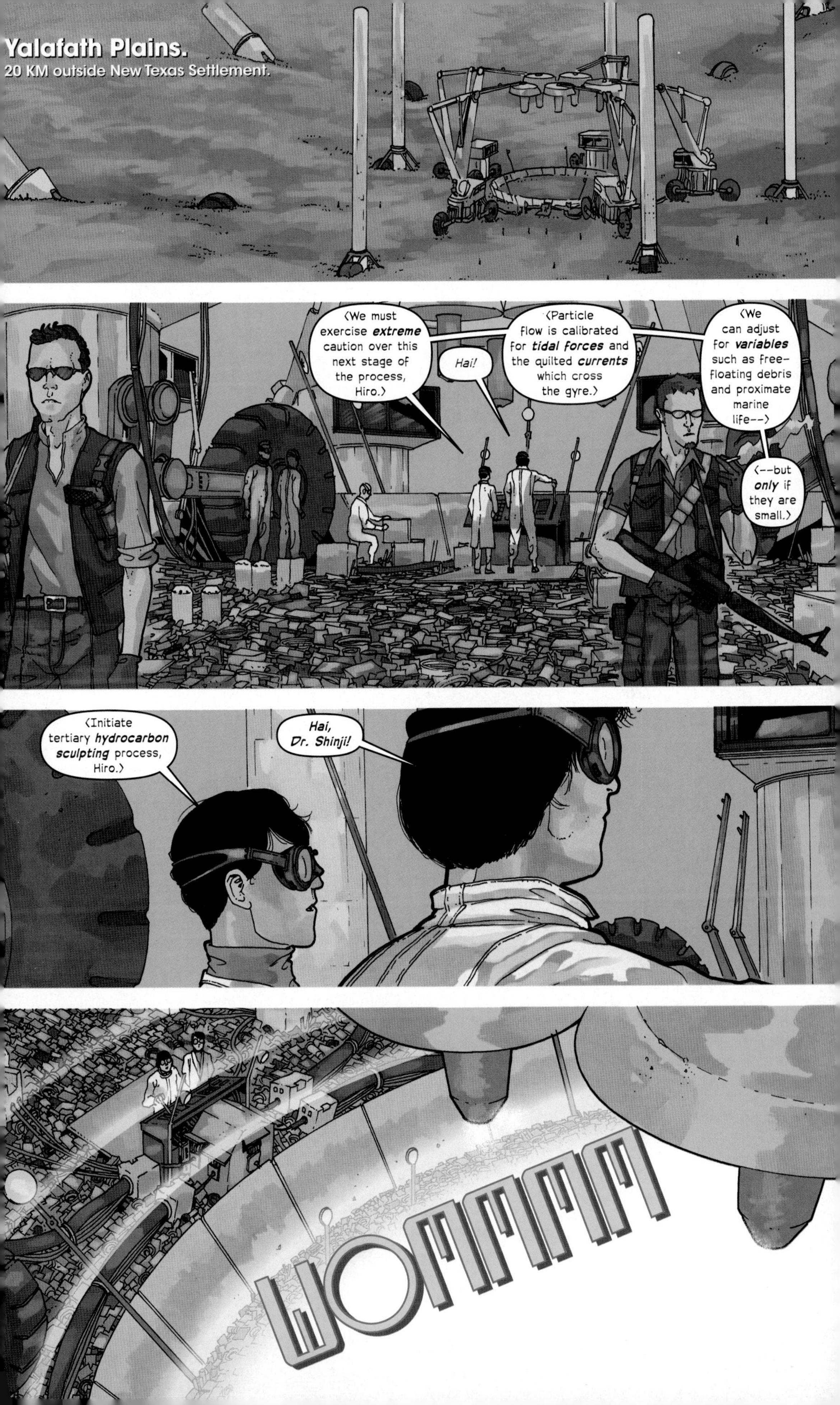
Yalafath Plains.
20 KM outside New Texas Settlement.
⟨We must exercise *extreme* caution over this next stage of the process, Hiro.⟩
Hai!
⟨Particle flow is calibrated for *tidal forces* and the quilted *currents* which cross the gyre.⟩
⟨We can adjust for *variables* such as free-floating debris and proximate marine life--⟩
⟨--but *only* if they are small.⟩
⟨Initiate tertiary *hydrocarbon sculpting* process, Hiro.⟩
Hai, Dr. Shinji!
WOMMM

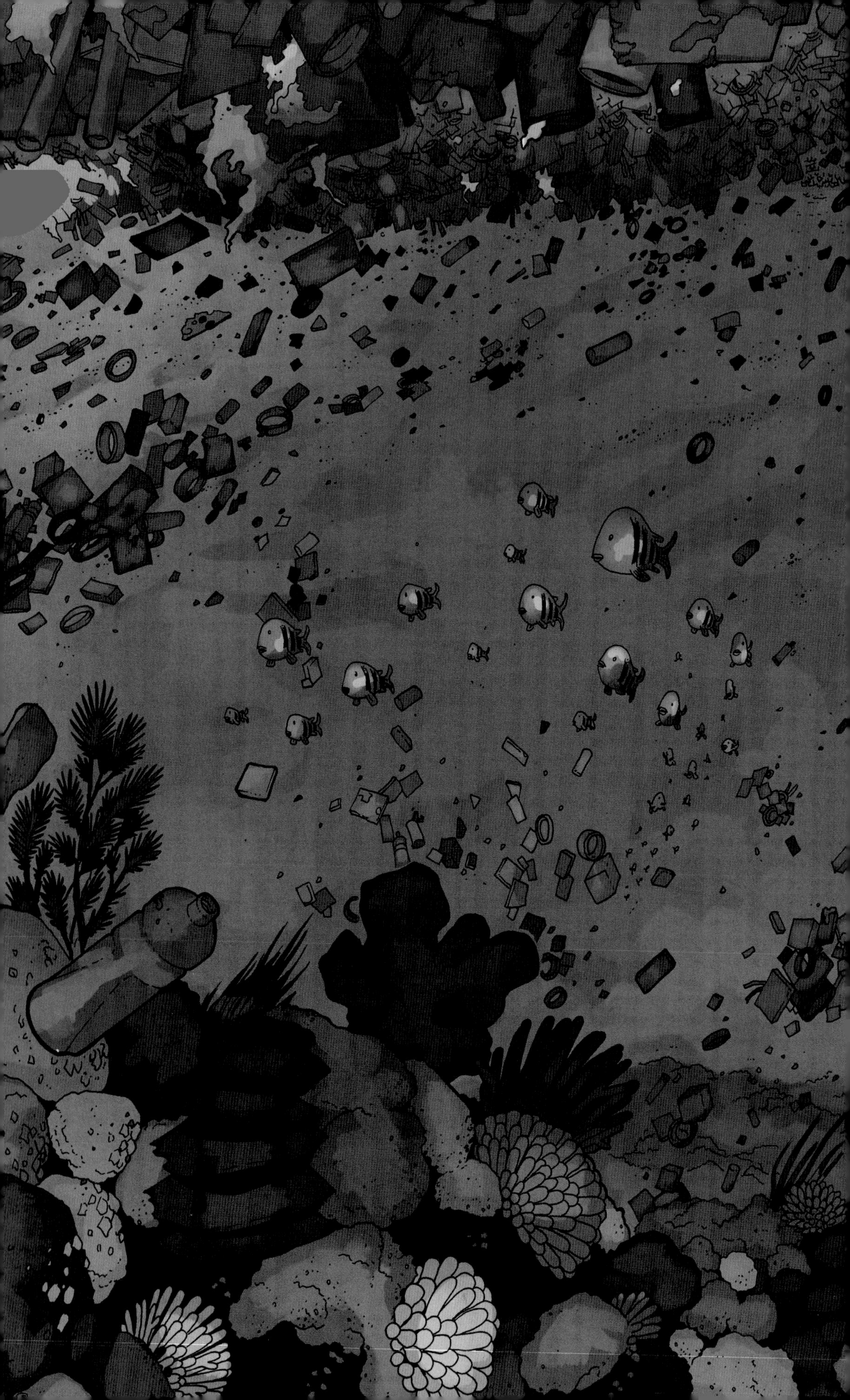

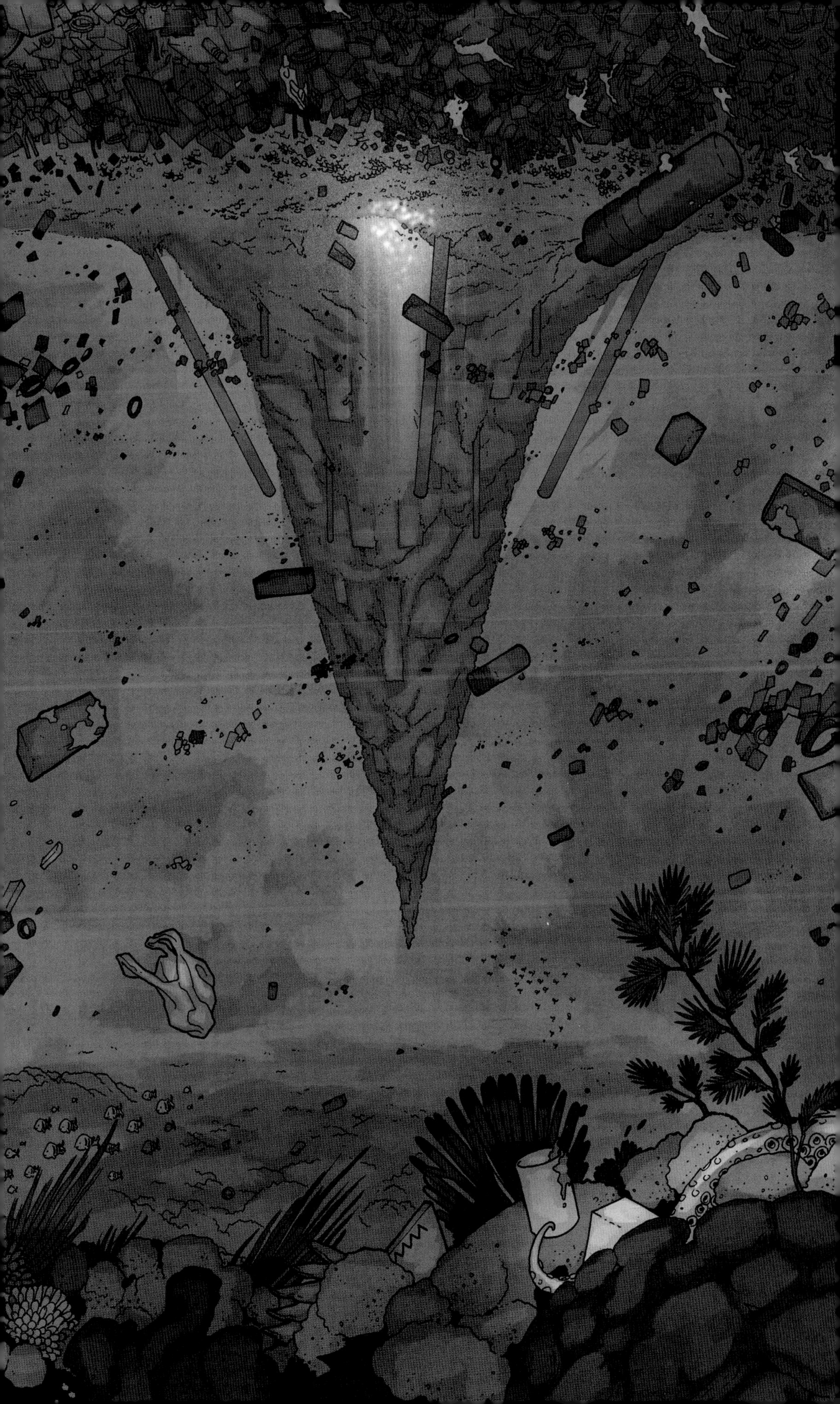

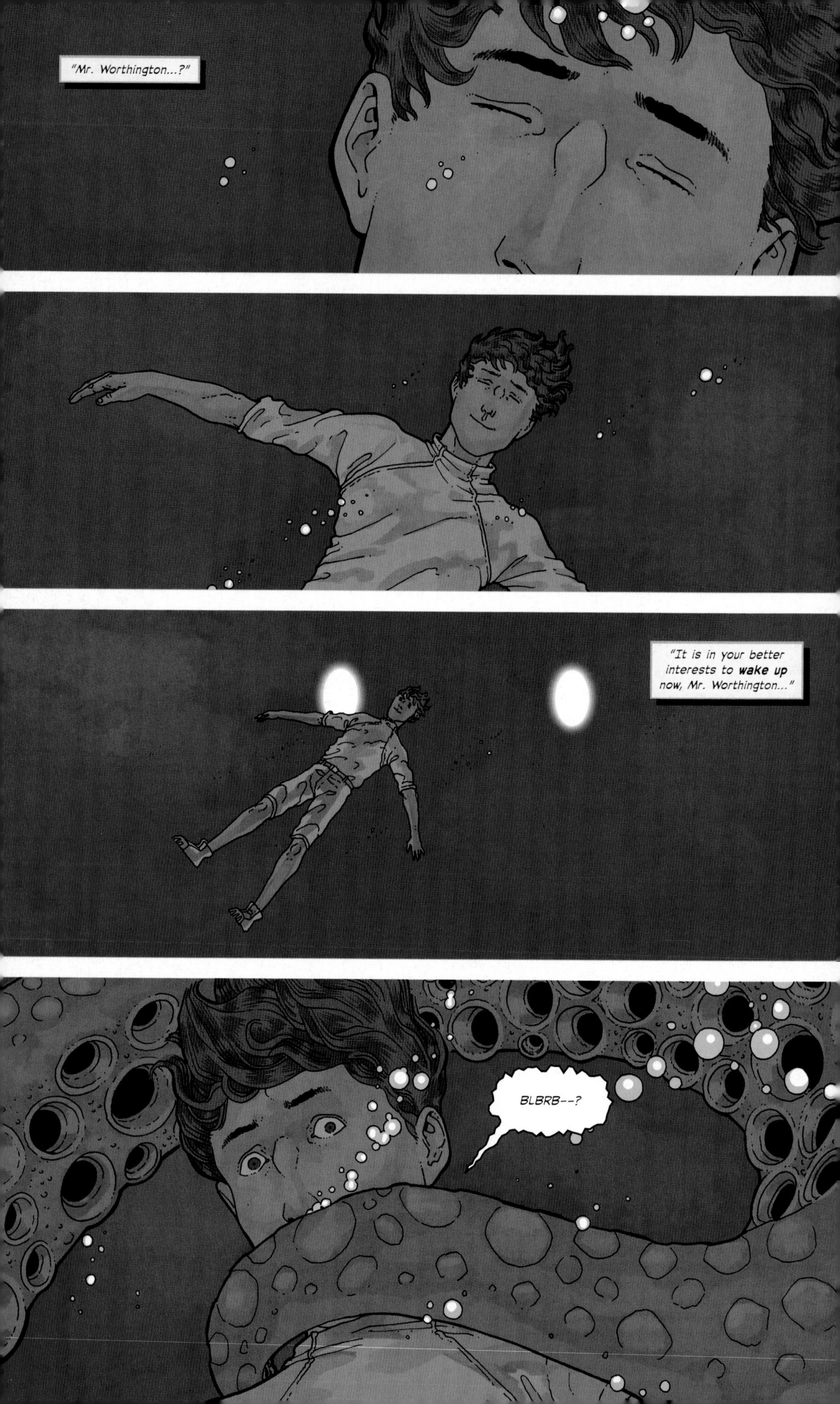
"Mr. Worthington...?"
"It is in your better interests to **wake up** now, Mr. Worthington..."
BLBRB--?

GASP

Please do not waste what time we have *left* together with questions or protestations.

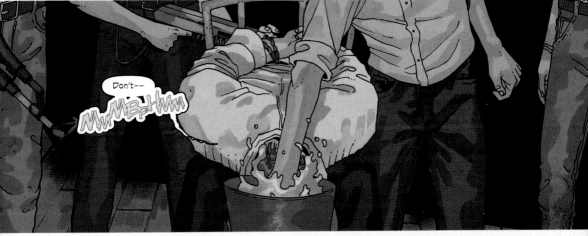

Don't--

MMMMBpHMM

Mr. Worthington...

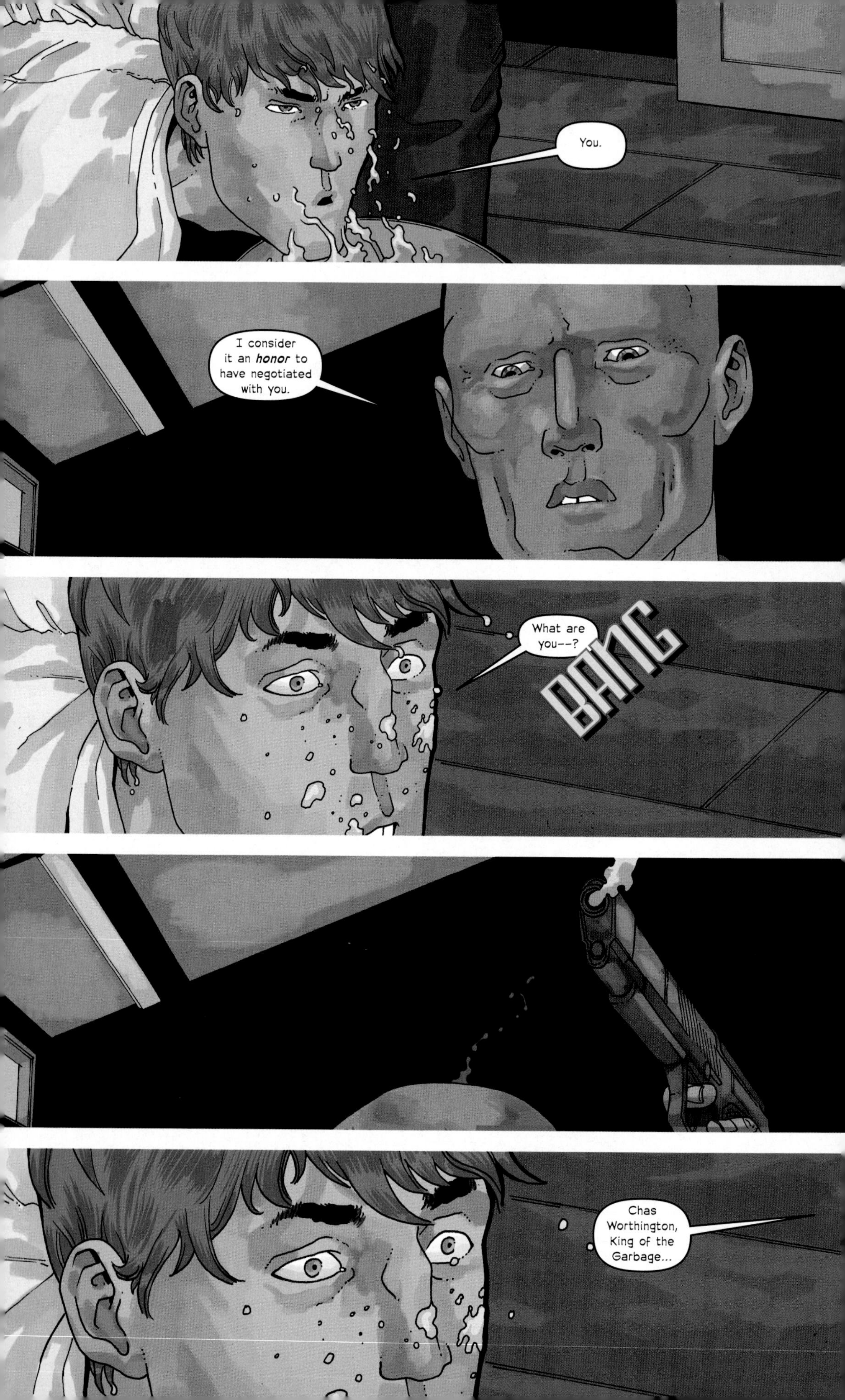
You.
I consider it an *honor* to have negotiated with you.
What are you--?
BANG
Chas Worthington, King of the Garbage...

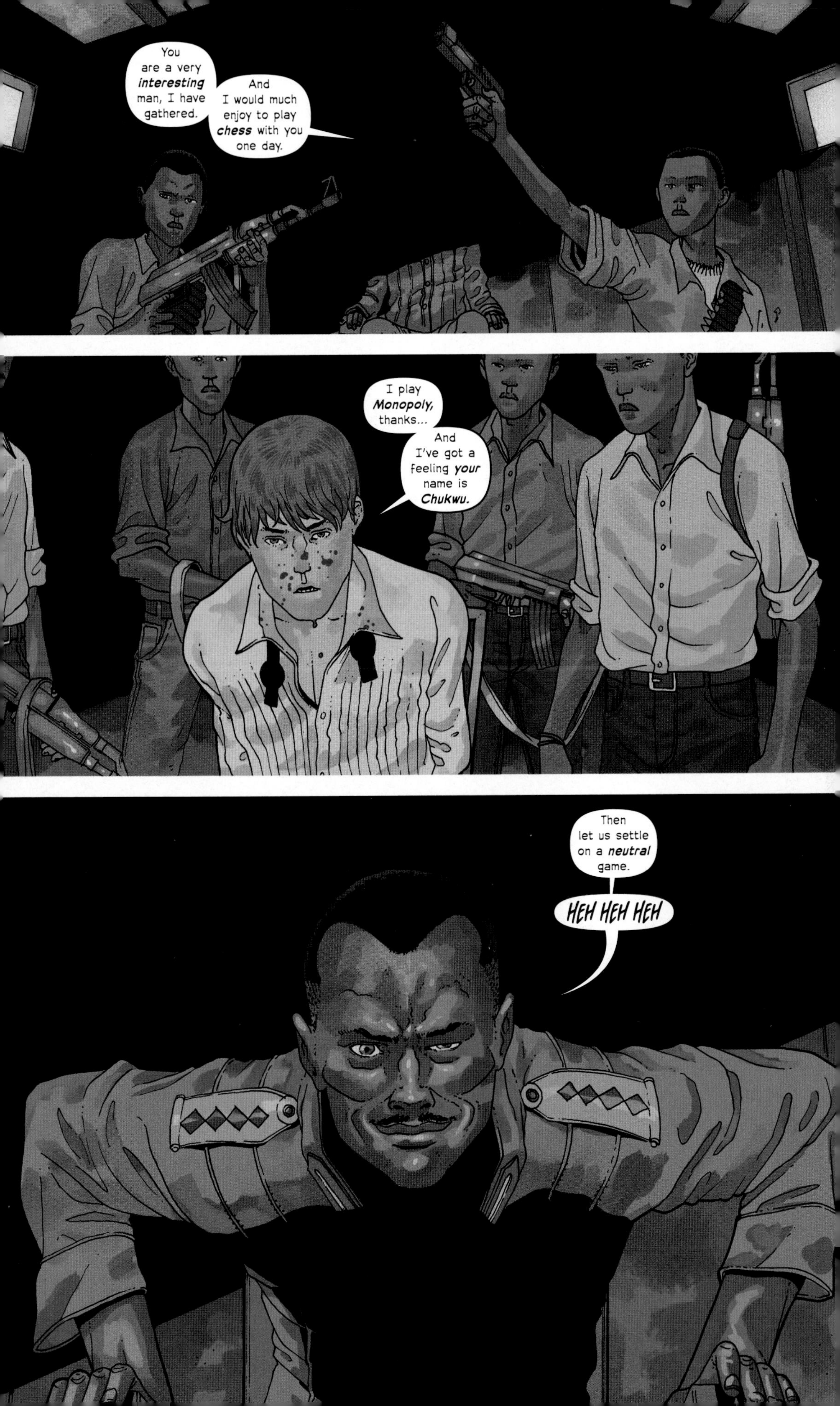
You are a very interesting man, I have gathered.
And I would much enjoy to play chess with you one day.
I play Monopoly, thanks...
And I've got a feeling your name is Chukwu.
Then let us settle on a neutral game.
HEH HEH HEH

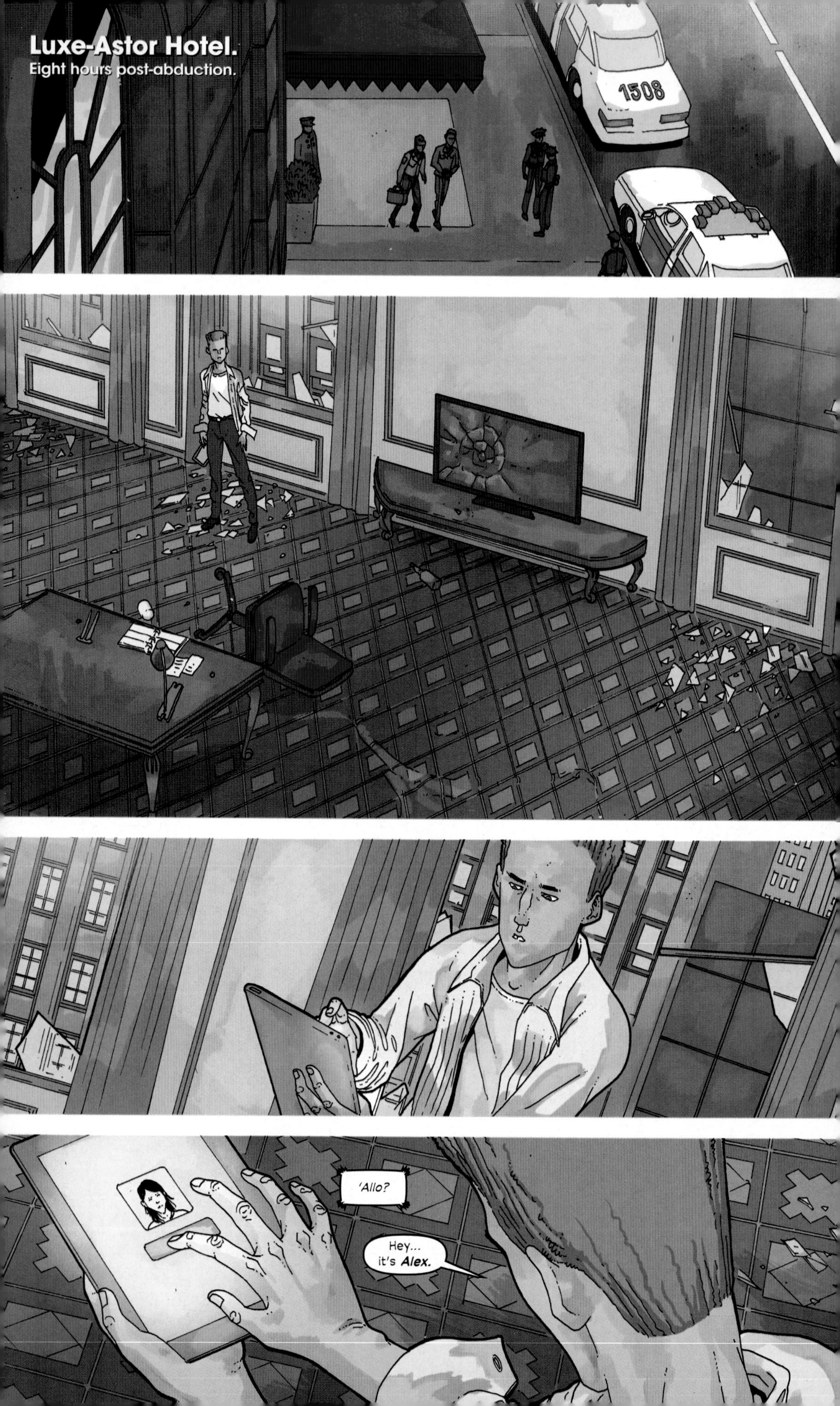
Luxe-Astor Hotel.
Eight hours post-abduction.
1508
'Allo?
Hey... it's Alex.

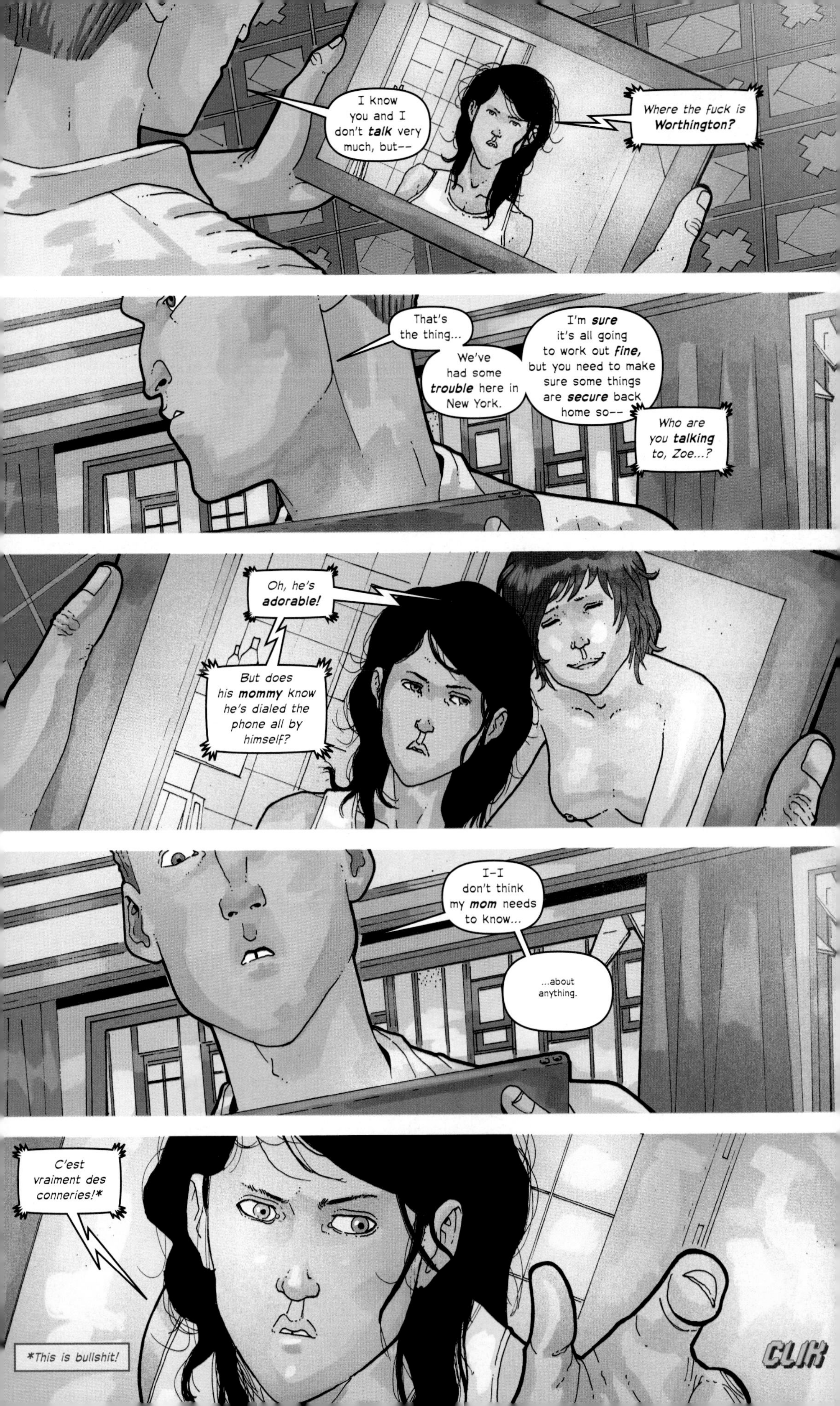
I know you and I don't *talk* very much, but--
Where the fuck is ***Worthington?***
That's the thing...
We've had some ***trouble*** here in New York.
I'm ***sure*** it's all going to work out ***fine,*** but you need to make sure some things are ***secure*** back home so--
Who are you ***talking*** *to, Zoe...?*
Oh, he's ***adorable!***
But does his ***mommy*** *know he's dialed the phone all by himself?*
I-I don't think my ***mom*** needs to know...
...about anything.
*C'est vraiment des conneries!**
**This is bullshit!*
CLIK

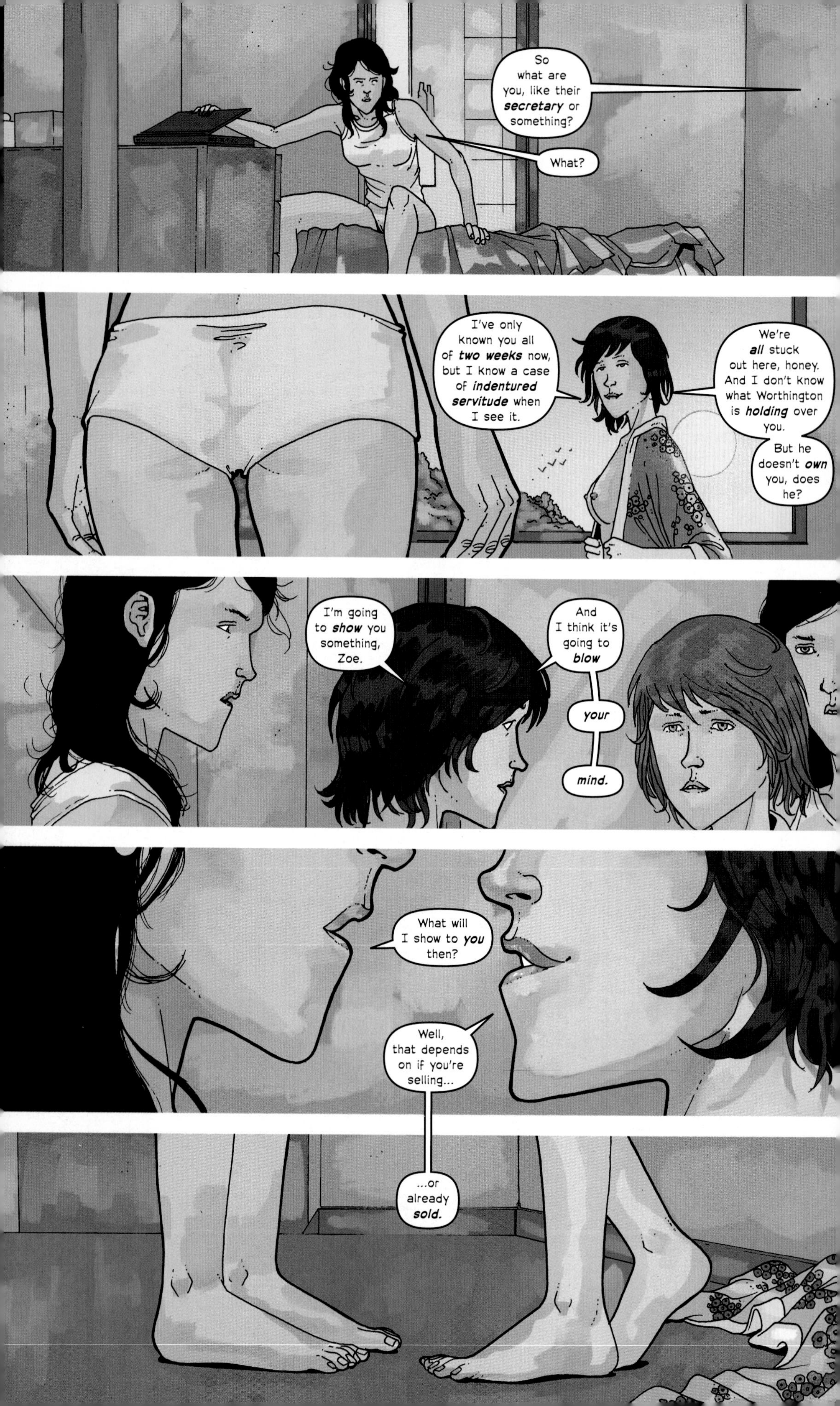
So what are you, like their secretary or something?
What?
I've only known you all of two weeks now, but I know a case of indentured servitude when I see it.
We're all stuck out here, honey. And I don't know what Worthington is holding over you.
But he doesn't own you, does he?
I'm going to show you something, Zoe.
And I think it's going to blow
your
mind.
What will I show to you then?
Well, that depends on if you're selling...
...or already sold.

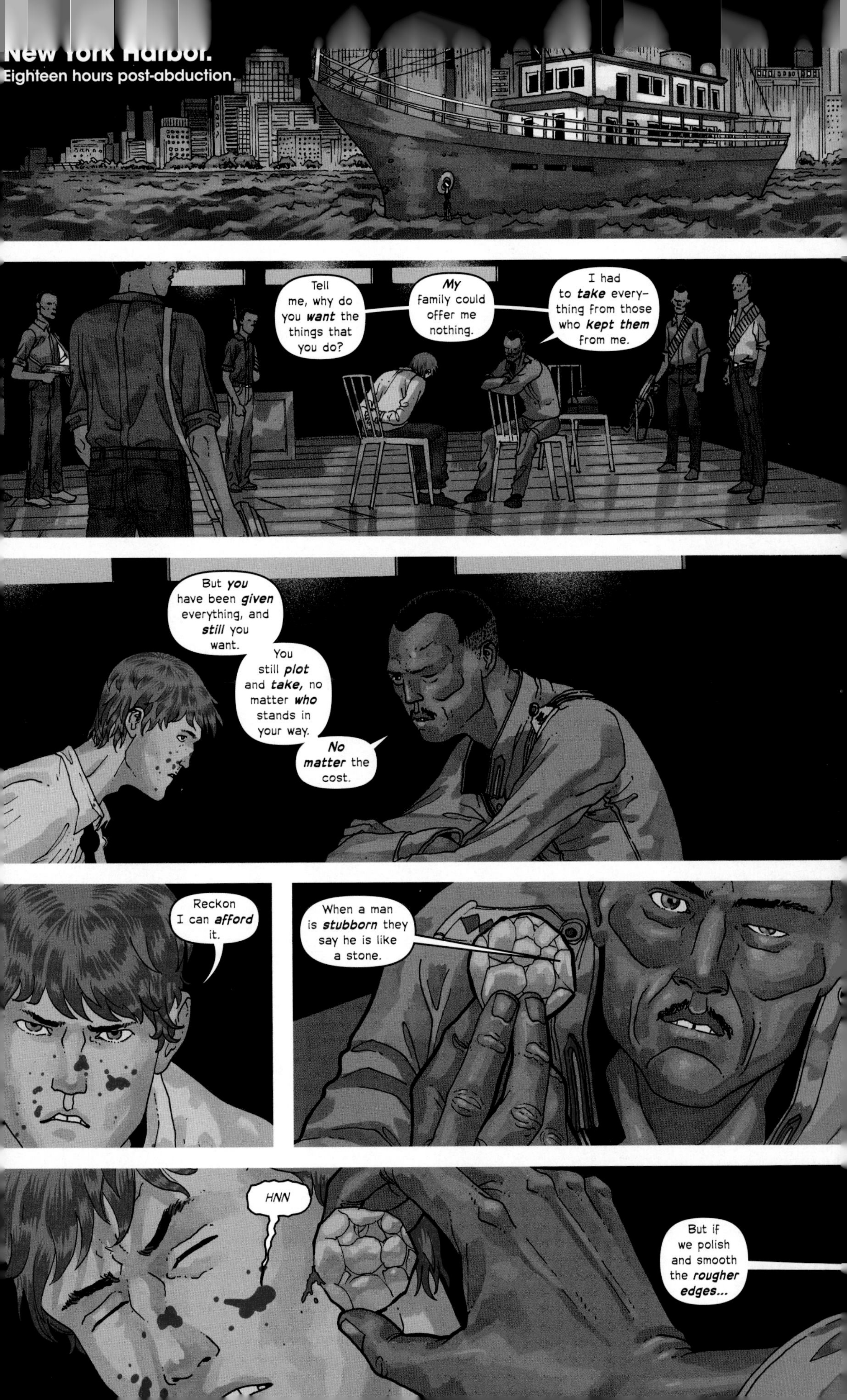
New York Harbor.
Eighteen hours post-abduction.
Tell me, why do you want the things that you do?
My family could offer me nothing.
I had to take everything from those who kept them from me.
But you have been given everything, and still you want.
You still plot and take, no matter who stands in your way.
No matter the cost.
Reckon I can afford it.
When a man is stubborn they say he is like a stone.
HNN
But if we polish and smooth the rougher edges...

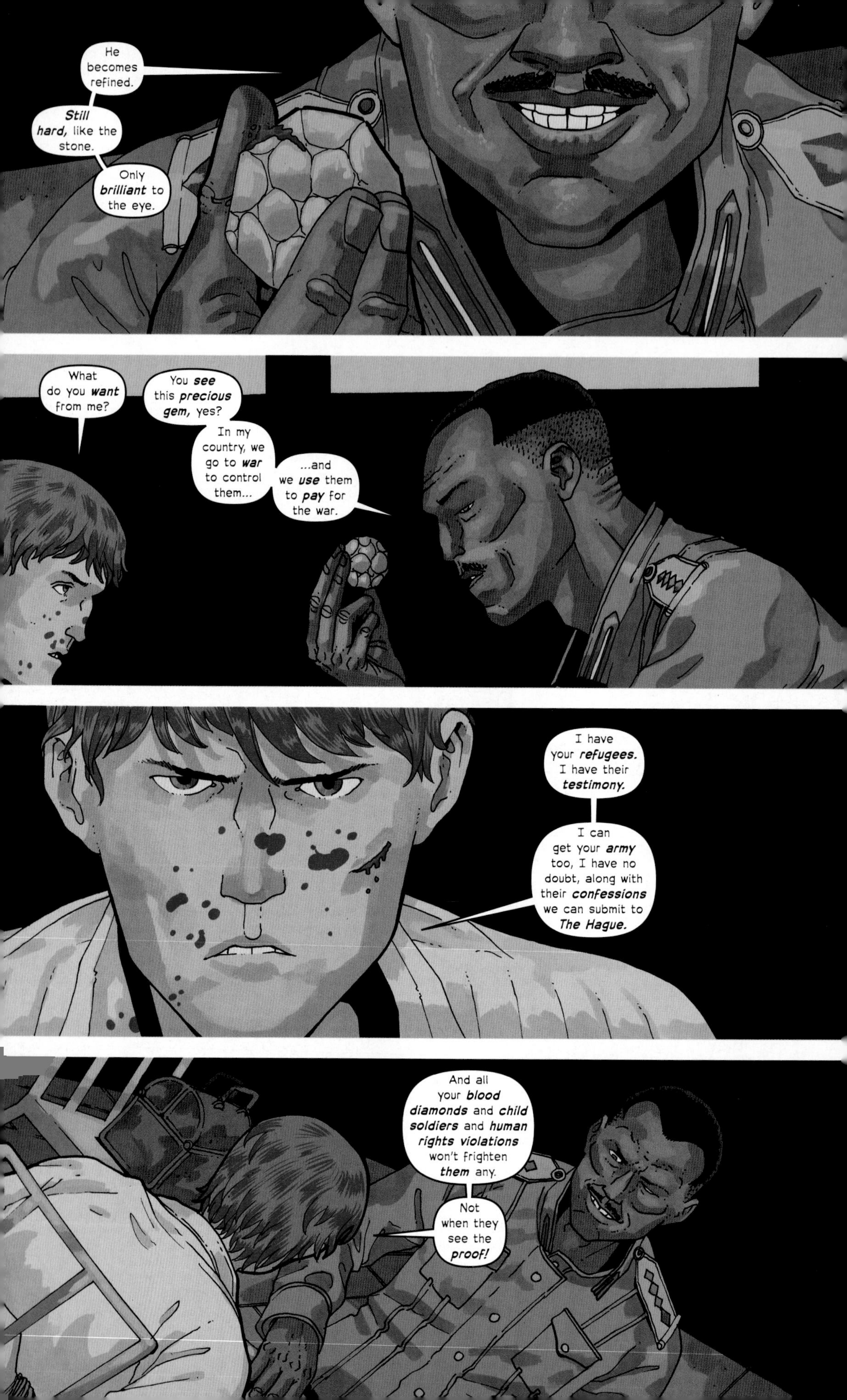
He becomes refined.
Still hard, like the stone.
Only brilliant to the eye.
What do you want from me?
You see this precious gem, yes?
In my country, we go to war to control them...
...and we use them to pay for the war.
I have your refugees. I have their testimony.
I can get your army too, I have no doubt, along with their confessions we can submit to The Hague.
And all your blood diamonds and child soldiers and human rights violations won't frighten them any.
Not when they see the proof!

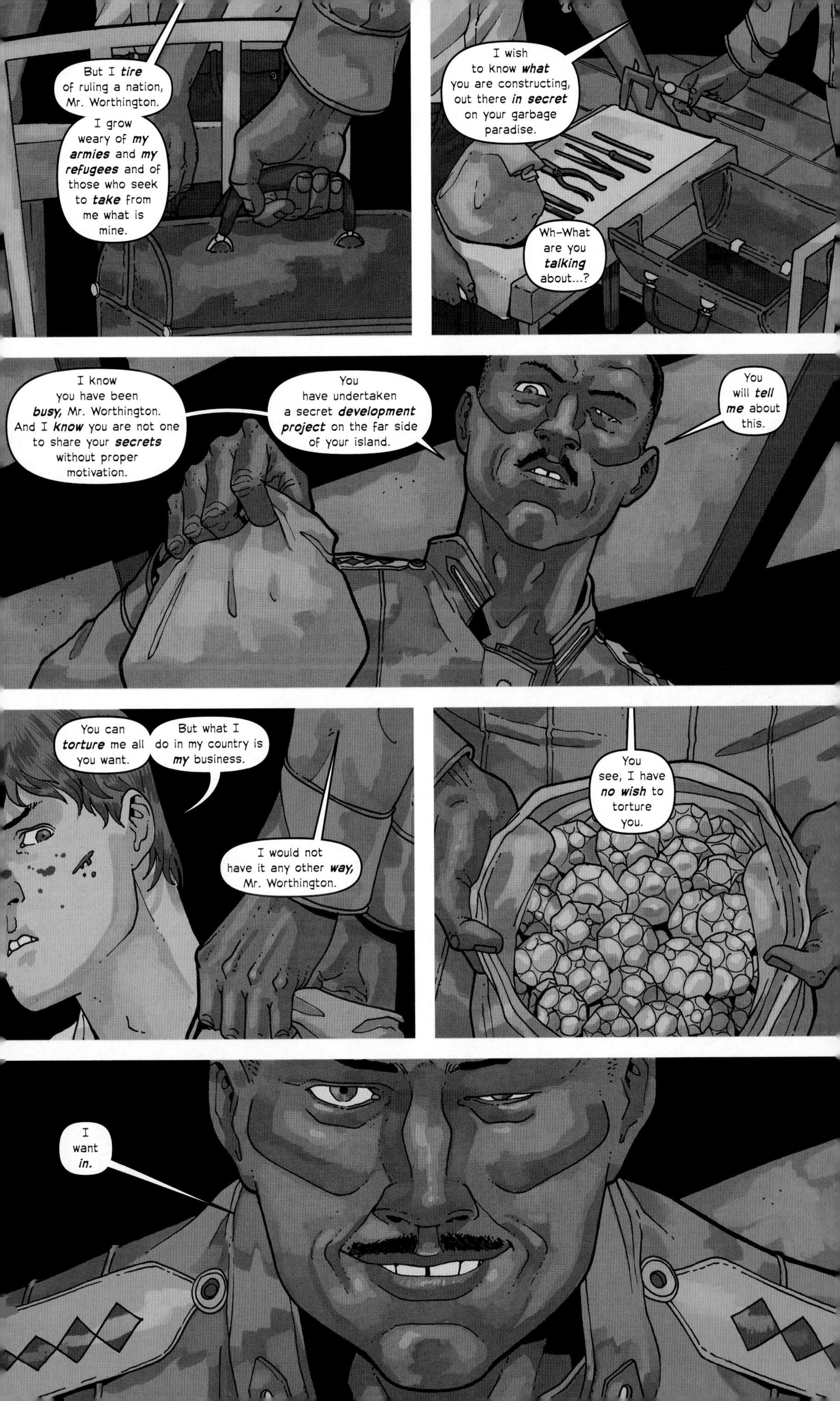
But I tire of ruling a nation, Mr. Worthington.
I grow weary of my armies and my refugees and of those who seek to take from me what is mine.
I wish to know what you are constructing, out there in secret on your garbage paradise.
Wh-What are you talking about...?
I know you have been busy, Mr. Worthington. And I know you are not one to share your secrets without proper motivation.
You have undertaken a secret development project on the far side of your island.
You will tell me about this.
You can torture me all you want.
But what I do in my country is my business.
I would not have it any other way, Mr. Worthington.
You see, I have no wish to torture you.
I want in.

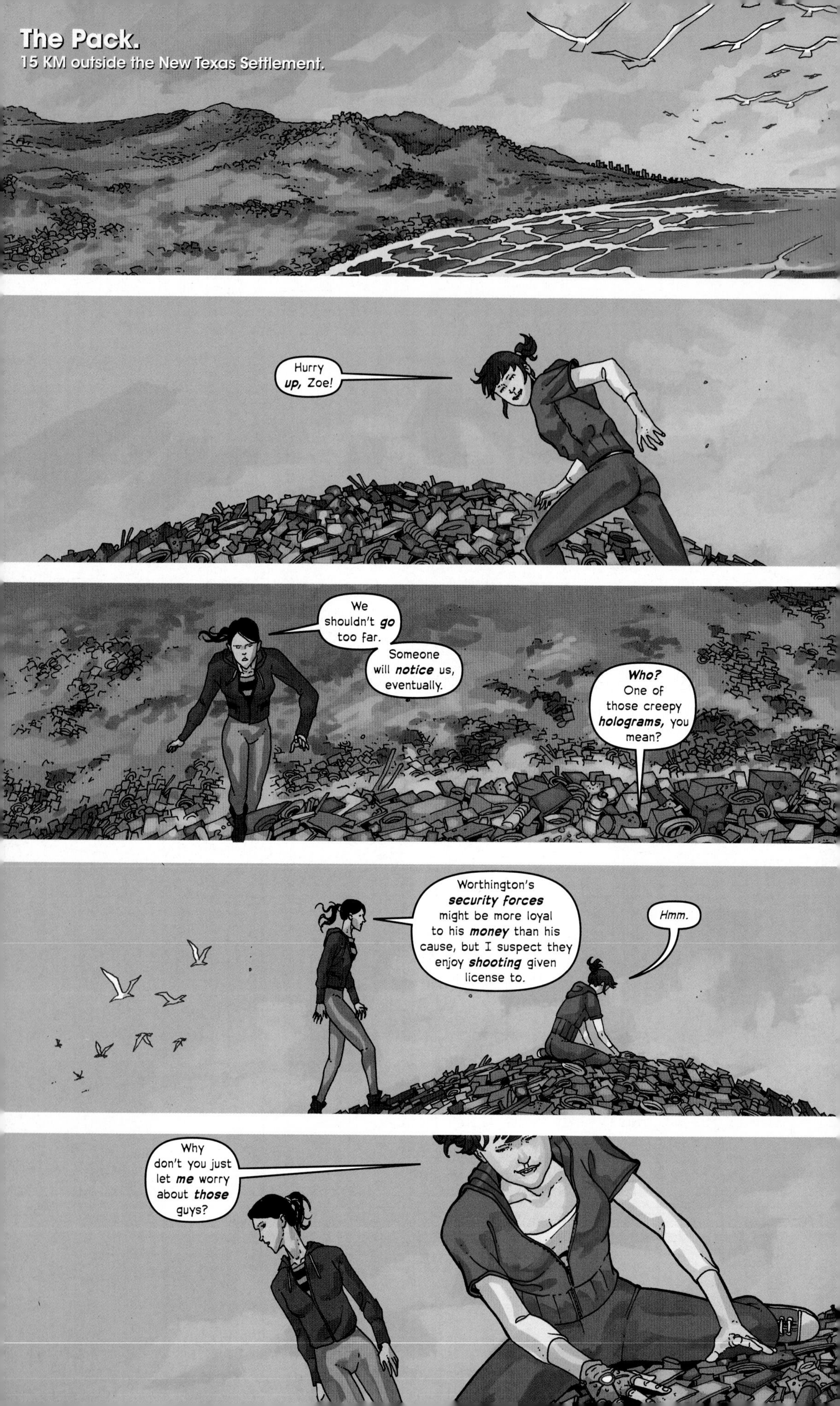

The Pack.
15 KM outside the New Texas Settlement.
Hurry up, Zoe!
We shouldn't go too far.
Someone will notice us, eventually.
Who? One of those creepy holograms, you mean?
Worthington's security forces might be more loyal to his money than his cause, but I suspect they enjoy shooting given license to.
Hmm.
Why don't you just let me worry about those guys?

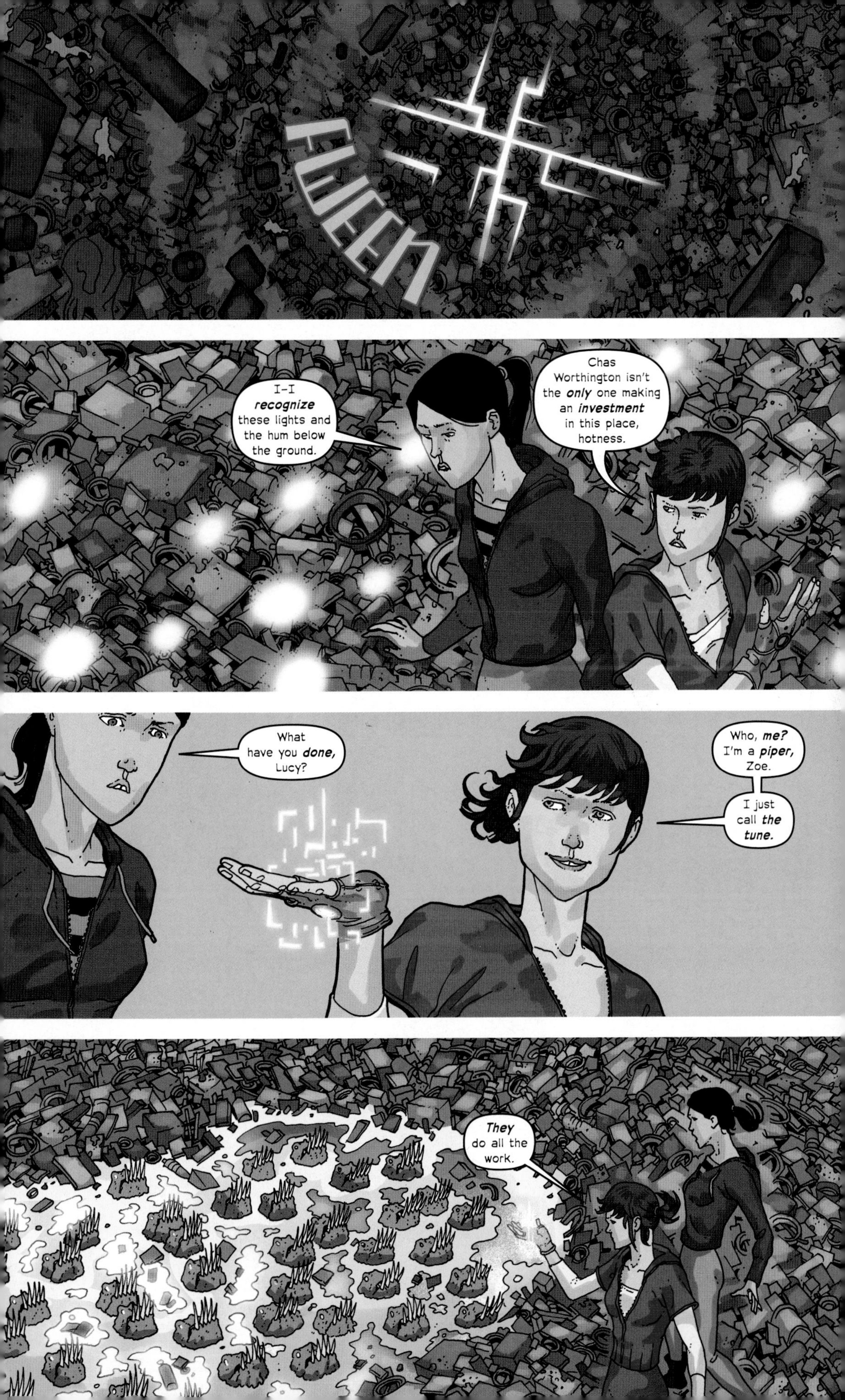
FWEEN
I-I *recognize* these lights and the hum below the ground.
Chas Worthington isn't the *only* one making an *investment* in this place, hotness.
What have you *done,* Lucy?
Who, *me?* I'm a *piper,* Zoe.
I just call *the tune.*
They do all the work.

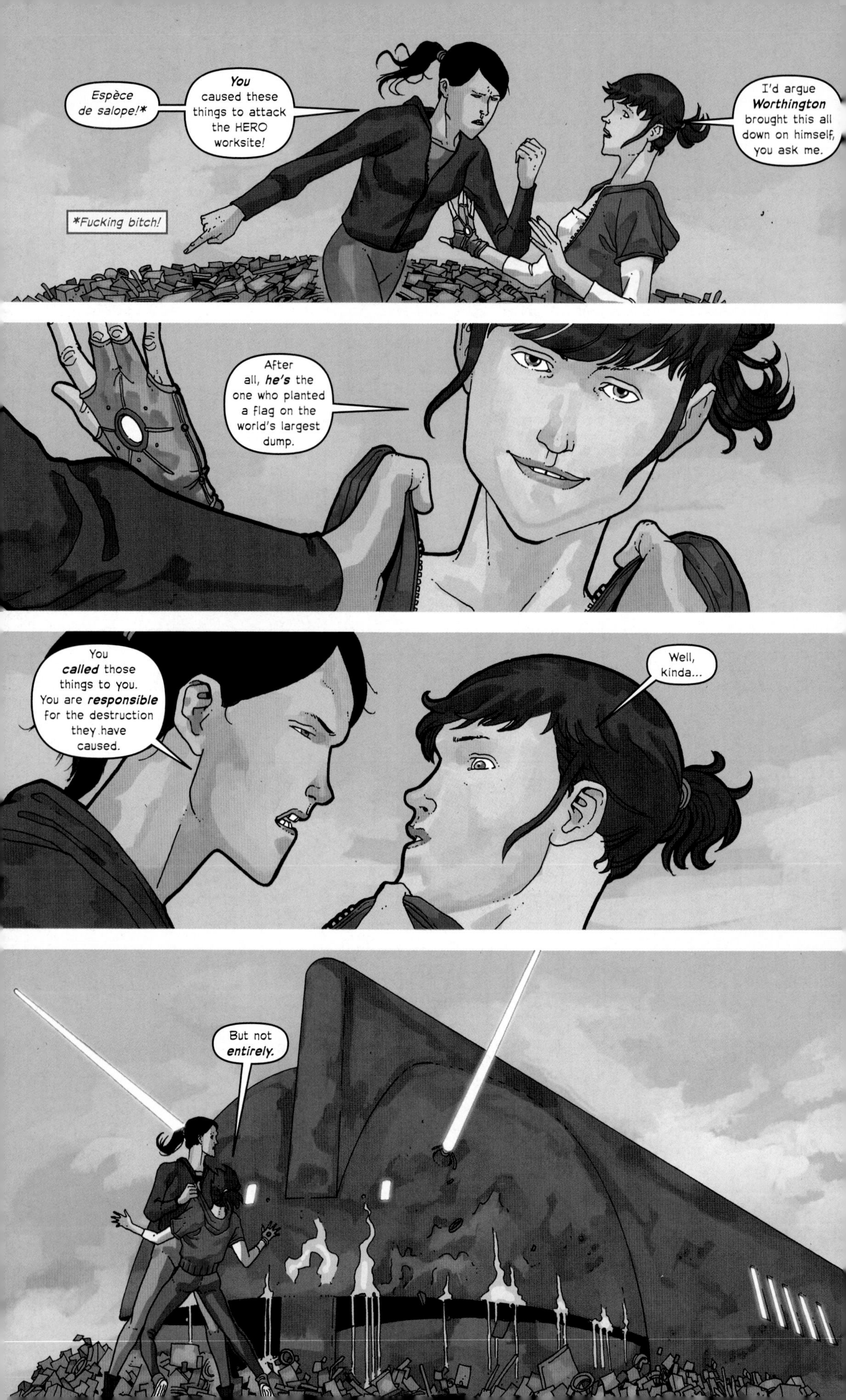
Espèce de salope!*
You caused these things to attack the HERO worksite!
*Fucking bitch!
I'd argue Worthington brought this all down on himself, you ask me.
After all, he's the one who planted a flag on the world's largest dump.
You called those things to you. You are responsible for the destruction they have caused.
Well, kinda...
But not entirely.

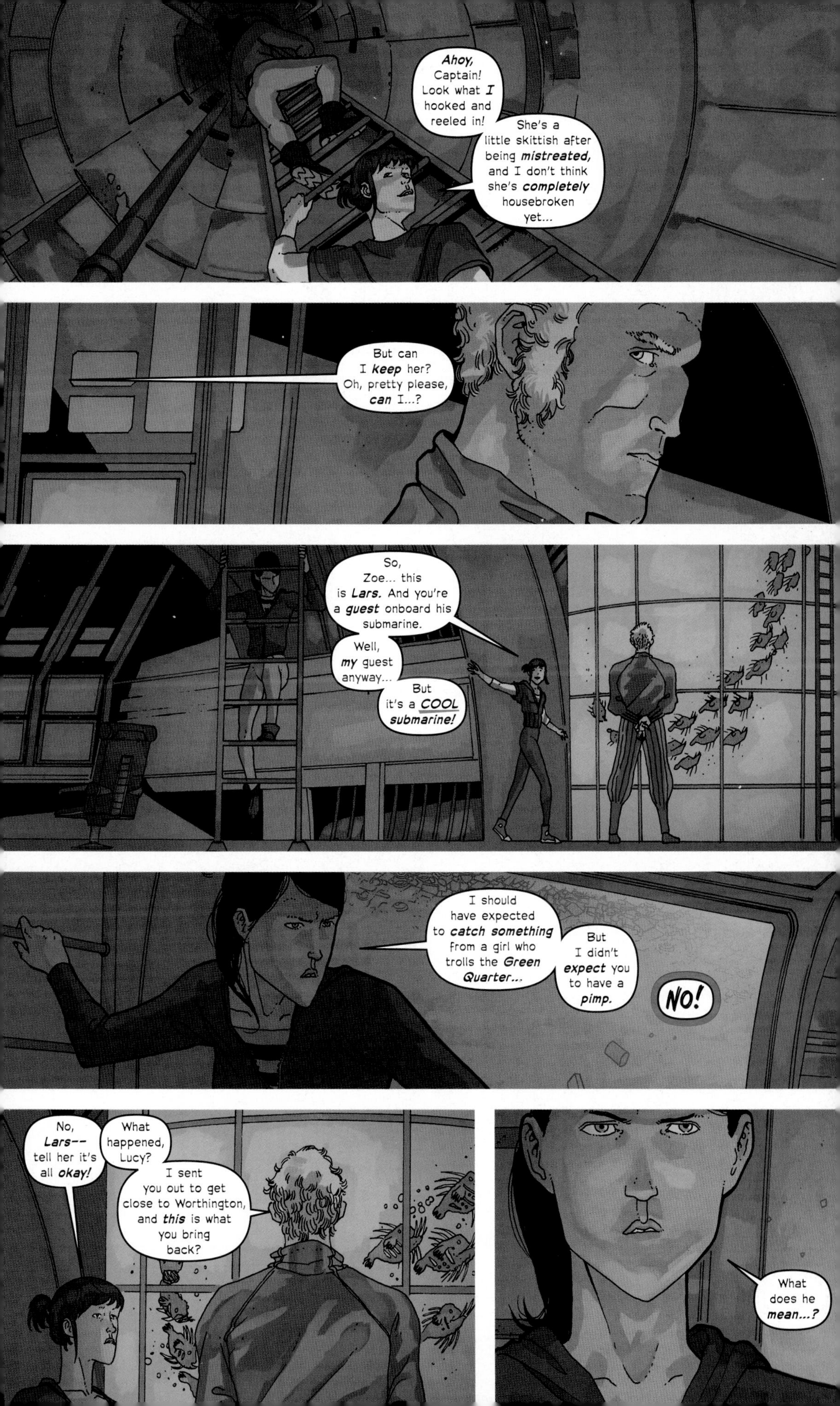

Ahoy, Captain! Look what I hooked and reeled in!
She's a little skittish after being mistreated, and I don't think she's completely housebroken yet...
But can I keep her? Oh, pretty please, can I...?
So, Zoe... this is Lars. And you're a guest onboard his submarine.
Well, my guest anyway...
But it's a COOL submarine!
I should have expected to catch something from a girl who trolls the Green Quarter...
But I didn't expect you to have a pimp.
NO!
No, Lars-- tell her it's all okay!
What happened, Lucy?
I sent you out to get close to Worthington, and this is what you bring back?
What does he mean...?

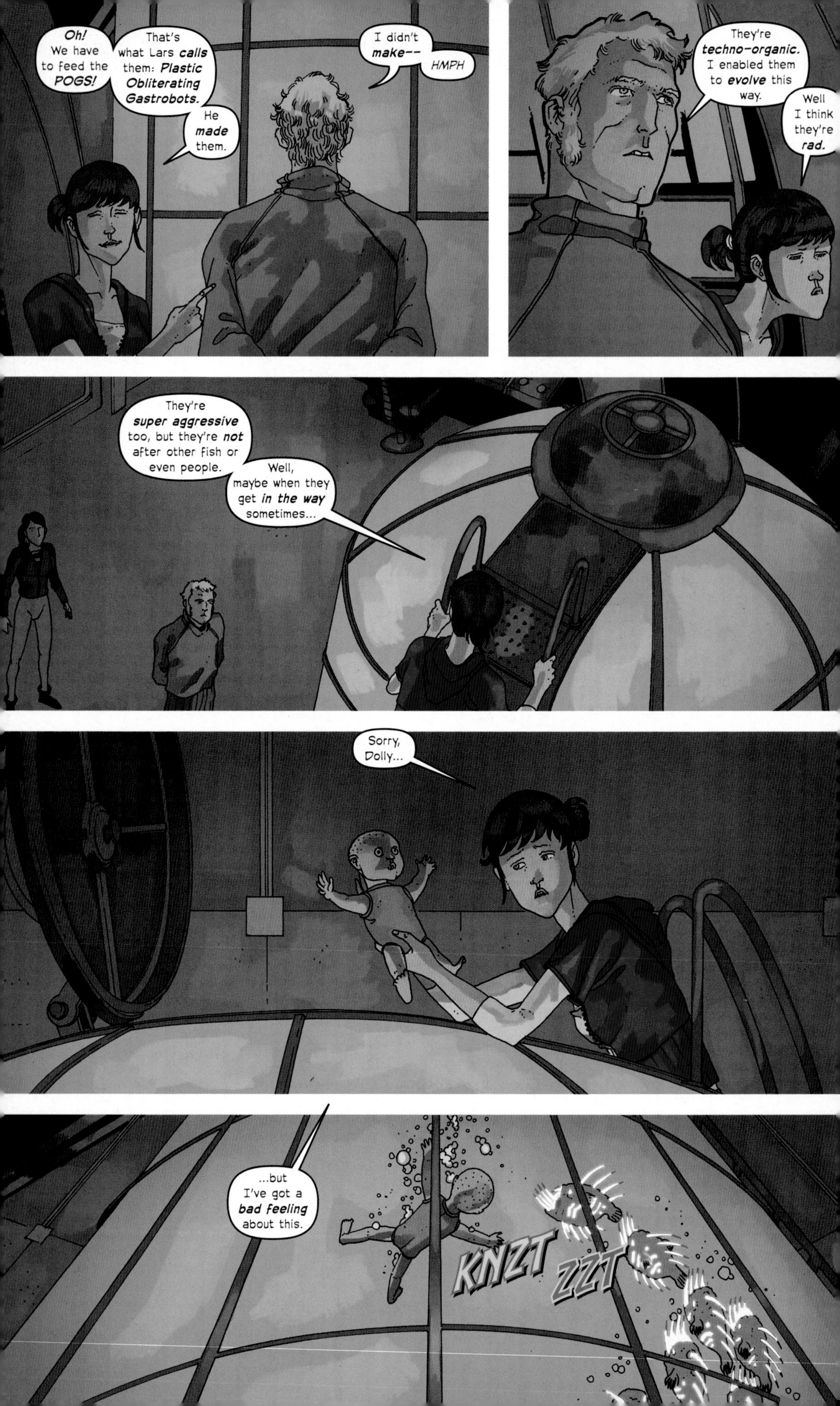

Oh! We have to feed the POGS!
That's what Lars calls them: Plastic Obliterating Gastrobots.
He made them.
I didn't make--
HMPH
They're techno-organic. I enabled them to evolve this way.
Well I think they're rad.
They're super aggressive too, but they're not after other fish or even people.
Well, maybe when they get in the way sometimes...
Sorry, Dolly...
...but I've got a bad feeling about this.
KNZT
ZZT

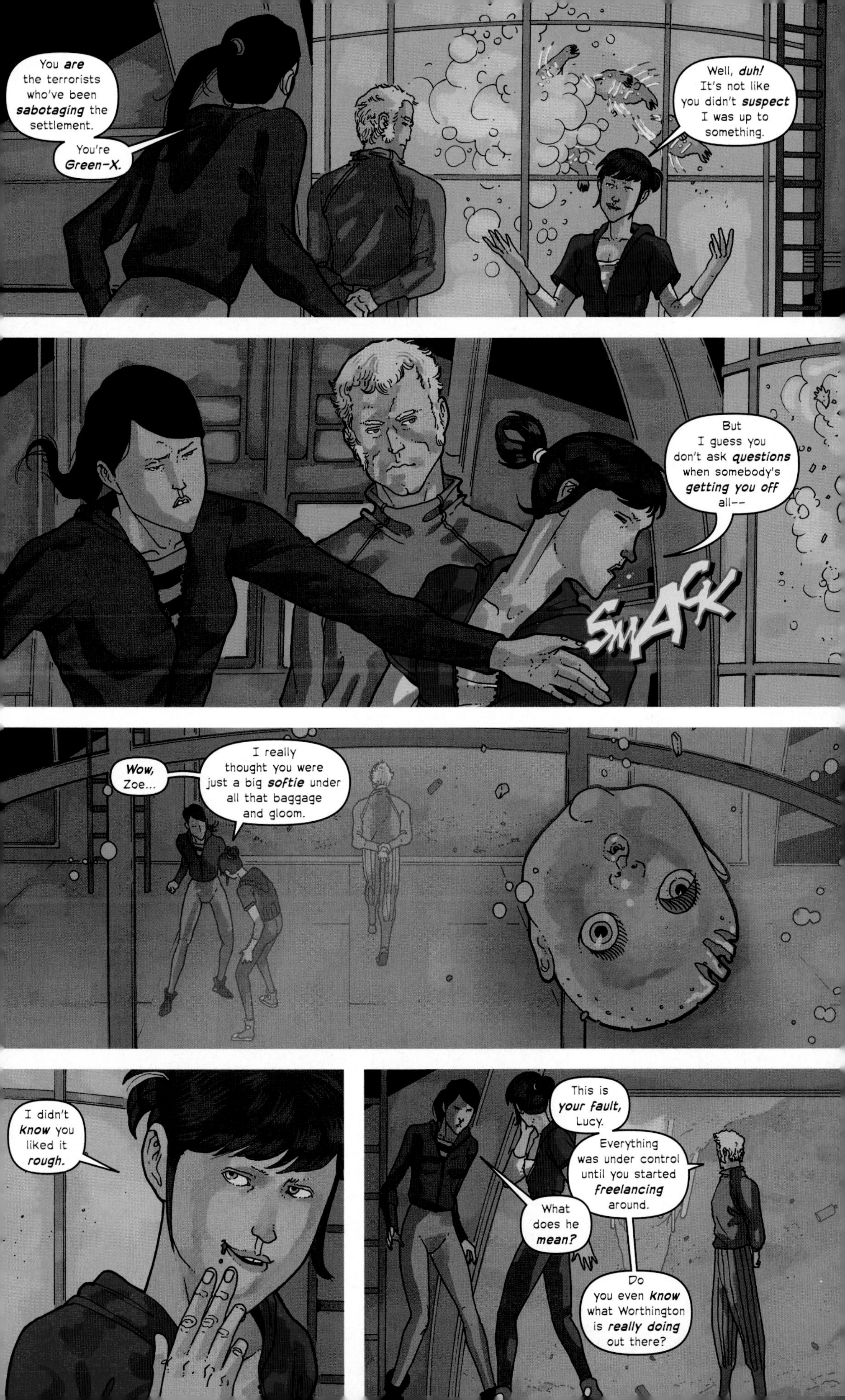

You are the terrorists who've been sabotaging the settlement.
You're Green-X.
Well, duh! It's not like you didn't suspect I was up to something.
But I guess you don't ask questions when somebody's getting you off all--
SMACK
Wow, Zoe...
I really thought you were just a big softie under all that baggage and gloom.
I didn't know you liked it rough.
This is your fault, Lucy.
Everything was under control until you started freelancing around.
What does he mean?
Do you even know what Worthington is really doing out there?

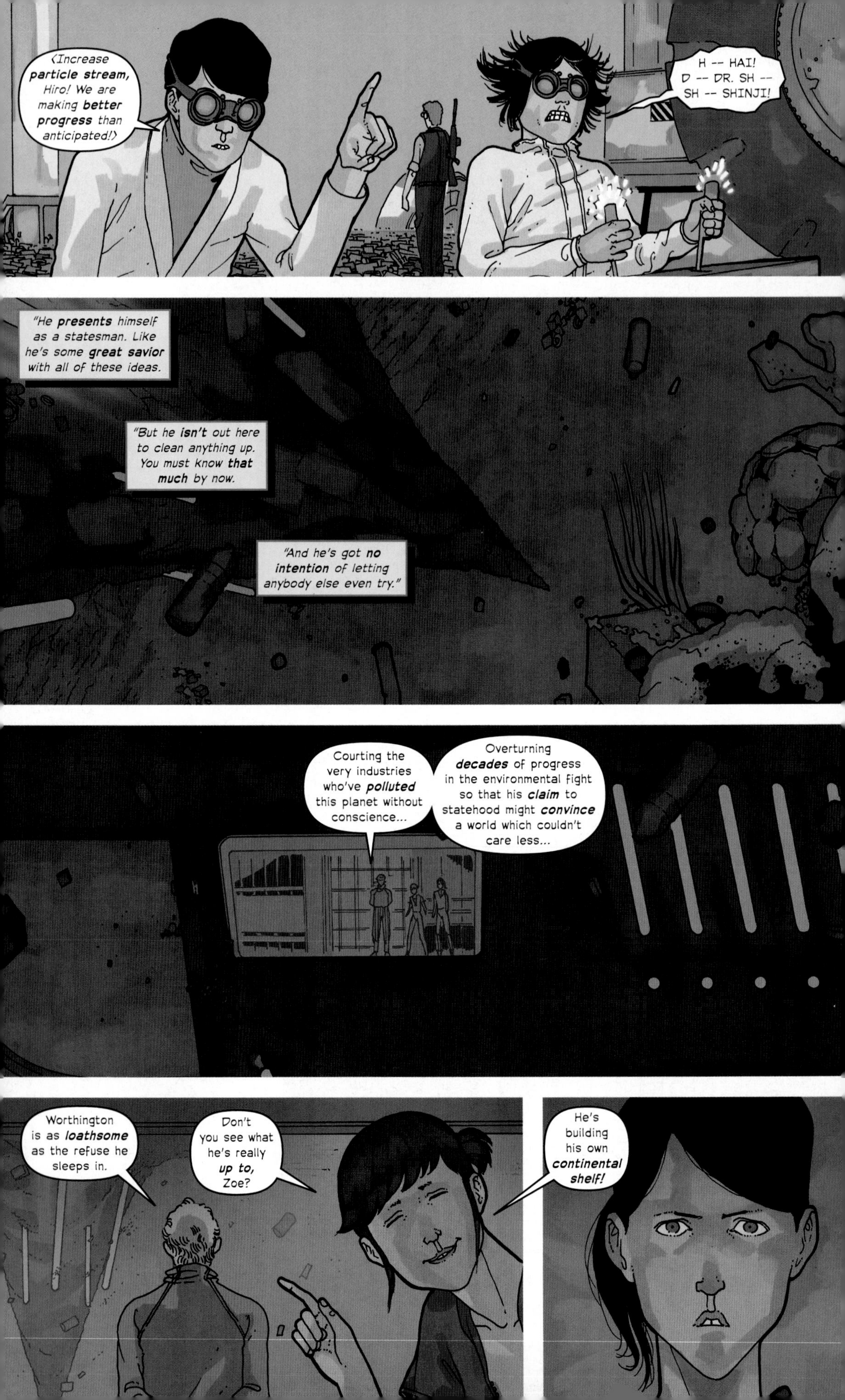
‹Increase particle stream, Hiro! We are making better progress than anticipated!›
H -- HAI! D -- DR. SH -- SH -- SHINJI!
"He presents himself as a statesman. Like he's some great savior with all of these ideas.
"But he isn't out here to clean anything up. You must know that much by now.
"And he's got no intention of letting anybody else even try."
Courting the very industries who've polluted this planet without conscience...
Overturning decades of progress in the environmental fight so that his claim to statehood might convince a world which couldn't care less...
Worthington is as loathsome as the refuse he sleeps in.
Don't you see what he's really up to, Zoe?
He's building his own continental shelf!

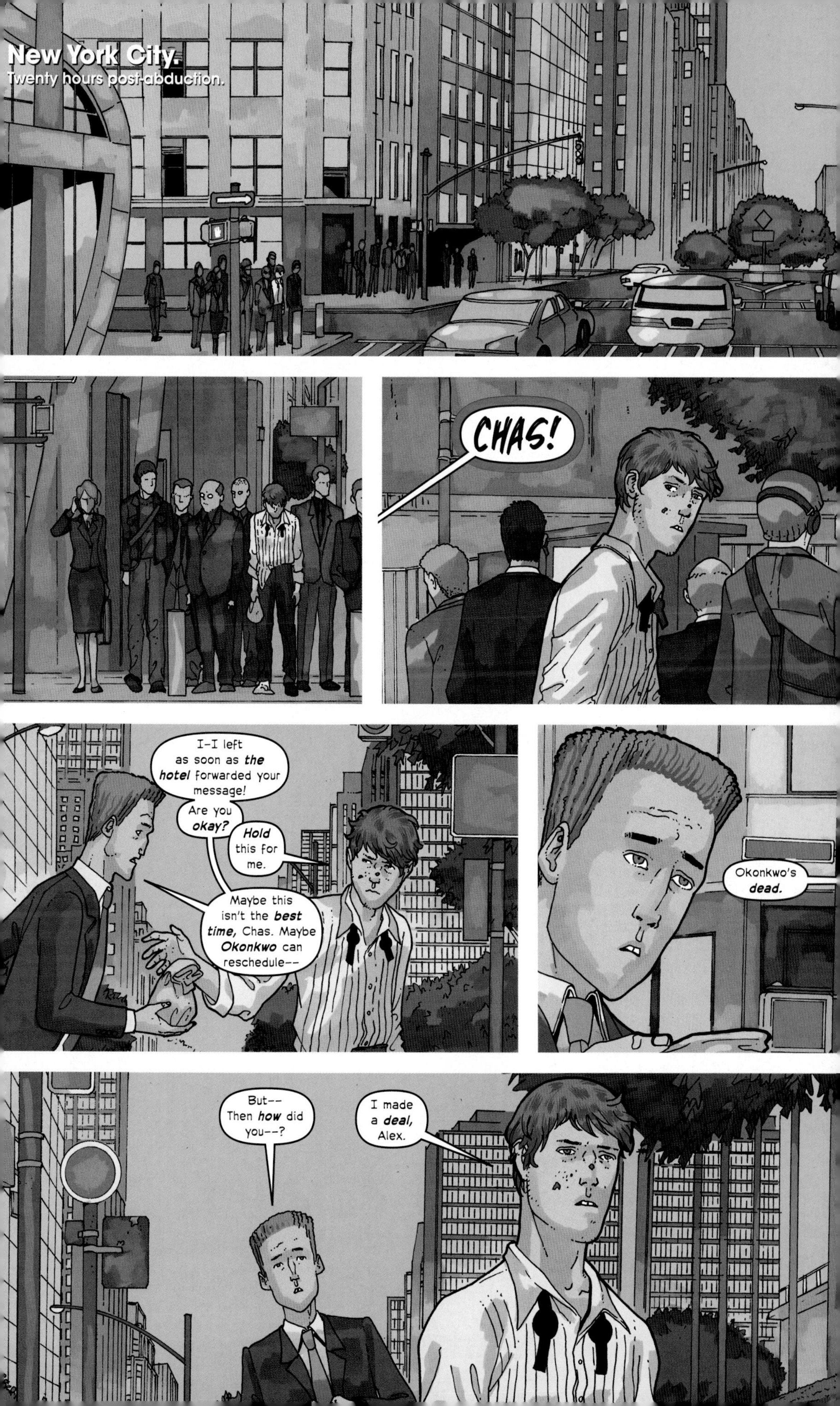
New York City.
Twenty hours post-abduction.
CHAS!
I-I left as soon as the hotel forwarded your message!
Are you okay?
Hold this for me.
Maybe this isn't the best time, Chas. Maybe Okonkwo can reschedule--
Okonkwo's dead.
But-- Then how did you--?
I made a deal, Alex.

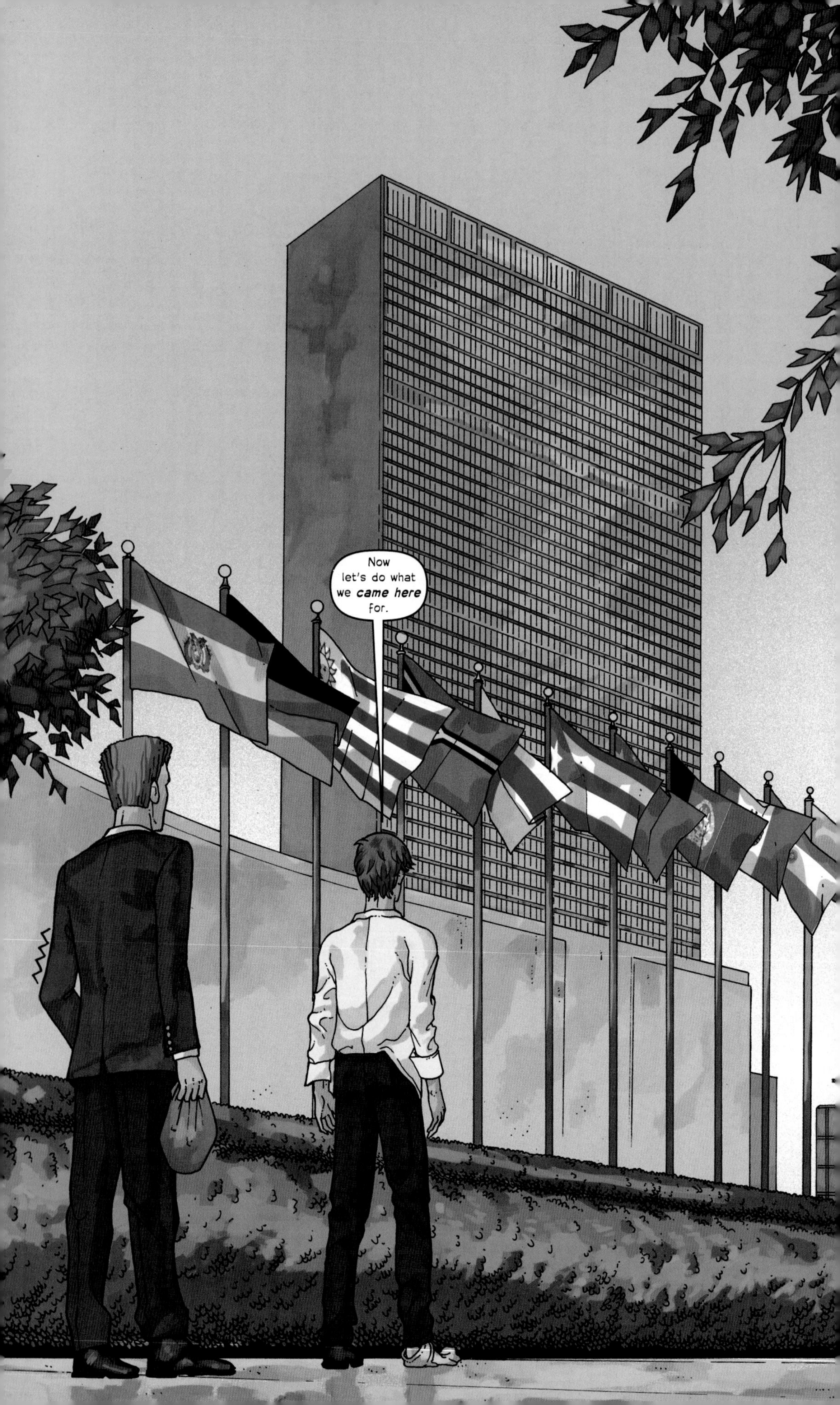
Now let's do what we **came here** for.

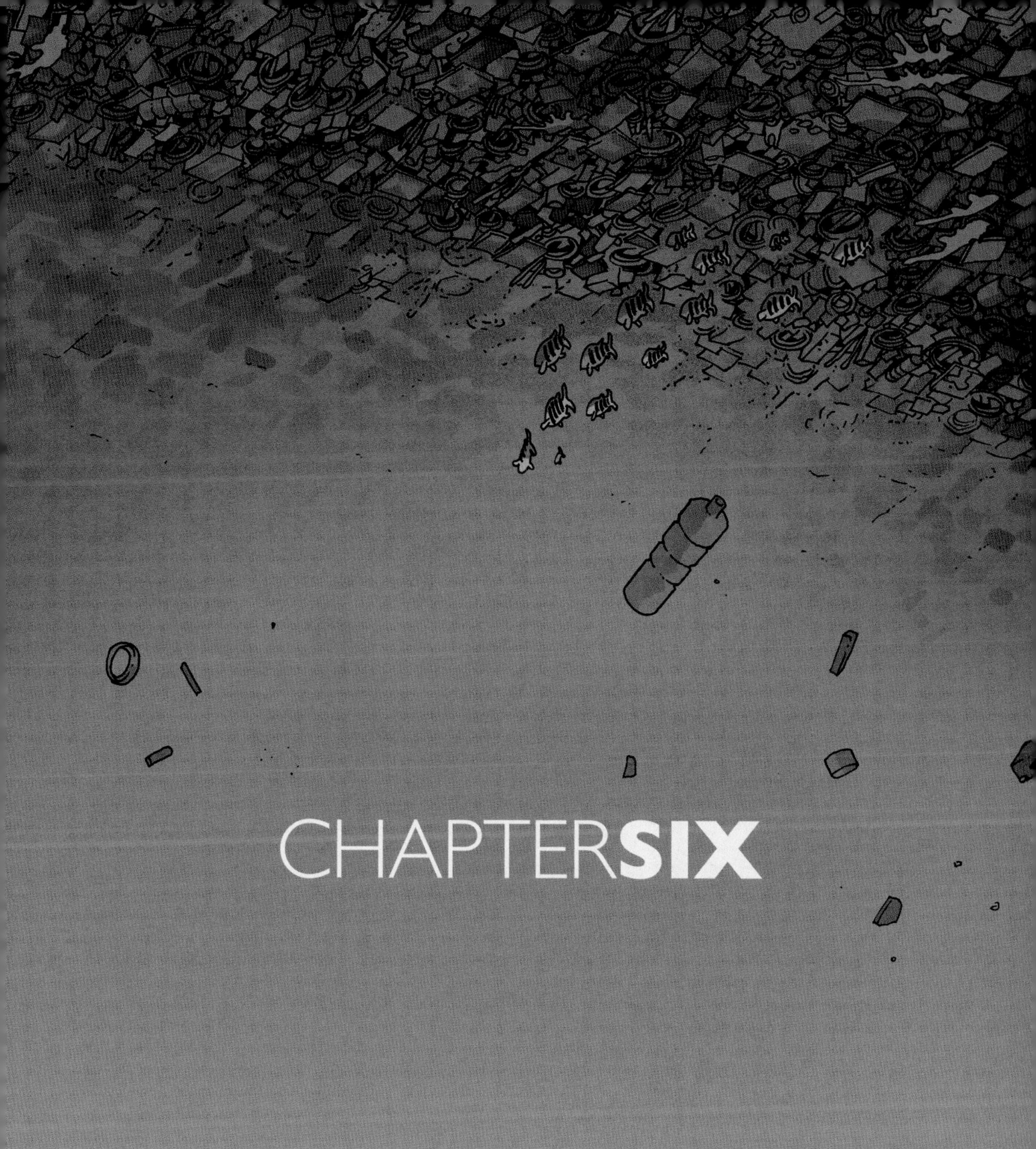

CHAPTER **SIX**

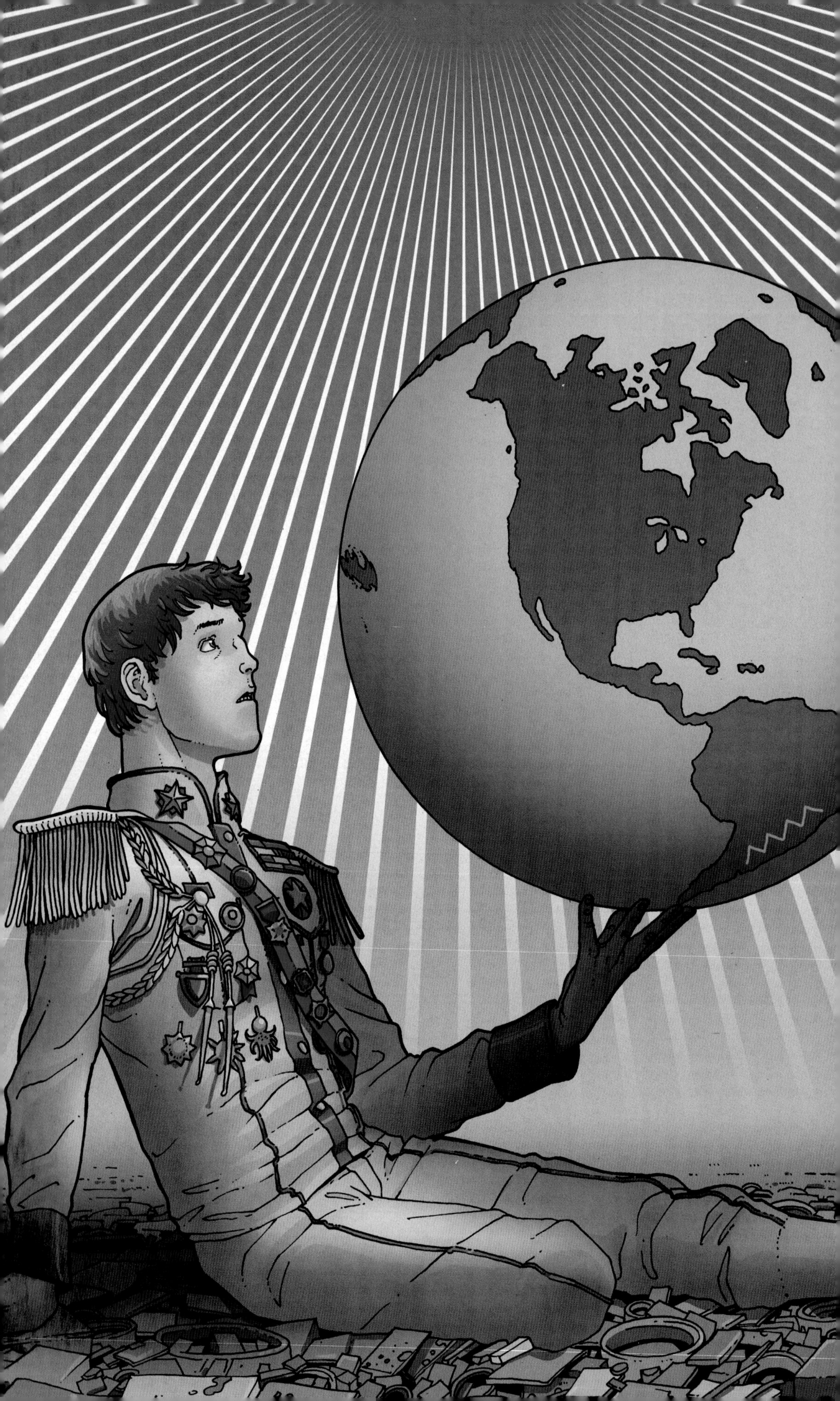

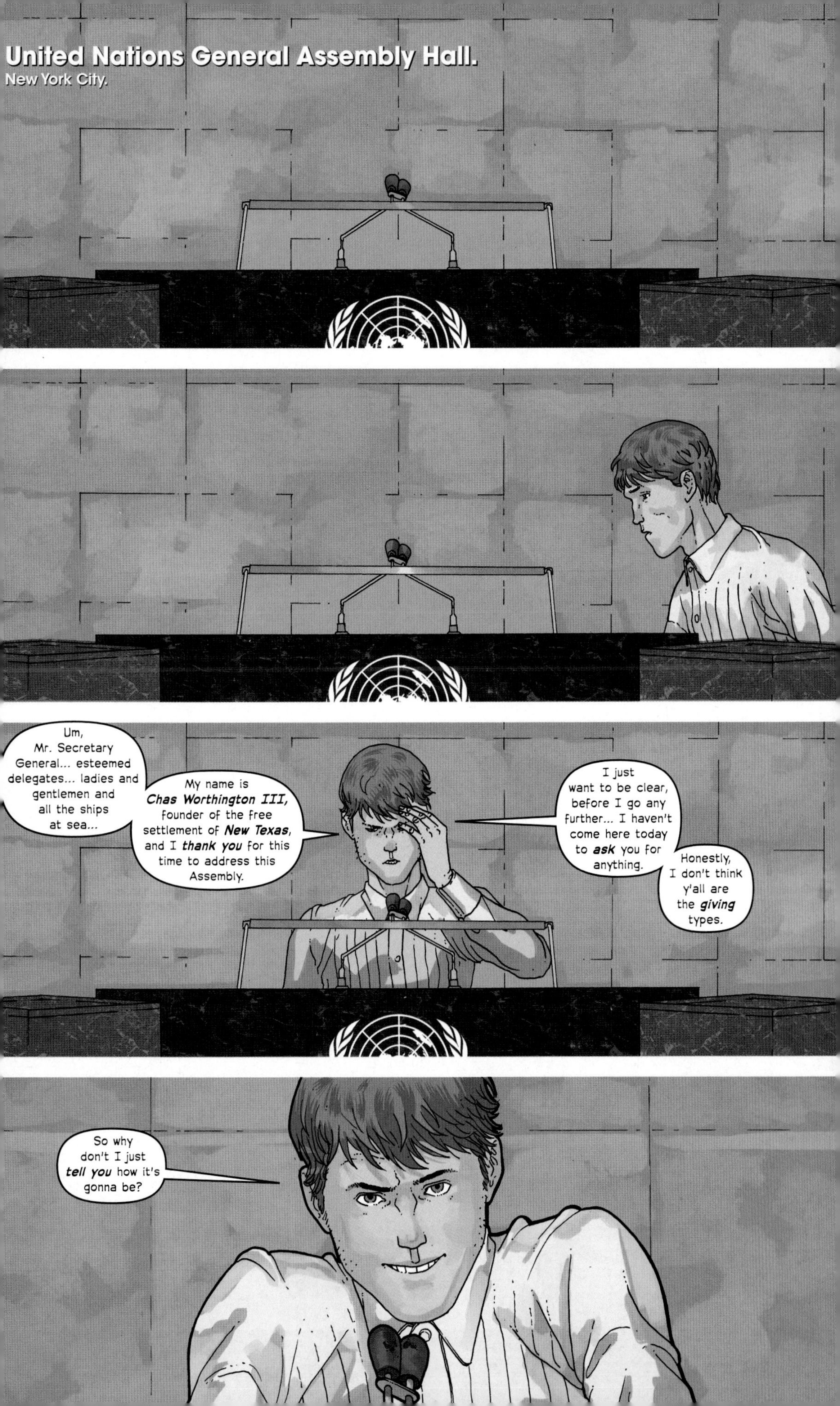

United Nations General Assembly Hall.
New York City.
Um, Mr. Secretary General... esteemed delegates... ladies and gentlemen and all the ships at sea...
My name is *Chas Worthington III,* founder of the free settlement of *New Texas*, and I *thank you* for this time to address this Assembly.
I just want to be clear, before I go any further... I haven't come here today to *ask* you for anything.
Honestly, I don't think y'all are the *giving* types.
So why don't I just *tell you* how it's gonna be?

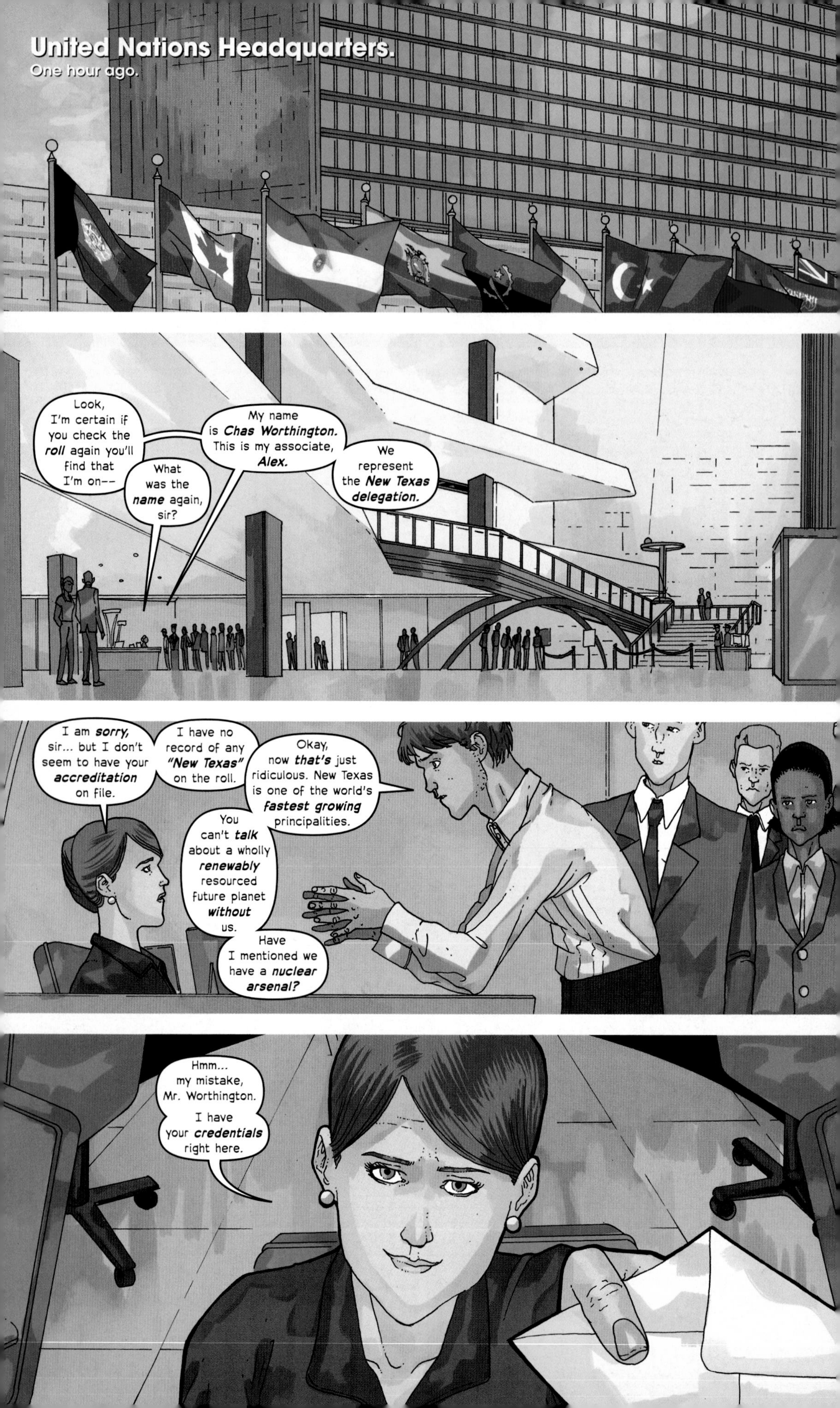
United Nations Headquarters.
One hour ago.
Look, I'm certain if you check the roll again you'll find that I'm on--
What was the name again, sir?
My name is Chas Worthington. This is my associate, Alex.
We represent the New Texas delegation.
I am sorry, sir... but I don't seem to have your accreditation on file.
I have no record of any "New Texas" on the roll.
Okay, now that's just ridiculous. New Texas is one of the world's fastest growing principalities.
You can't talk about a wholly renewably resourced future planet without us.
Have I mentioned we have a nuclear arsenal?
Hmm... my mistake, Mr. Worthington.
I have your credentials right here.

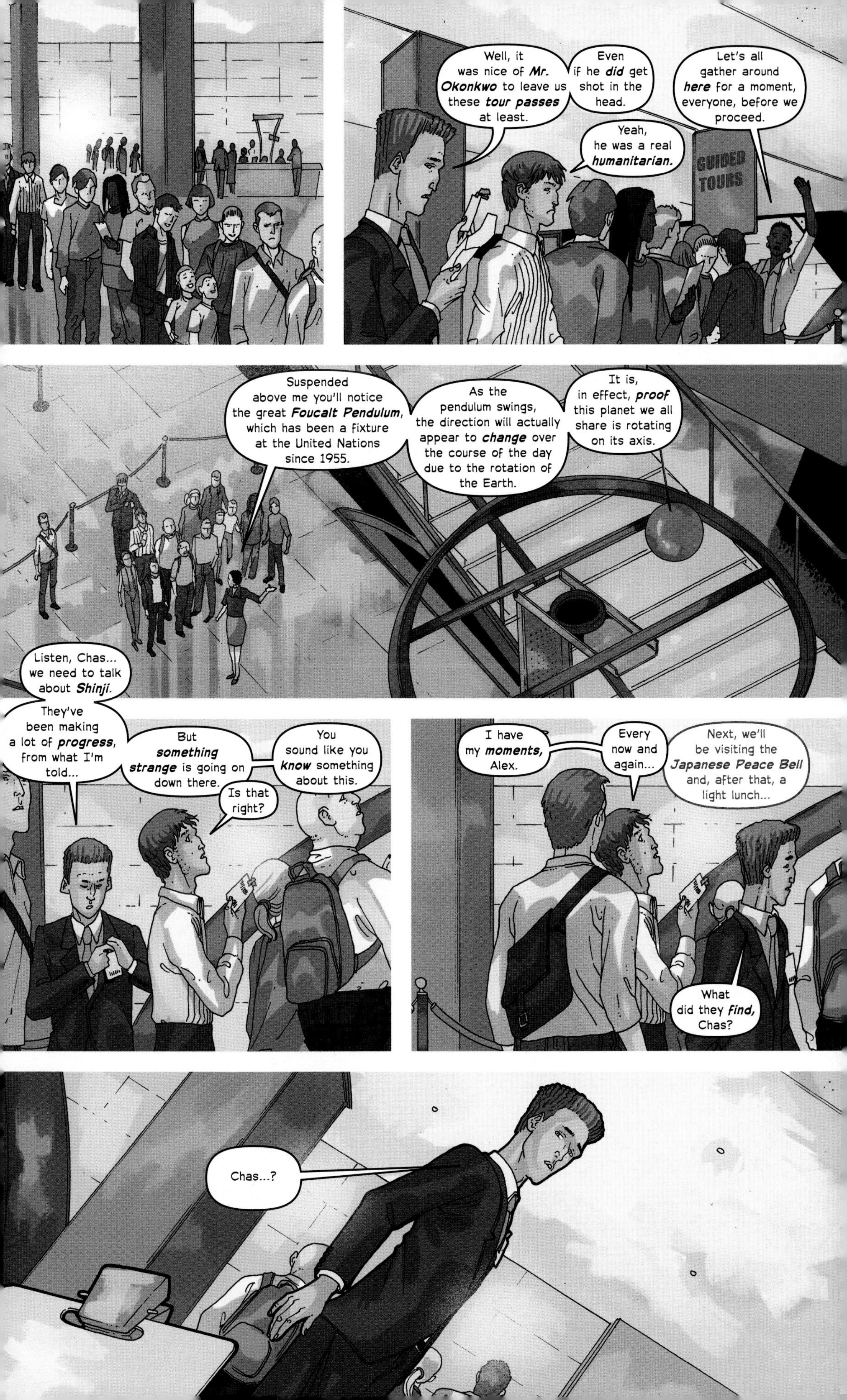
Well, it was nice of Mr. Okonkwo to leave us these tour passes at least.
Even if he did get shot in the head.
Yeah, he was a real humanitarian.
Let's all gather around here for a moment, everyone, before we proceed.
GUIDED TOURS
Suspended above me you'll notice the great Foucalt Pendulum, which has been a fixture at the United Nations since 1955.
As the pendulum swings, the direction will actually appear to change over the course of the day due to the rotation of the Earth.
It is, in effect, proof this planet we all share is rotating on its axis.
Listen, Chas... we need to talk about Shinji.
They've been making a lot of progress, from what I'm told...
But something strange is going on down there.
Is that right?
You sound like you know something about this.
I have my moments, Alex.
Every now and again...
Next, we'll be visiting the Japanese Peace Bell and, after that, a light lunch...
What did they find, Chas?
Chas...?

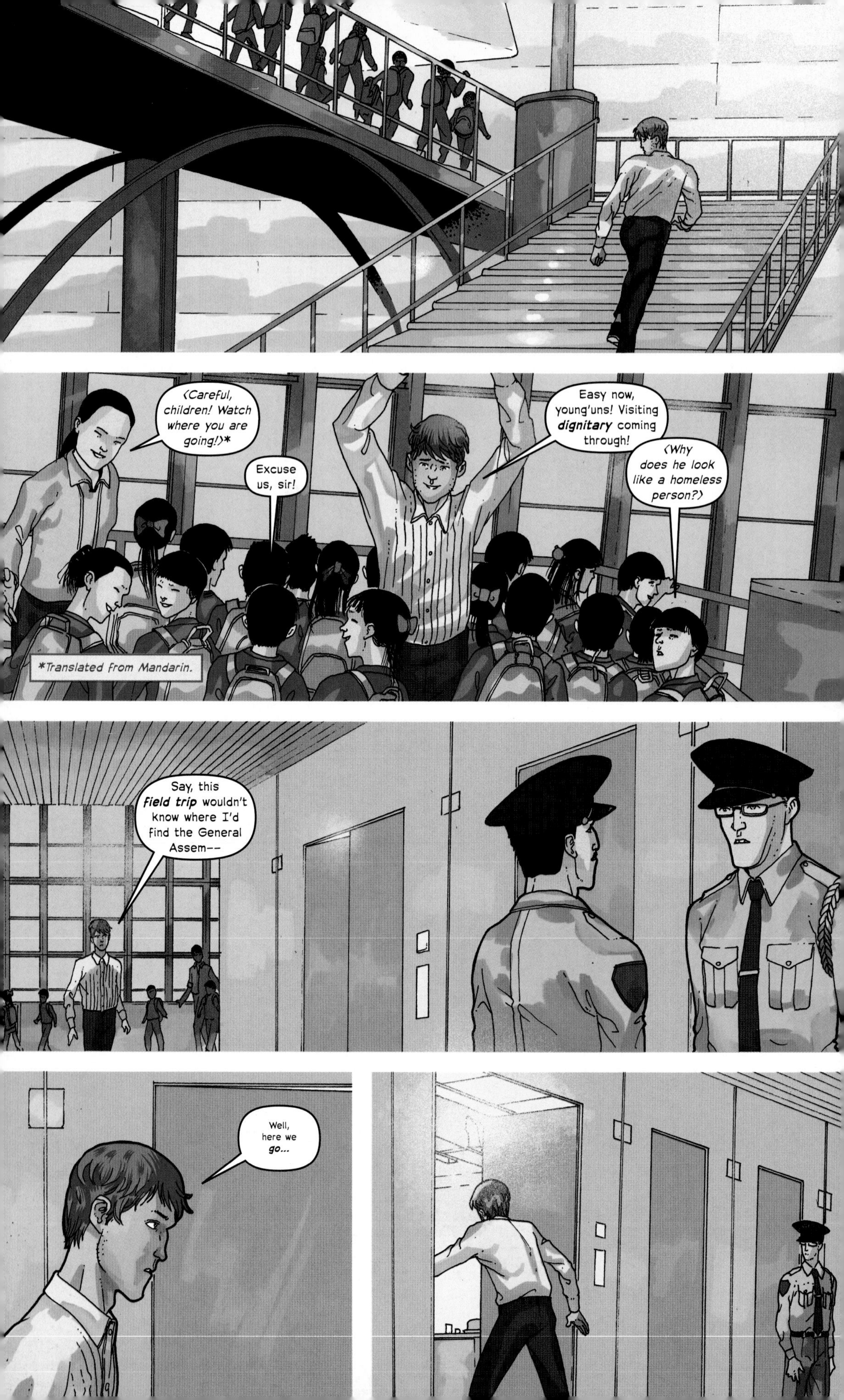

‹Careful, children! Watch where you are going!›*
Excuse us, sir!
Easy now, young'uns! Visiting **dignitary** coming through!
‹Why does he look like a homeless person?›
*Translated from Mandarin.
Say, this **field trip** wouldn't know where I'd find the General Assem--
Well, here we **go...**

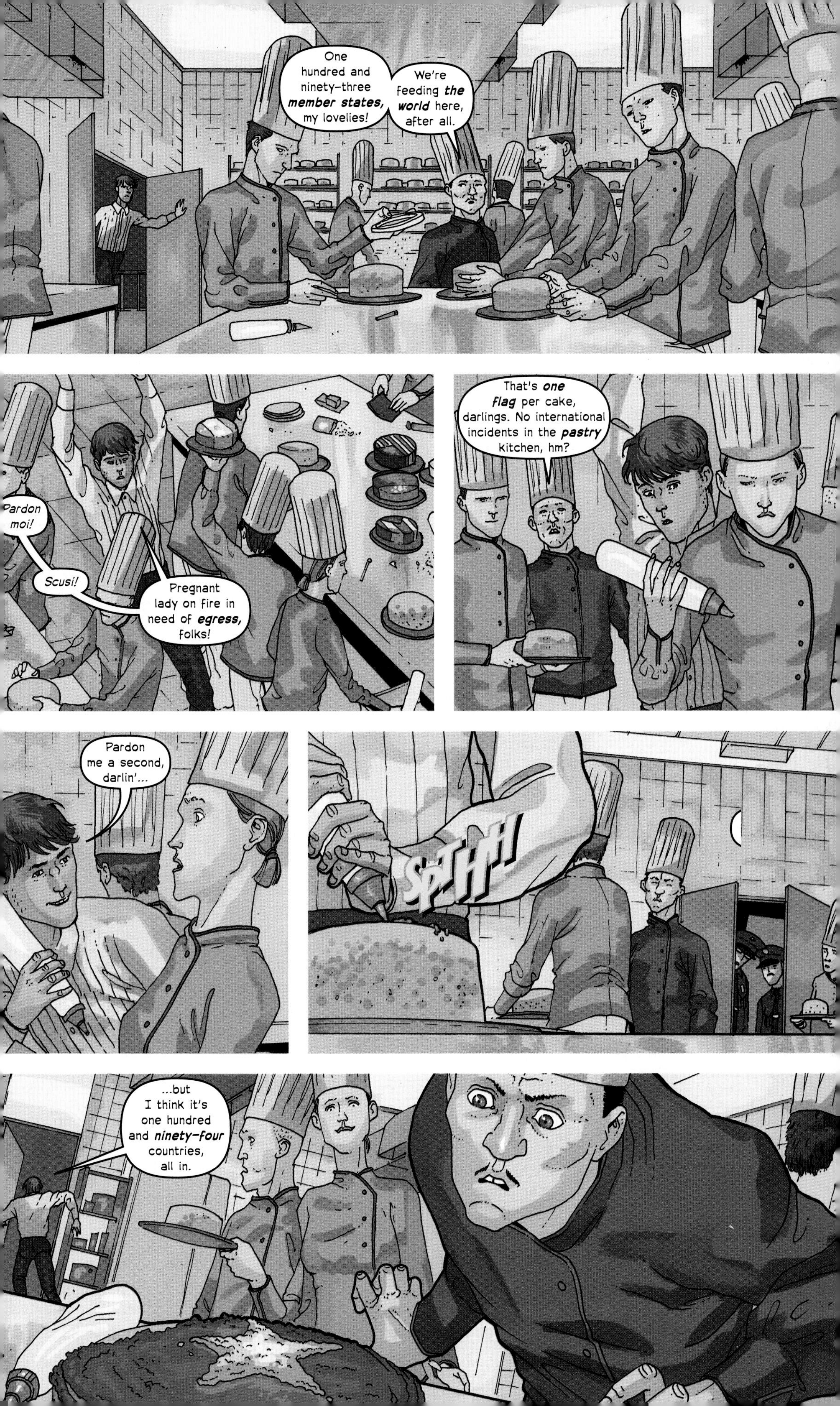
One hundred and ninety-three ***member states,*** my lovelies!
We're feeding ***the world*** here, after all.
Pardon moi!
Scusi!
Pregnant lady on fire in need of ***egress,*** folks!
That's ***one flag*** per cake, darlings. No international incidents in the ***pastry*** kitchen, hm?
Pardon me a second, darlin'...
SPTHHH
...but I think it's one hundred and ***ninety-four*** countries, all in.

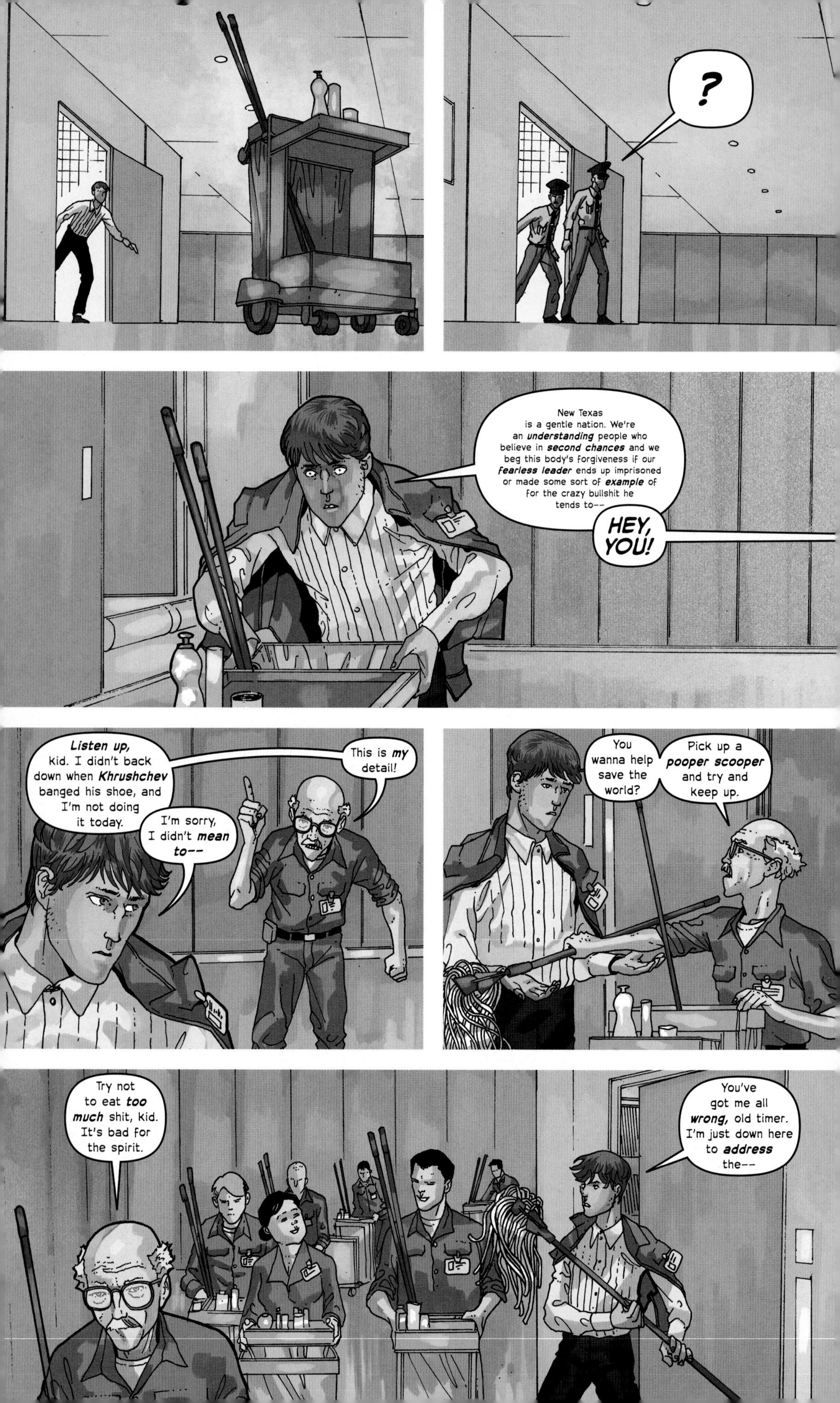
?
New Texas is a gentle nation. We're an *understanding* people who believe in *second chances* and we beg this body's forgiveness if our *fearless leader* ends up imprisoned or made some sort of *example* of for the crazy bullshit he tends to--
HEY, YOU!
Listen up, kid. I didn't back down when *Khrushchev* banged his shoe, and I'm not doing it today.
This is *my* detail!
I'm sorry, I didn't *mean to--*
You wanna help save the world?
Pick up a *pooper scooper* and try and keep up.
Try not to eat *too much* shit, kid. It's bad for the spirit.
You've got me all *wrong,* old timer. I'm just down here to *address* the--

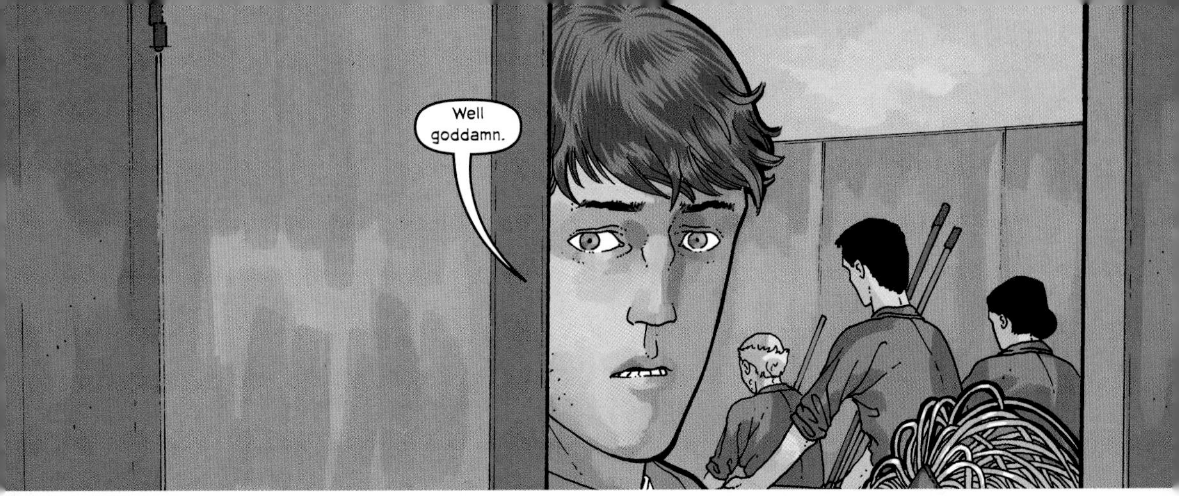
Well goddamn.

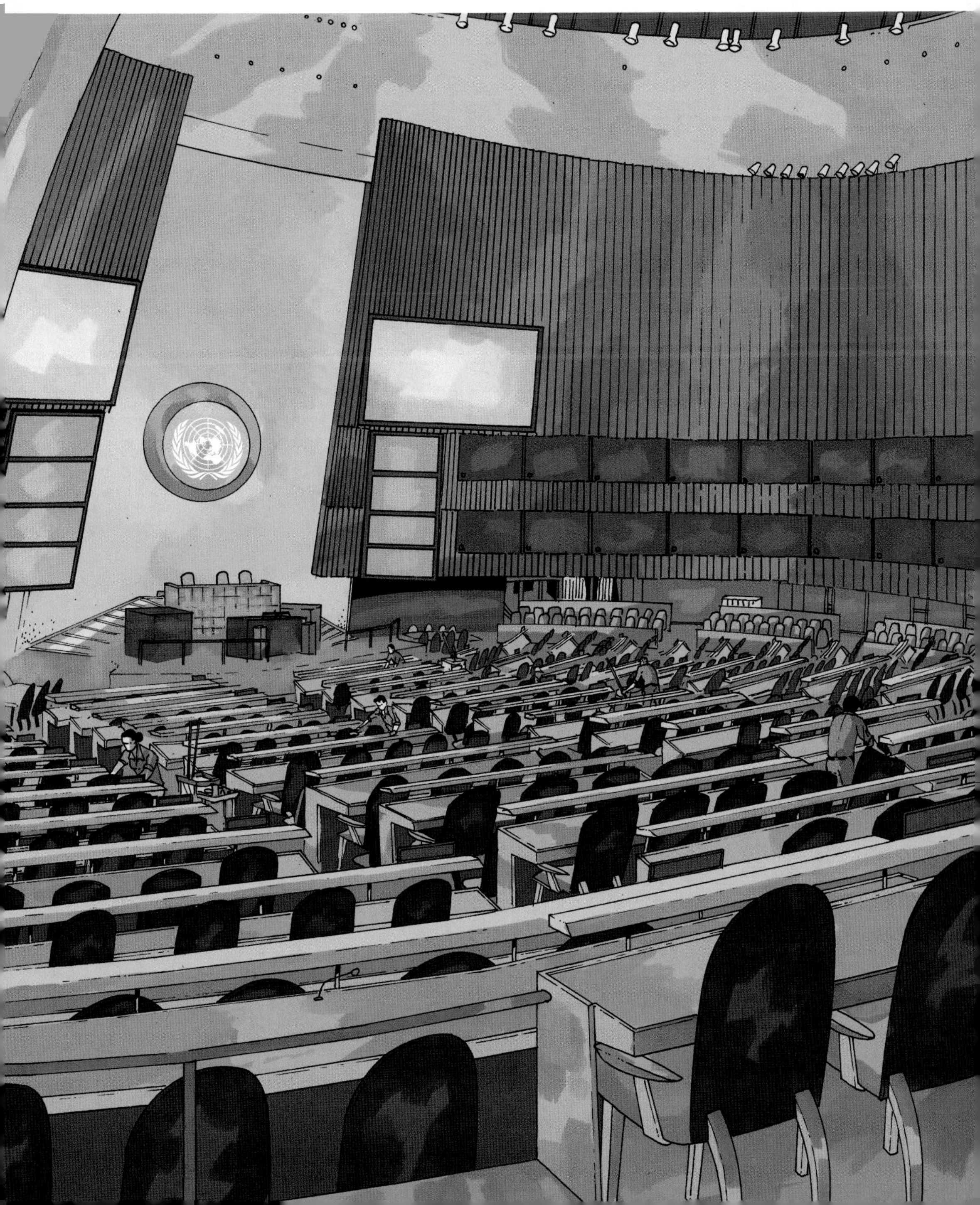

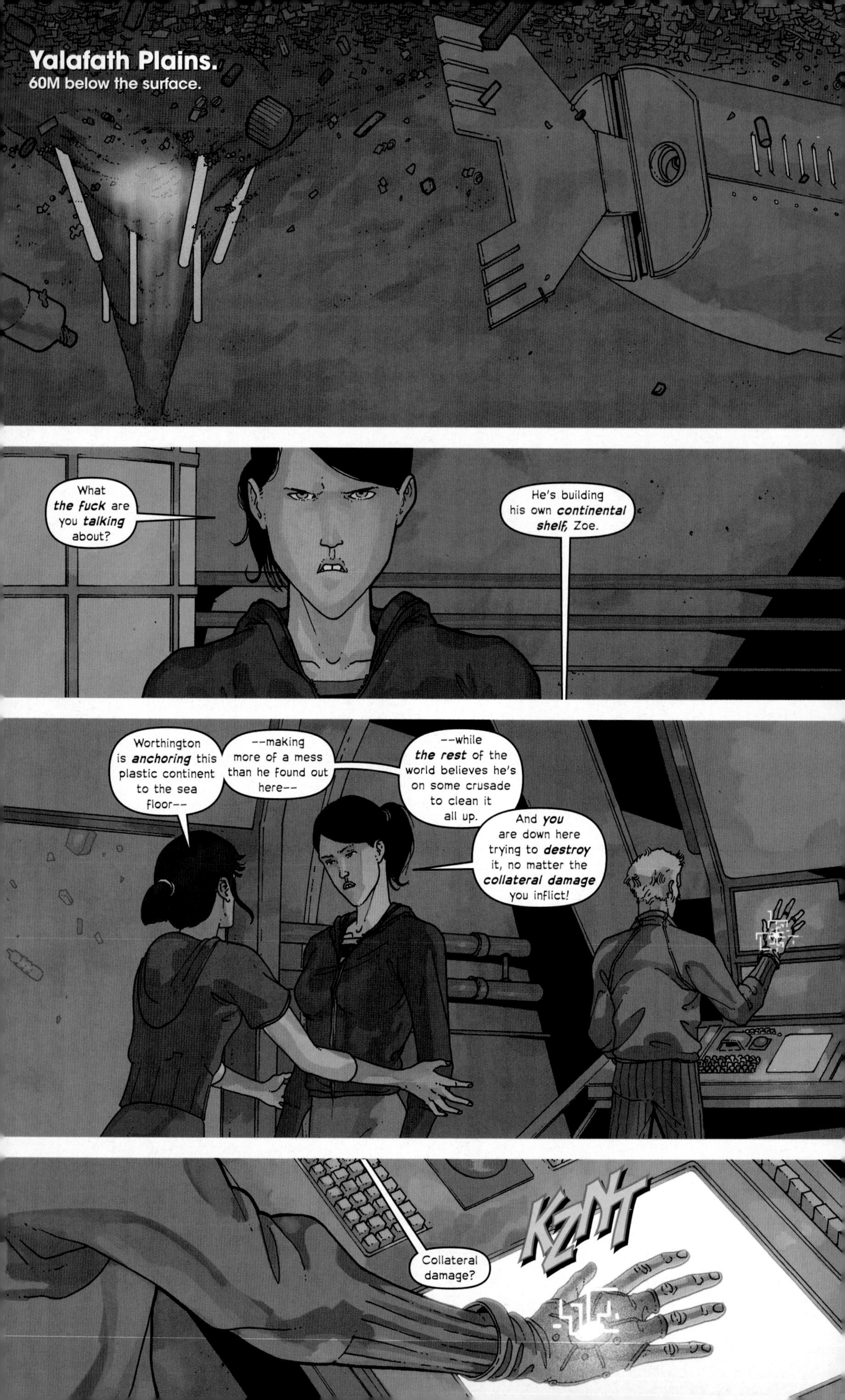

Yalafath Plains.
60M below the surface.
What the fuck are you talking about?
He's building his own continental shelf, Zoe.
Worthington is anchoring this plastic continent to the sea floor--
--making more of a mess than he found out here--
--while the rest of the world believes he's on some crusade to clean it all up.
And you are down here trying to destroy it, no matter the collateral damage you inflict!
KZNT
Collateral damage?

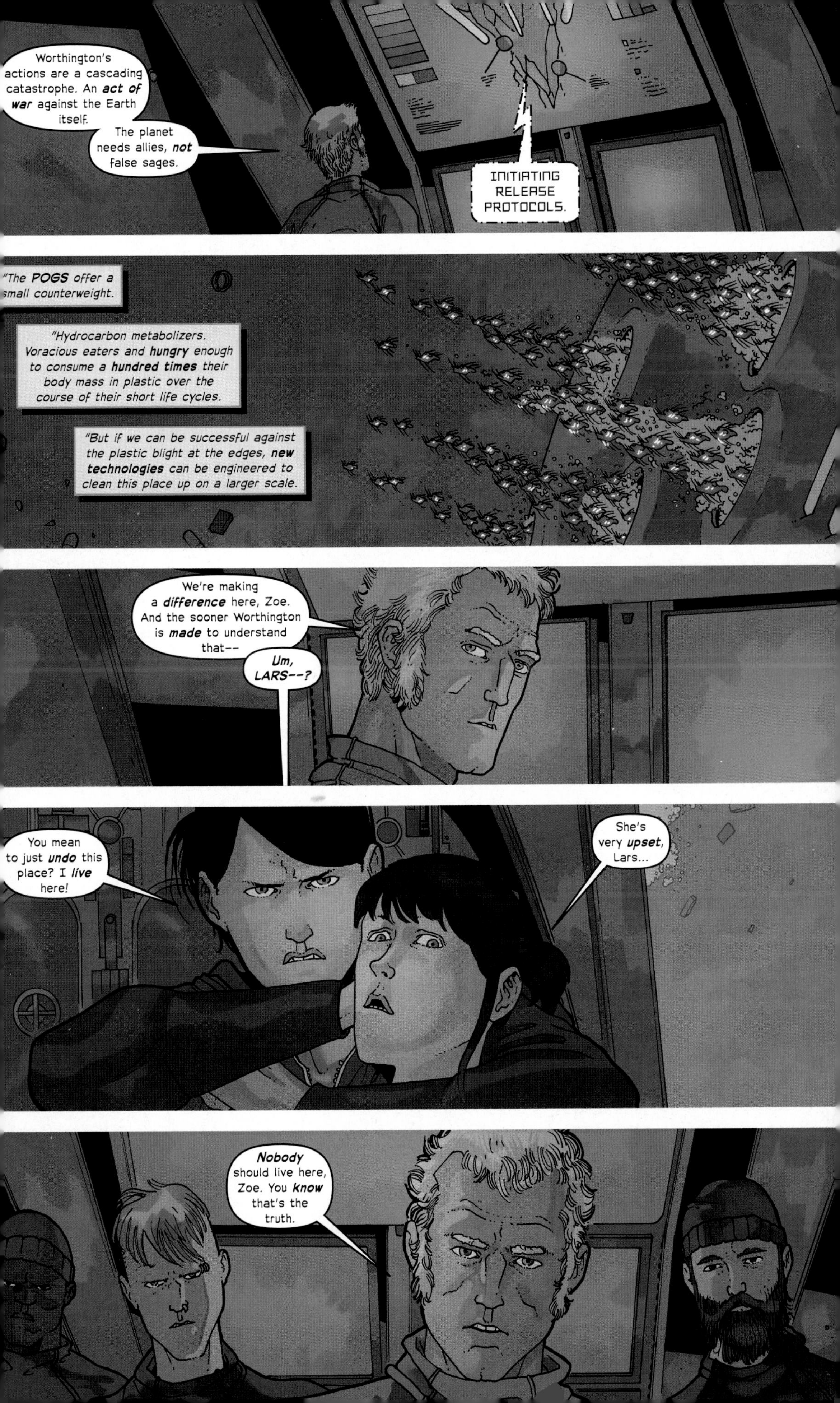
Worthington's actions are a cascading catastrophe. An **act of war** against the Earth itself.
The planet needs allies, **not** false sages.
INITIATING RELEASE PROTOCOLS.
"The **POGS** offer a small counterweight.
"Hydrocarbon metabolizers. Voracious eaters and **hungry** enough to consume a **hundred times** their body mass in plastic over the course of their short life cycles.
"But if we can be successful against the plastic blight at the edges, **new technologies** can be engineered to clean this place up on a larger scale.
We're making a **difference** here, Zoe. And the sooner Worthington is **made** to understand that--
Um, **LARS--?**
You mean to just **undo** this place? I **live** here!
She's very **upset**, Lars...
Nobody should live here, Zoe. You **know** that's the truth.

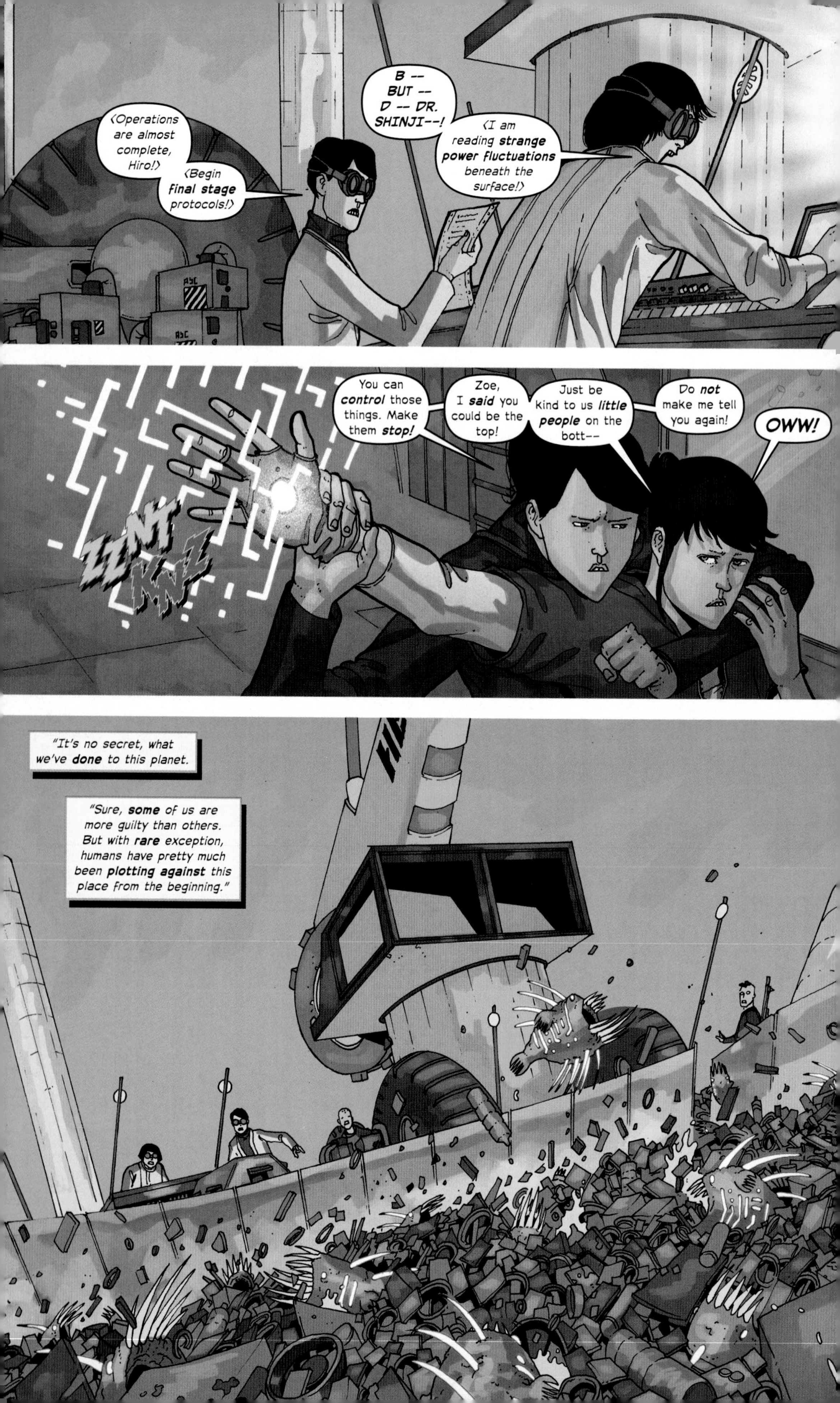
‹Operations are almost complete, Hiro!›
‹Begin final stage protocols!›
B -- BUT -- D -- DR. SHINJI--!
‹I am reading strange power fluctuations beneath the surface!›
You can control those things. Make them stop!
Zoe, I said you could be the top!
Just be kind to us little people on the bott--
Do not make me tell you again!
OWW!
ZZNT
KNZ
"It's no secret, what we've done to this planet.
"Sure, some of us are more guilty than others. But with rare exception, humans have pretty much been plotting against this place from the beginning."

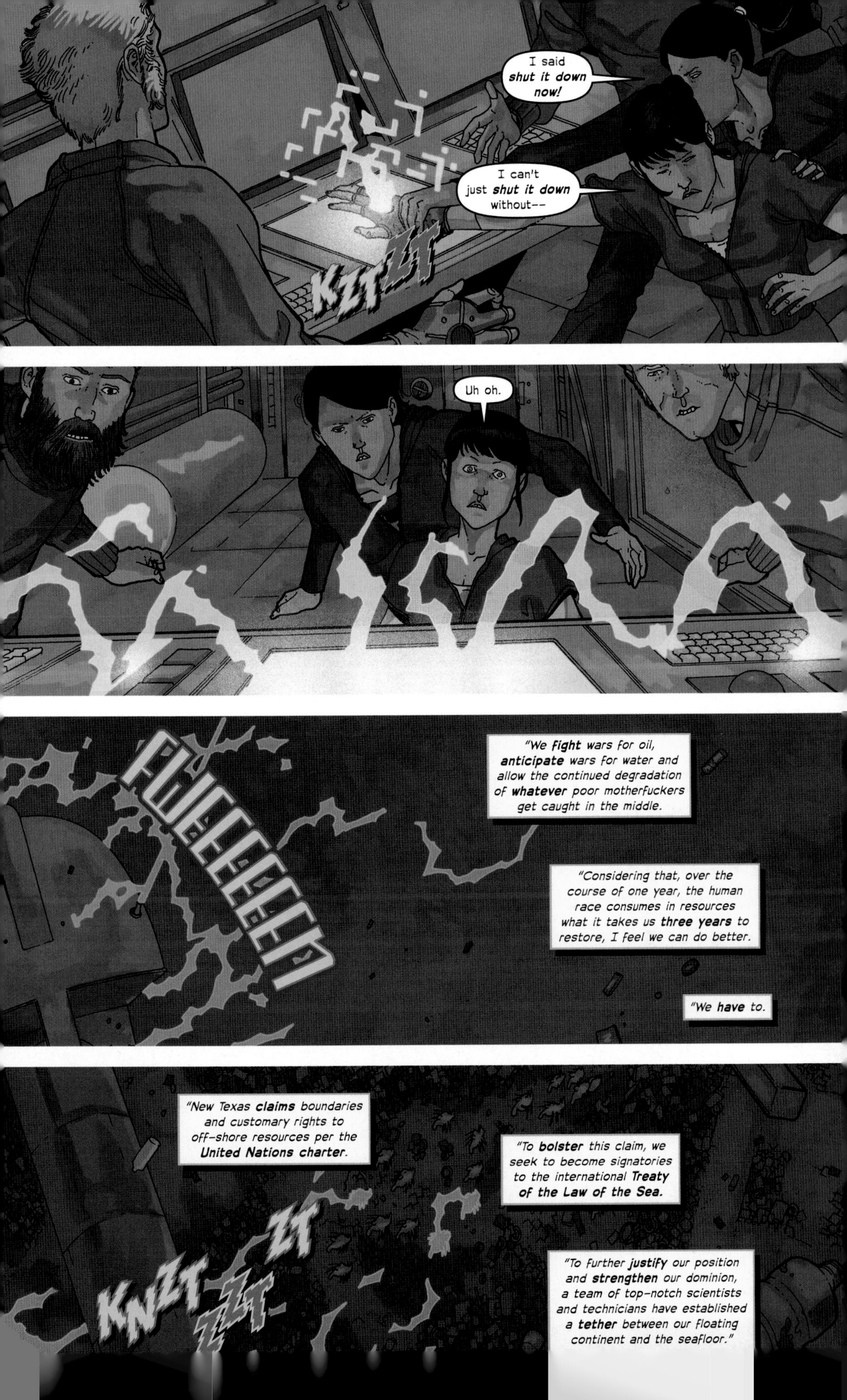
I said *shut it down now!*
I can't just *shut it down* without--
KZTZT
Uh oh.
FWEEEEEEM
"We **fight** wars for oil, **anticipate** wars for water and allow the continued degradation of **whatever** poor motherfuckers get caught in the middle.
"Considering that, over the course of one year, the human race consumes in resources what it takes us **three years** to restore, I feel we can do better.
"We **have** to.
"New Texas **claims** boundaries and customary rights to off-shore resources per the **United Nations charter**.
"To **bolster** this claim, we seek to become signatories to the international **Treaty of the Law of the Sea.**
KNZZT ZZT ZT
"To further **justify** our position and **strengthen** our dominion, a team of top-notch scientists and technicians have established a **tether** between our floating continent and the seafloor."

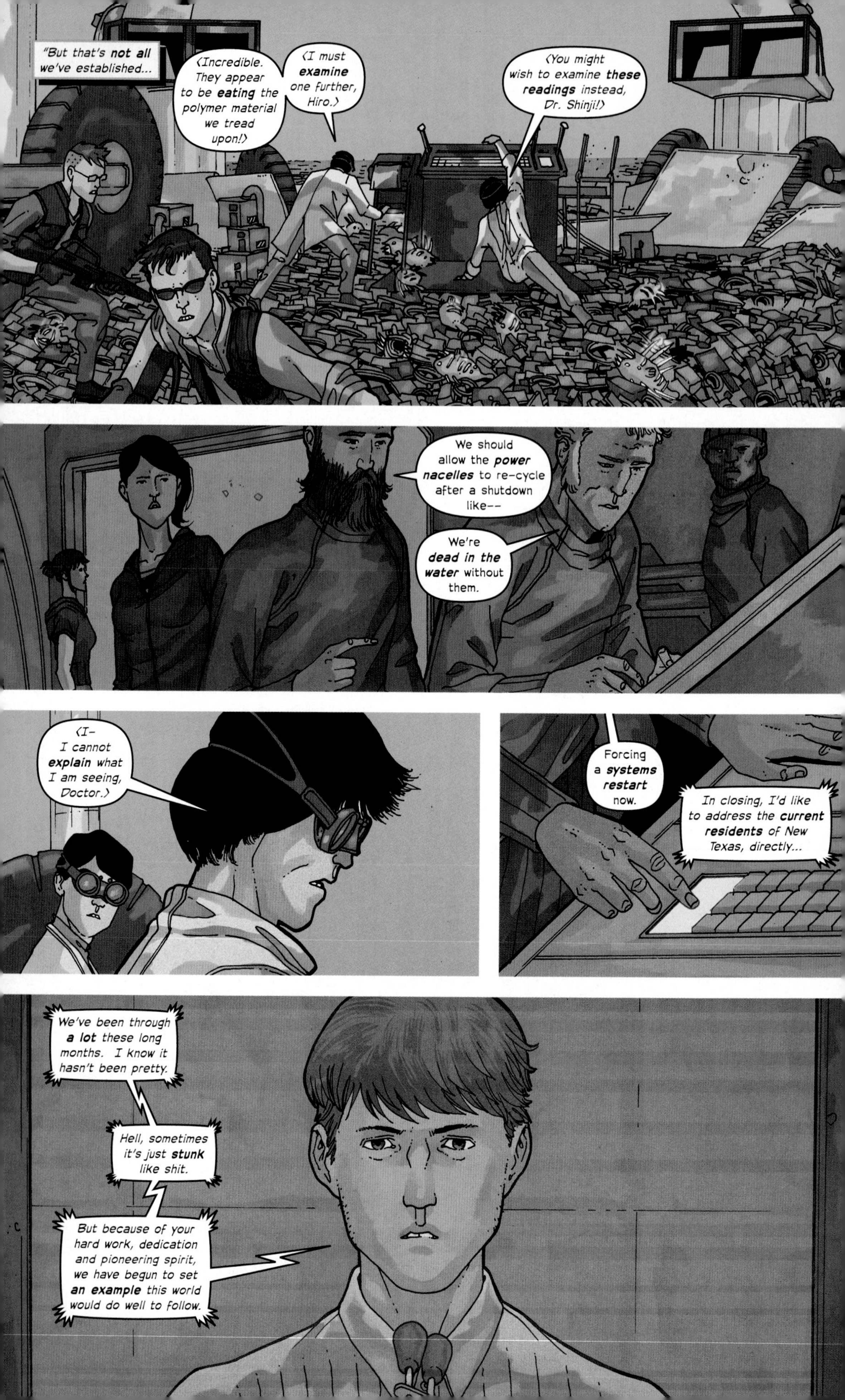

"But that's **not all** we've established...
‹Incredible. They appear to be **eating** the polymer material we tread upon!›
‹I must **examine** one further, Hiro.›
‹You might wish to examine **these readings** instead, Dr. Shinji!›
We should allow the ***power nacelles*** to re-cycle after a shutdown like--
We're ***dead in the water*** without them.
‹I- I cannot **explain** what I am seeing, Doctor.›
Forcing a ***systems restart*** now.
In closing, I'd like to address the **current residents** of New Texas, directly...
We've been through **a lot** these long months. I know it hasn't been pretty.
Hell, sometimes it's just **stunk** like shit.
But because of your hard work, dedication and pioneering spirit, we have begun to set **an example** this world would do well to follow.

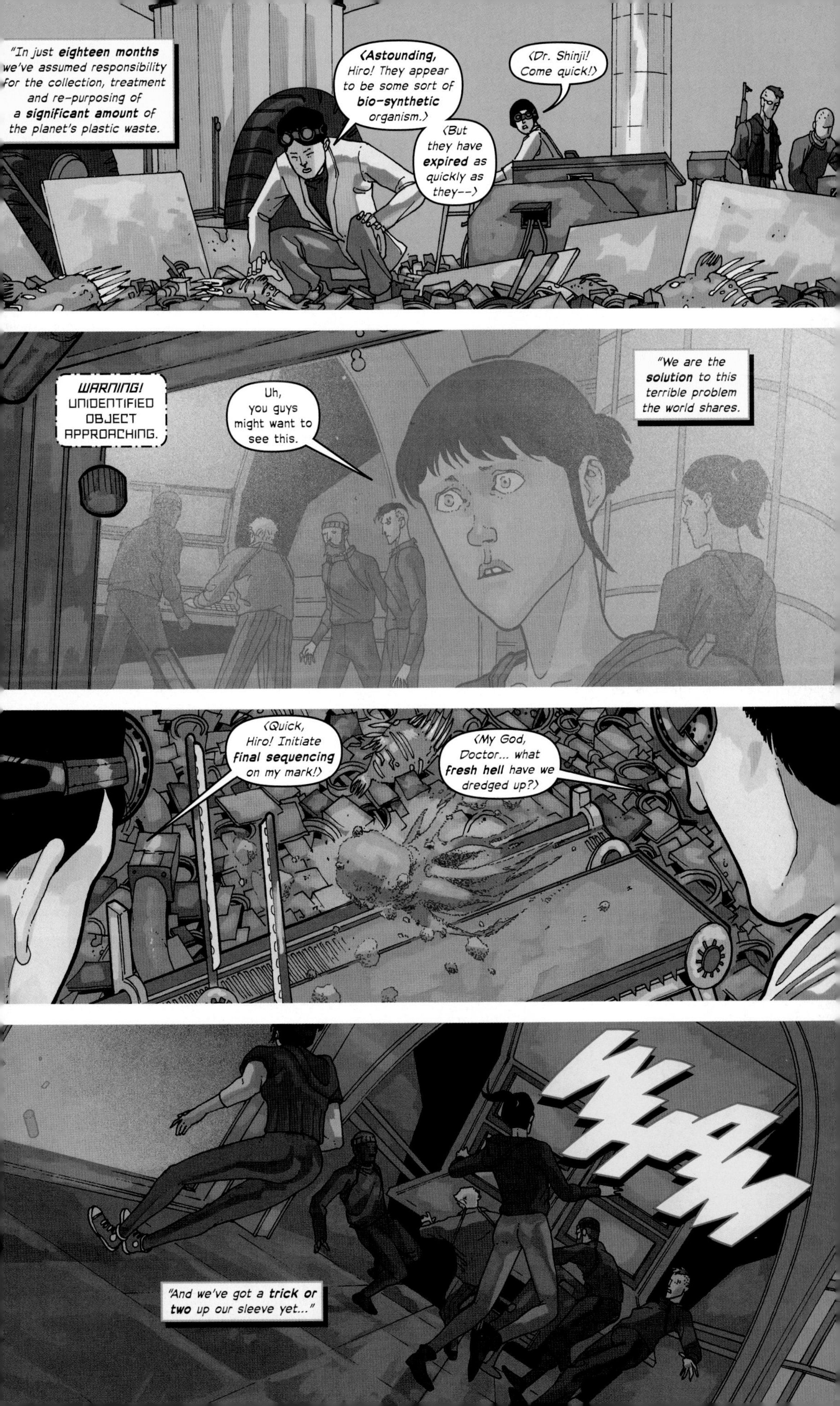
"In just **eighteen months** we've assumed responsibility for the collection, treatment and re-purposing of a **significant amount** of the planet's plastic waste.
‹**Astounding,** Hiro! They appear to be some sort of **bio-synthetic** organism.›
‹But they have **expired** as quickly as they--›
‹Dr. Shinji! Come quick!›
WARNING! UNIDENTIFIED OBJECT APPROACHING.
Uh, you guys might want to see this.
"We are the **solution** to this terrible problem the world shares.
‹Quick, Hiro! Initiate **final sequencing** on my mark!›
‹My God, Doctor... what **fresh hell** have we dredged up?›
"And we've got a **trick or two** up our sleeve yet..."

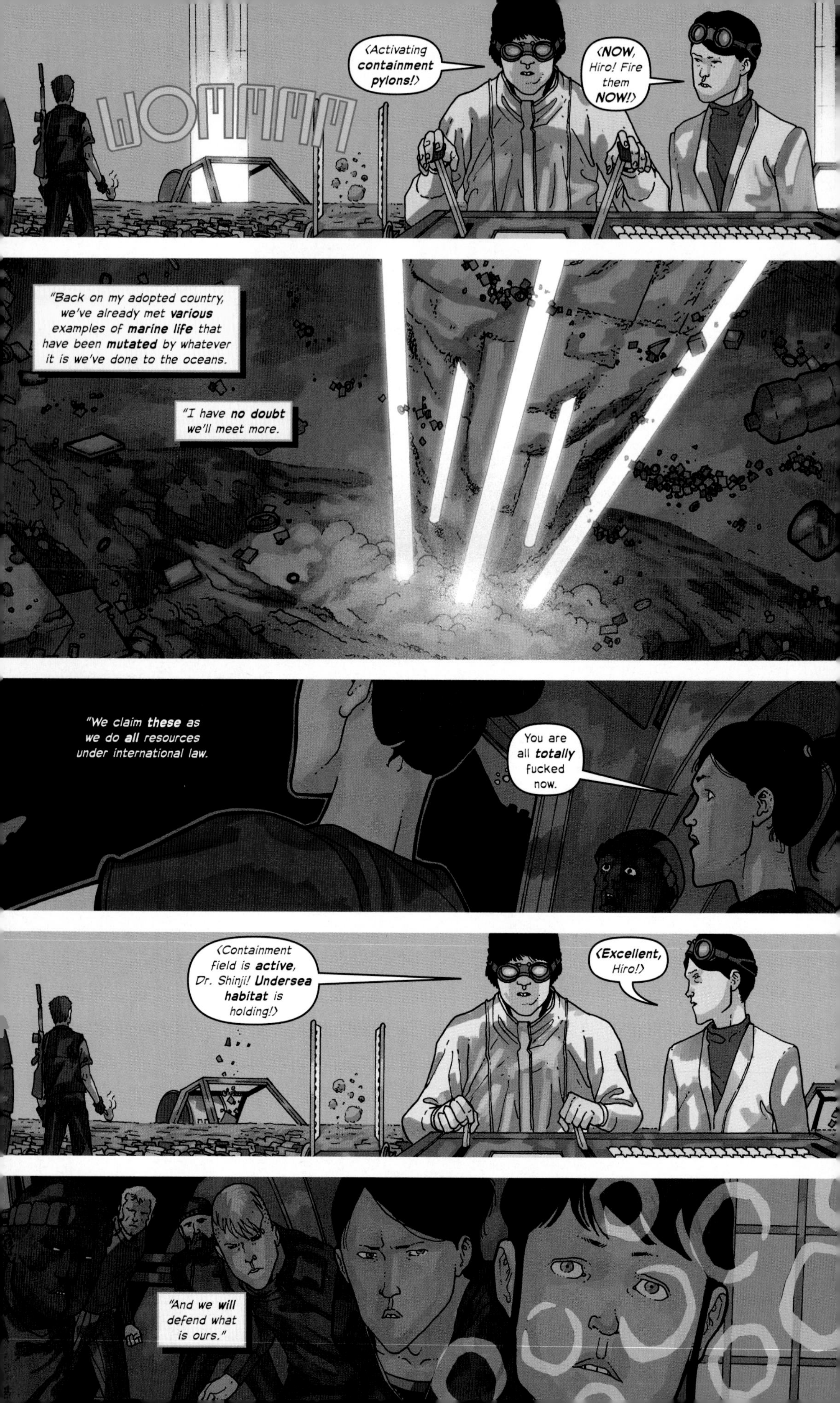
WOMMMM
‹Activating containment pylons!›
‹NOW, Hiro! Fire them NOW!›
"Back on my adopted country, we've already met various examples of marine life that have been mutated by whatever it is we've done to the oceans.
"I have no doubt we'll meet more.
"We claim these as we do all resources under international law.
You are all totally fucked now.
‹Containment field is active, Dr. Shinji! Undersea habitat is holding!›
‹Excellent, Hiro!›
"And we will defend what is ours."

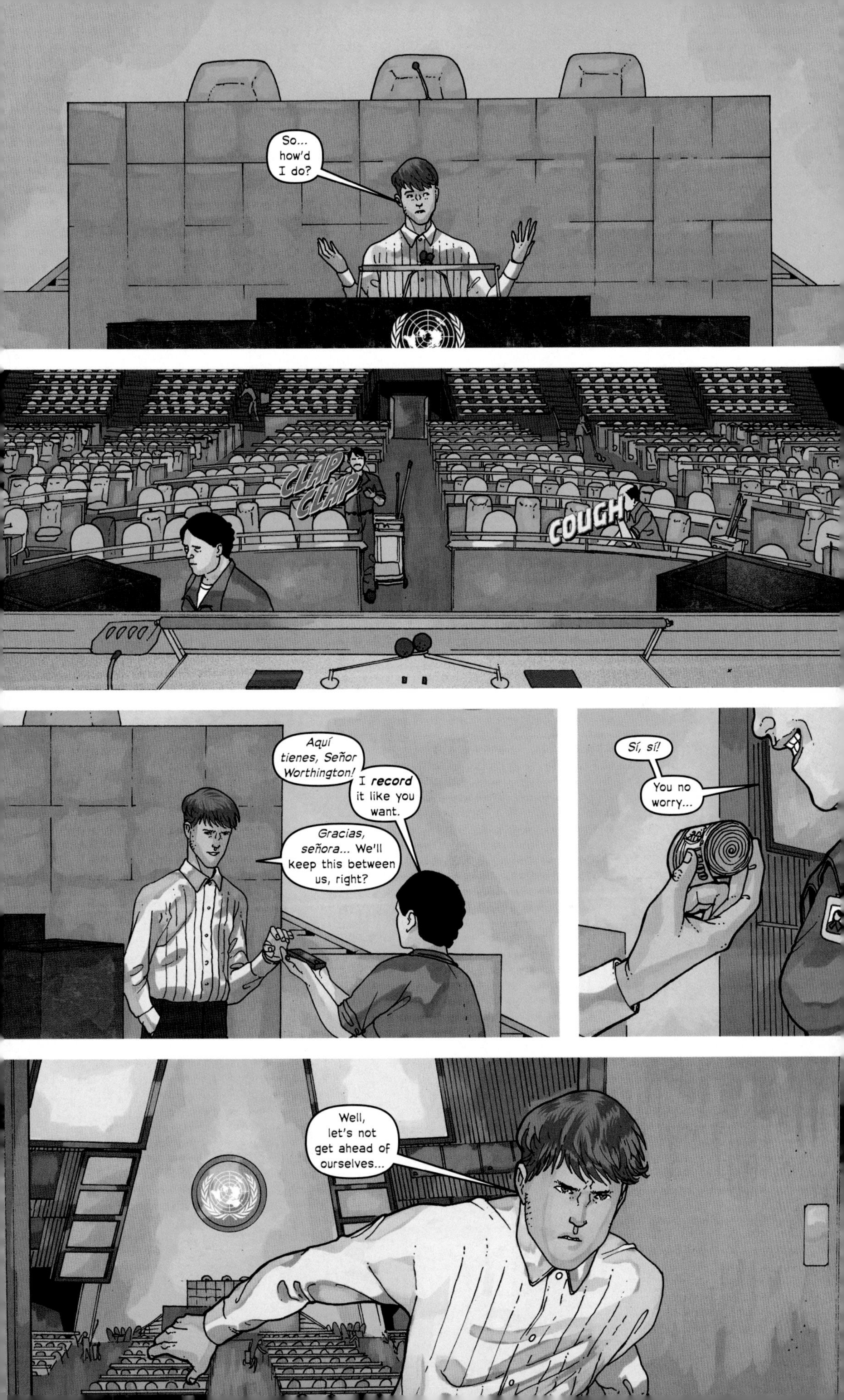
So... how'd I do?
CLAP CLAP
COUGH
Aquí tienes, Señor Worthington!
I **record** it like you want.
Gracias, señora... We'll keep this between us, right?
Sí, sí!
You no worry...
Well, let's not get ahead of ourselves...

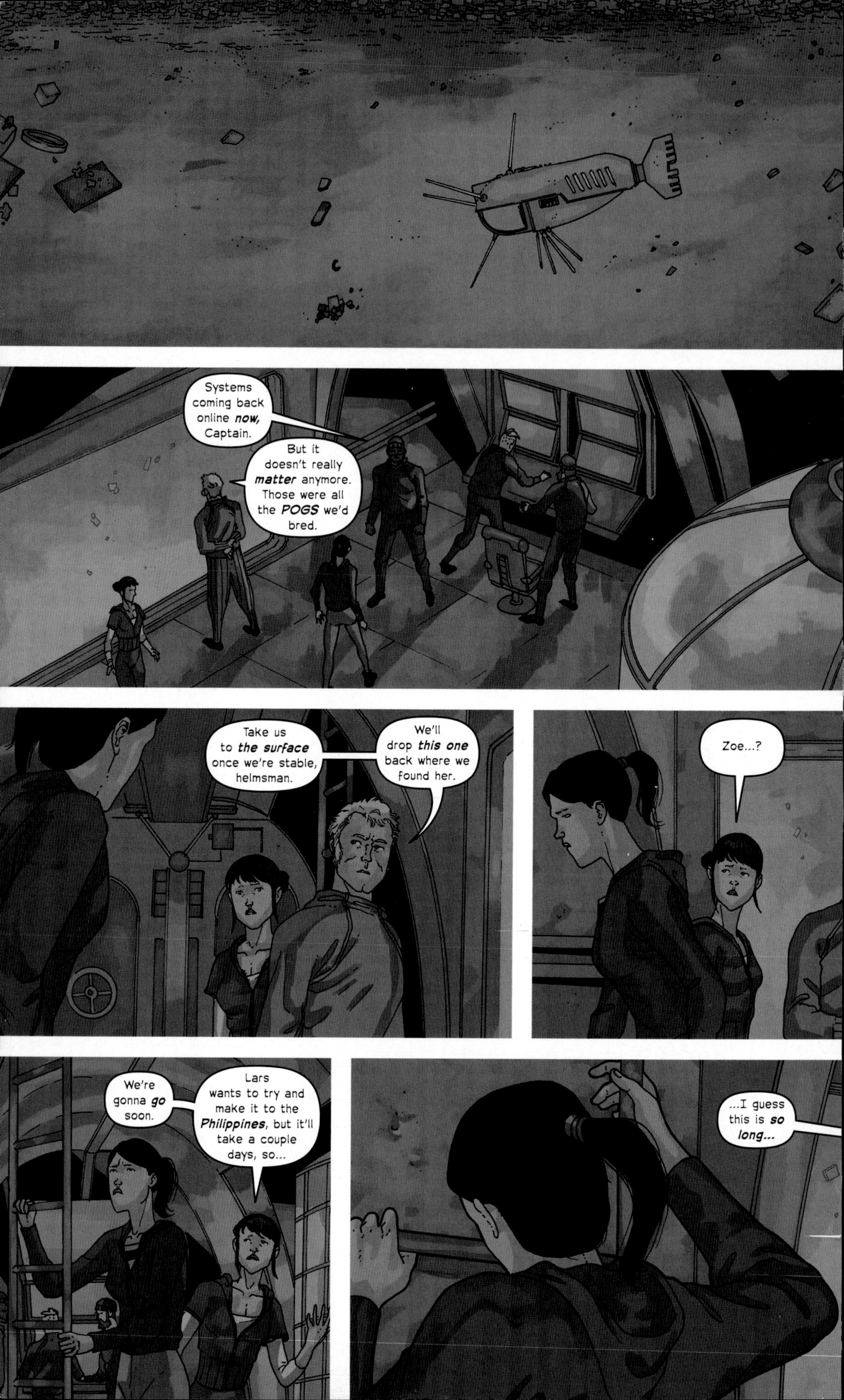
Systems coming back online *now,* Captain.
But it doesn't really *matter* anymore. Those were all the *POGS* we'd bred.
Take us to *the surface* once we're stable, helmsman.
We'll drop *this one* back where we found her.
Zoe...?
We're gonna *go* soon.
Lars wants to try and make it to the *Philippines*, but it'll take a couple days, so...
...I guess this is *so long...*

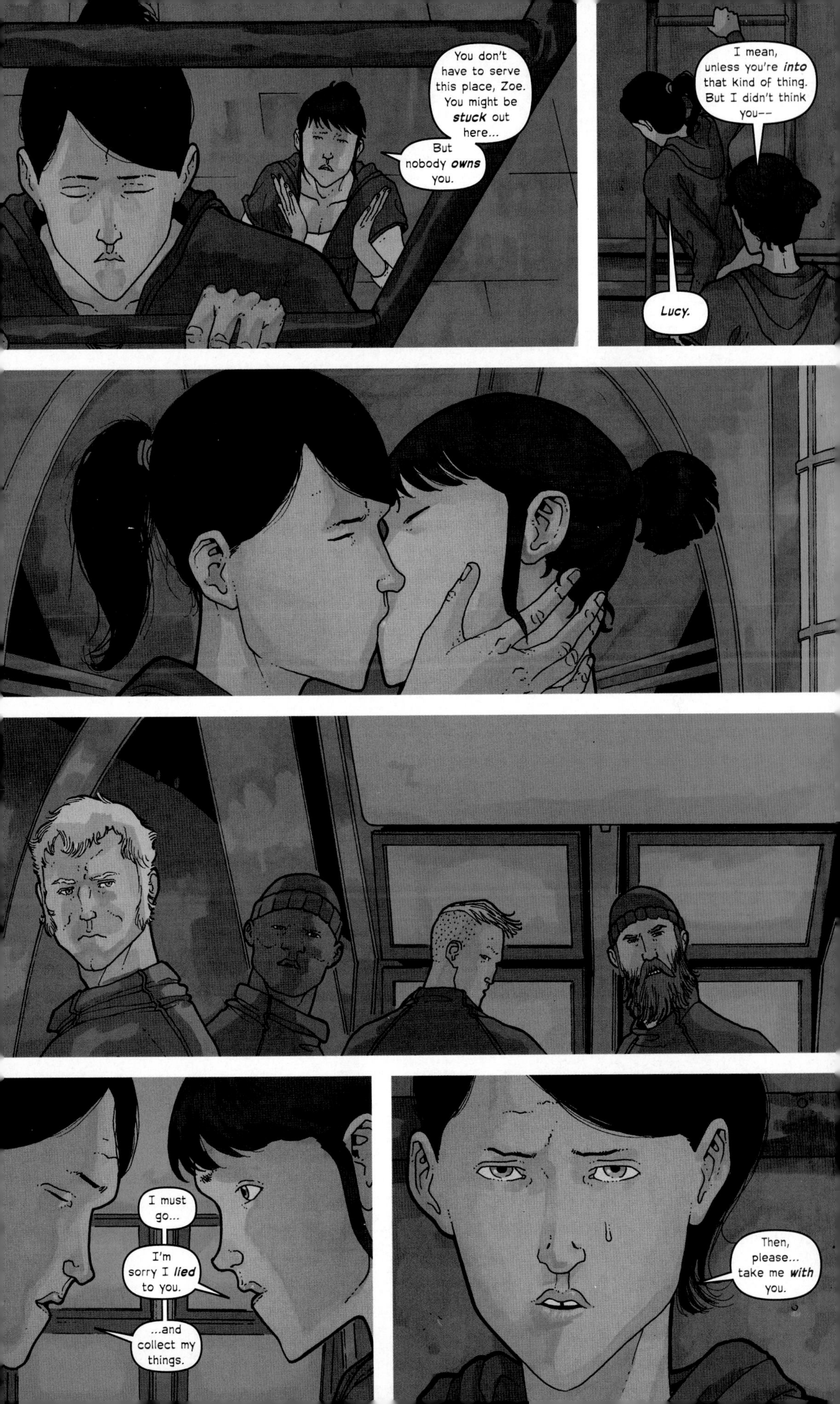
You don't have to serve this place, Zoe. You might be *stuck* out here...
But nobody *owns* you.
I mean, unless you're *into* that kind of thing. But I didn't think you--
Lucy.
I must go...
I'm sorry I *lied* to you.
...and collect my things.
Then, please... take me *with* you.

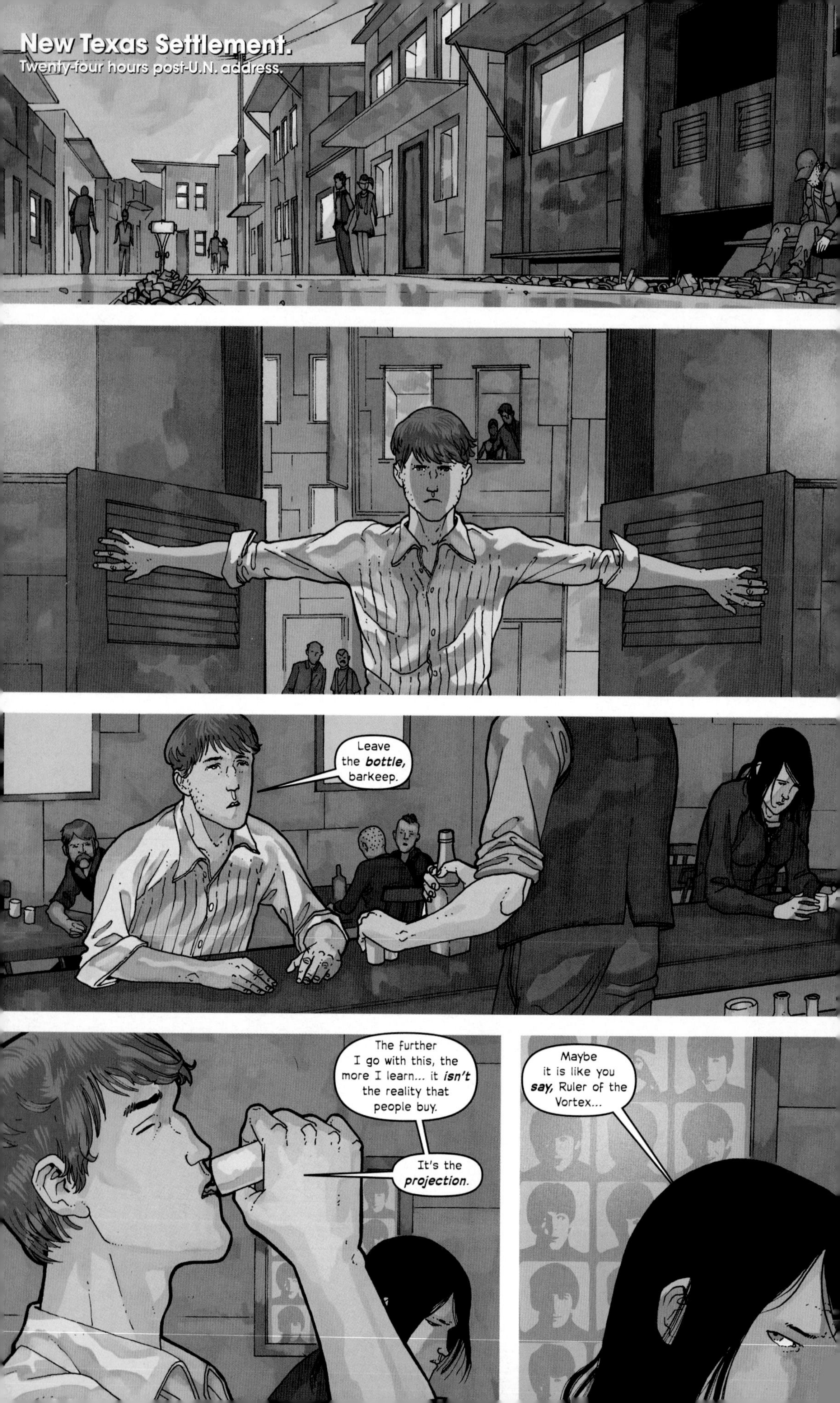

New Texas Settlement.
Twenty-four hours post-U.N. address.
Leave the **bottle,** barkeep.
The further I go with this, the more I learn... it ***isn't*** the reality that people buy.
It's the ***projection***.
Maybe it is like you ***say,*** Ruler of the Vortex...

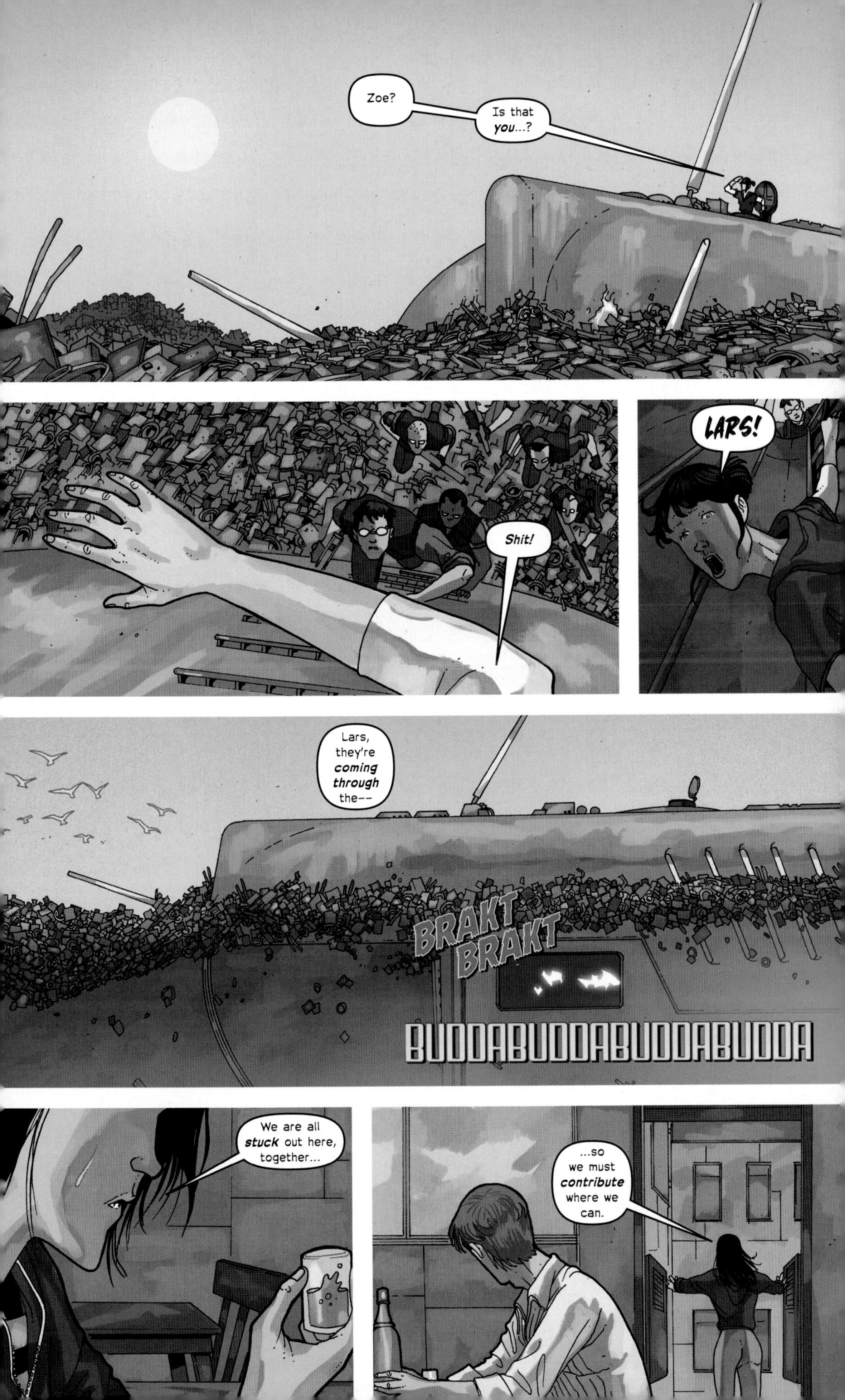
Zoe?
Is that *you*...?
Shit!
LARS!
Lars, they're *coming through* the--
BRAKT BRAKT
BUDDABUDDABUDDABUDDA
We are all *stuck* out here, together...
...so we must *contribute* where we can.

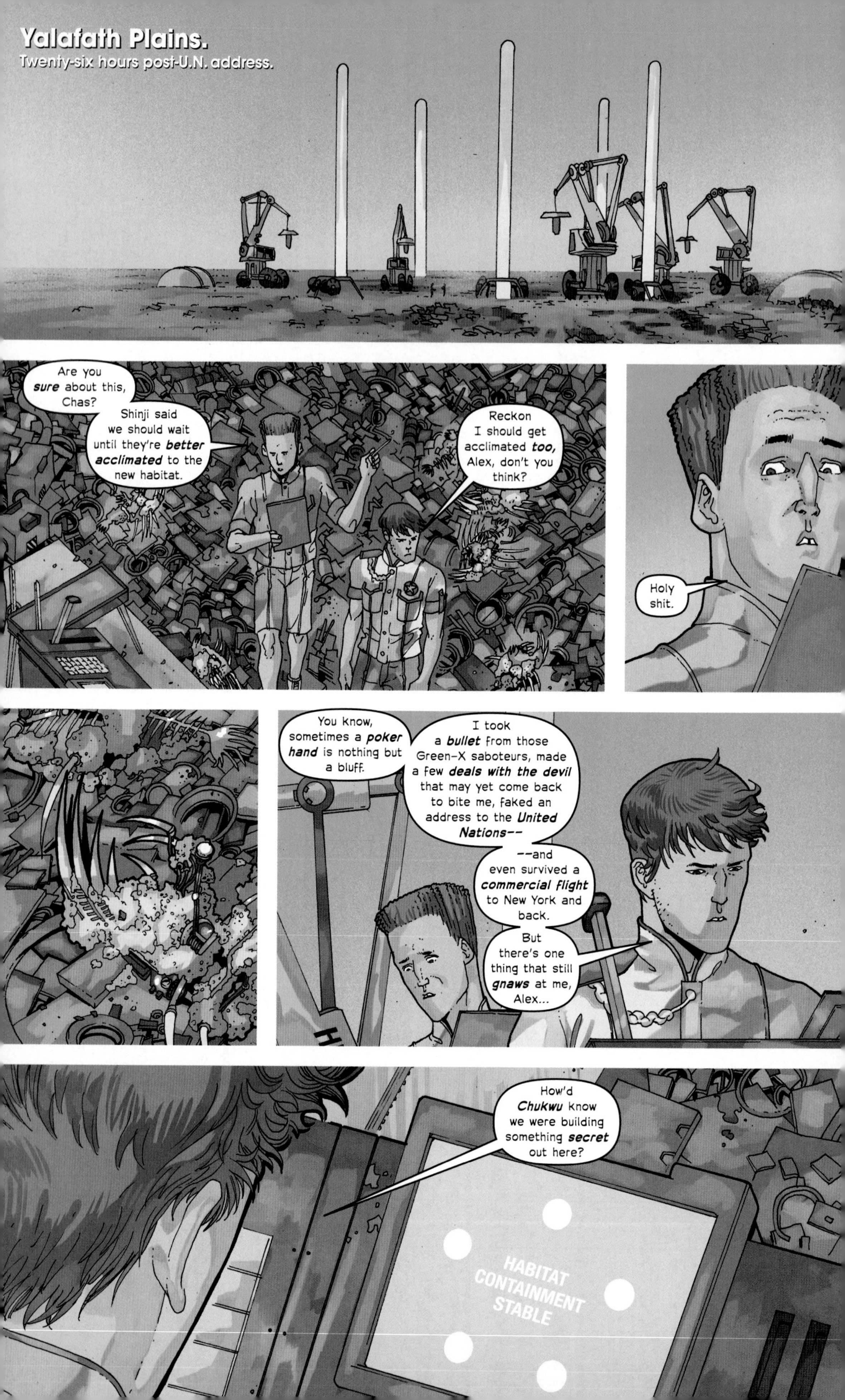
Yalafath Plains.
Twenty-six hours post-U.N. address.
Are you sure about this, Chas?
Shinji said we should wait until they're better acclimated to the new habitat.
Reckon I should get acclimated too, Alex, don't you think?
Holy shit.
You know, sometimes a poker hand is nothing but a bluff.
I took a bullet from those Green-X saboteurs, made a few deals with the devil that may yet come back to bite me, faked an address to the United Nations--
--and even survived a commercial flight to New York and back.
But there's one thing that still gnaws at me, Alex...
How'd Chukwu know we were building something secret out here?
HABITAT CONTAINMENT STABLE

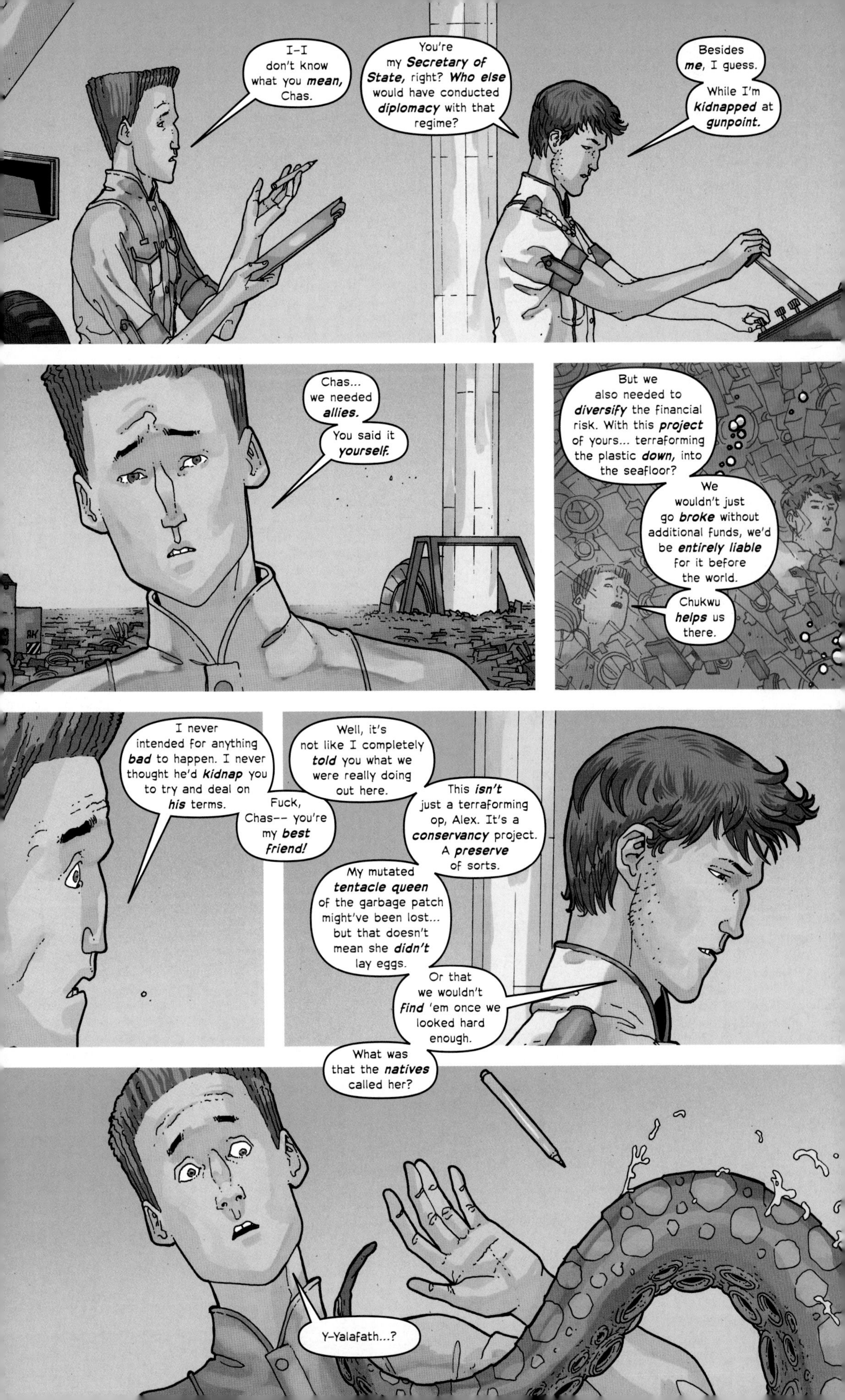
I-I don't know what you mean, Chas.
You're my Secretary of State, right? Who else would have conducted diplomacy with that regime?
Besides me, I guess.
While I'm kidnapped at gunpoint.
Chas... we needed allies.
You said it yourself.
But we also needed to diversify the financial risk. With this project of yours... terraforming the plastic down, into the seafloor?
We wouldn't just go broke without additional funds, we'd be entirely liable for it before the world.
Chukwu helps us there.
I never intended for anything bad to happen. I never thought he'd kidnap you to try and deal on his terms.
Fuck, Chas-- you're my best friend!
Well, it's not like I completely told you what we were really doing out here.
This isn't just a terraforming op, Alex. It's a conservancy project. A preserve of sorts.
My mutated tentacle queen of the garbage patch might've been lost... but that doesn't mean she didn't lay eggs.
Or that we wouldn't find 'em once we looked hard enough.
What was that the natives called her?
Y-Yalafath...?

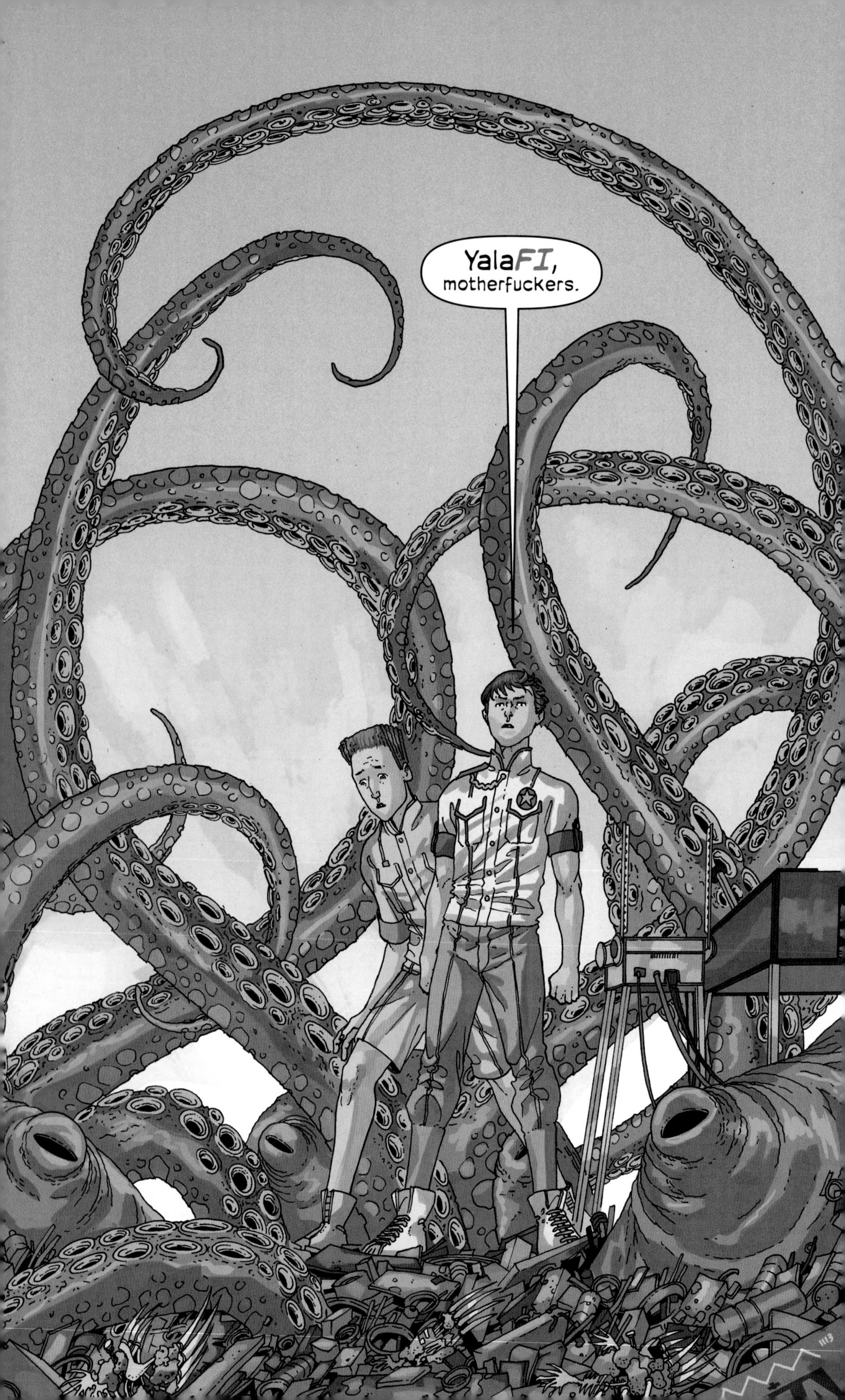
YalaFI, motherfuckers.

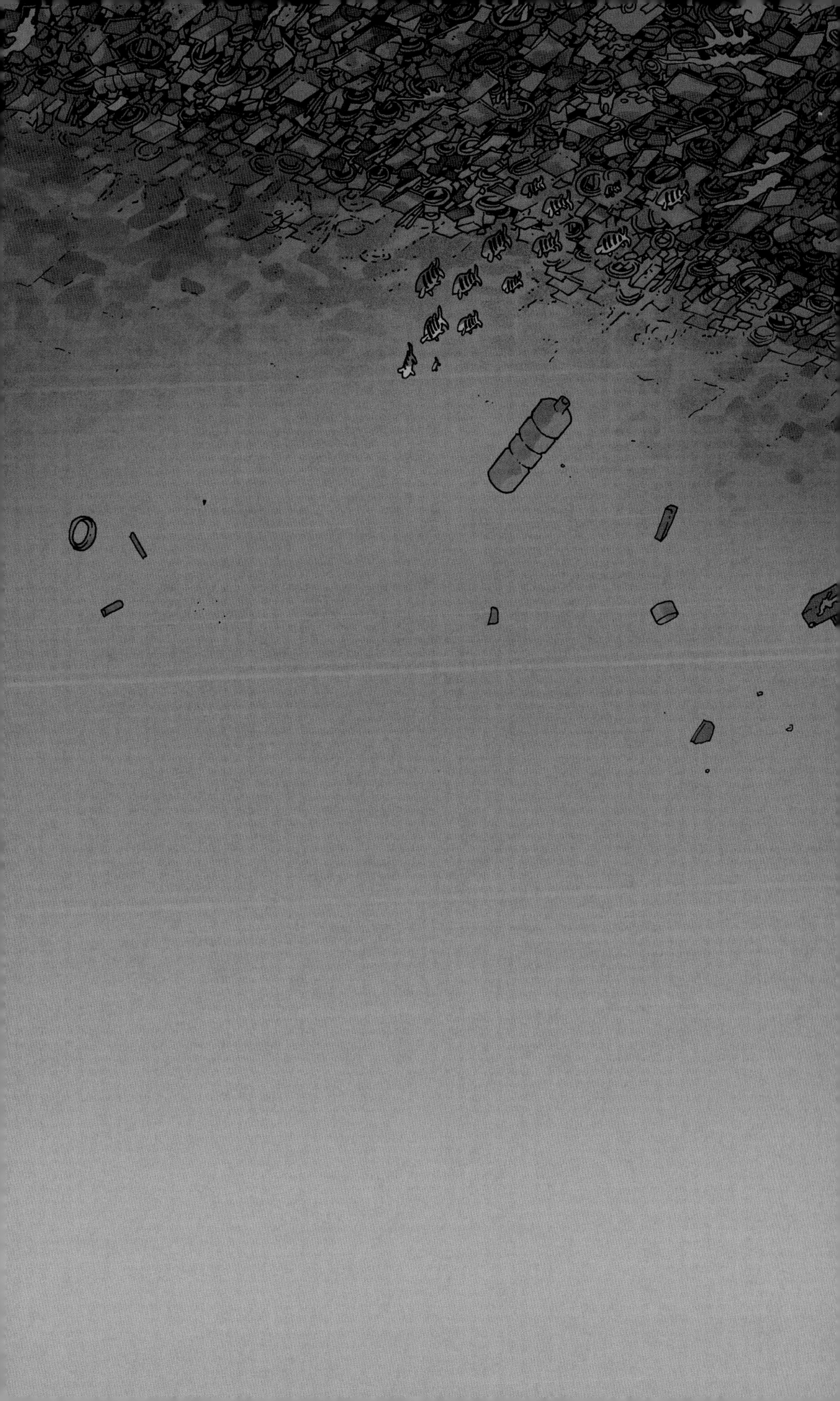

JOE HARRIS is the creator and writer of myriad comics and graphic novels such as the Hitchcockian portrait of spontaneous human combustion, *Spontaneous* and the fantasy graphic novel, *Wars In Toyland* for Oni Press, along with the fan-favorite, monthly paranormal investigations of Agents Mulder and Scully in *The X-Files: Season 10* for IDW.

His supernatural thriller, *Ghost Projekt* was also published by Oni. Lauded by Ain't It Cool News as "one of the finest" miniseries of the year, the tense tale of ghosts, gambits and Cold War secrets is being actively developed for television by NBC.

Harris conceived, and co-wrote the screenplay for, the hit Sony Pictures horror film, *Darkness Falls*, as well as the politically-themed slasher movie and Fox release, *The Tripper*.

A native New Yorker, he lives in Manhattan.

MARTIN MORAZZO is an artist based in Argentina who first came to the attention of US comics readers through his gorgeous artwork on the award-winning webcomic Absolute Magnitude, which was published via DC's now defunct online imprint, Zuda. Morazzo lives in Buenos Aires, and when he isn't spending every waking minute drawing GREAT PACIFIC, he likes to spend time at the beach with his lovely wife, Victoria and his two children.

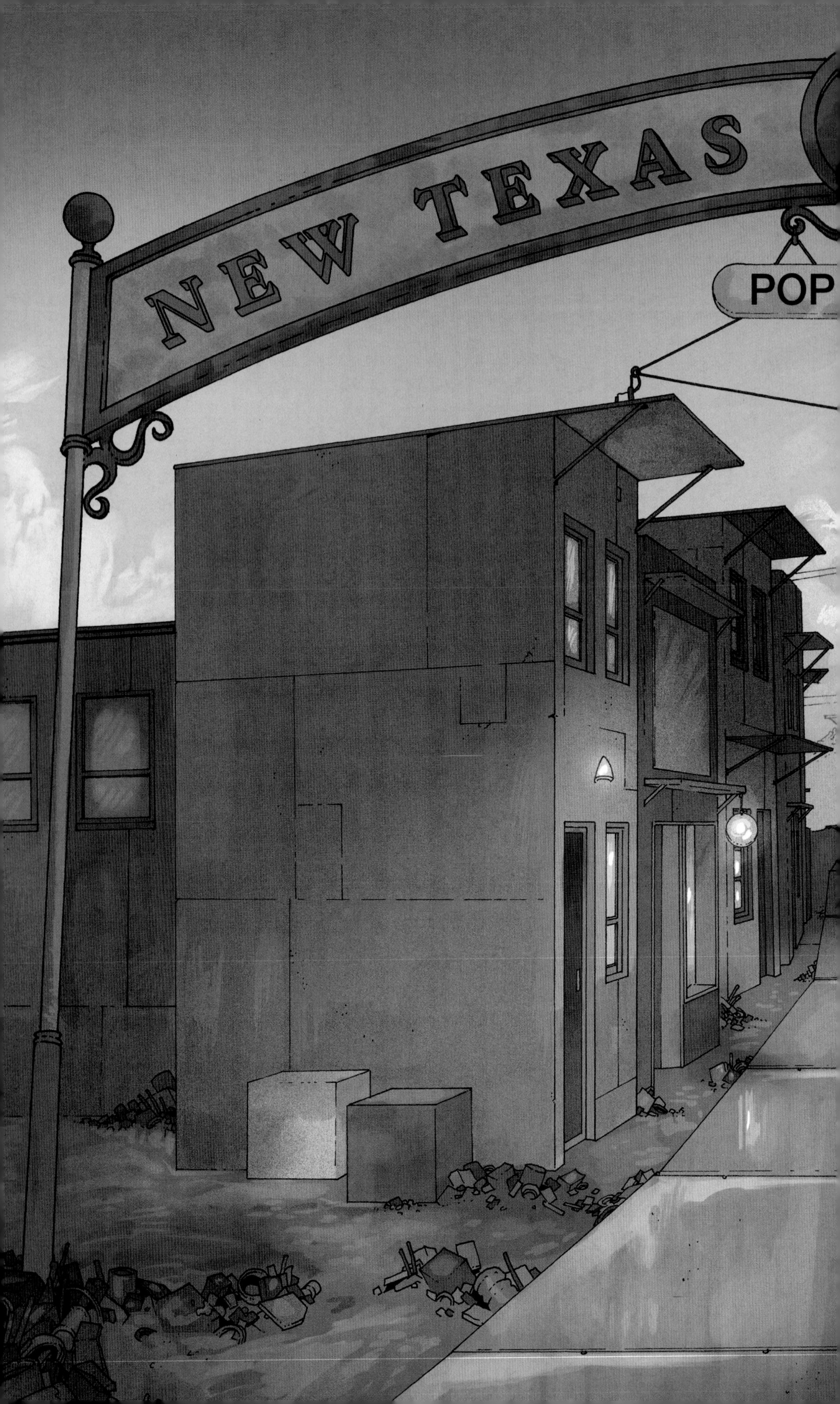
NEW TEXAS
POP

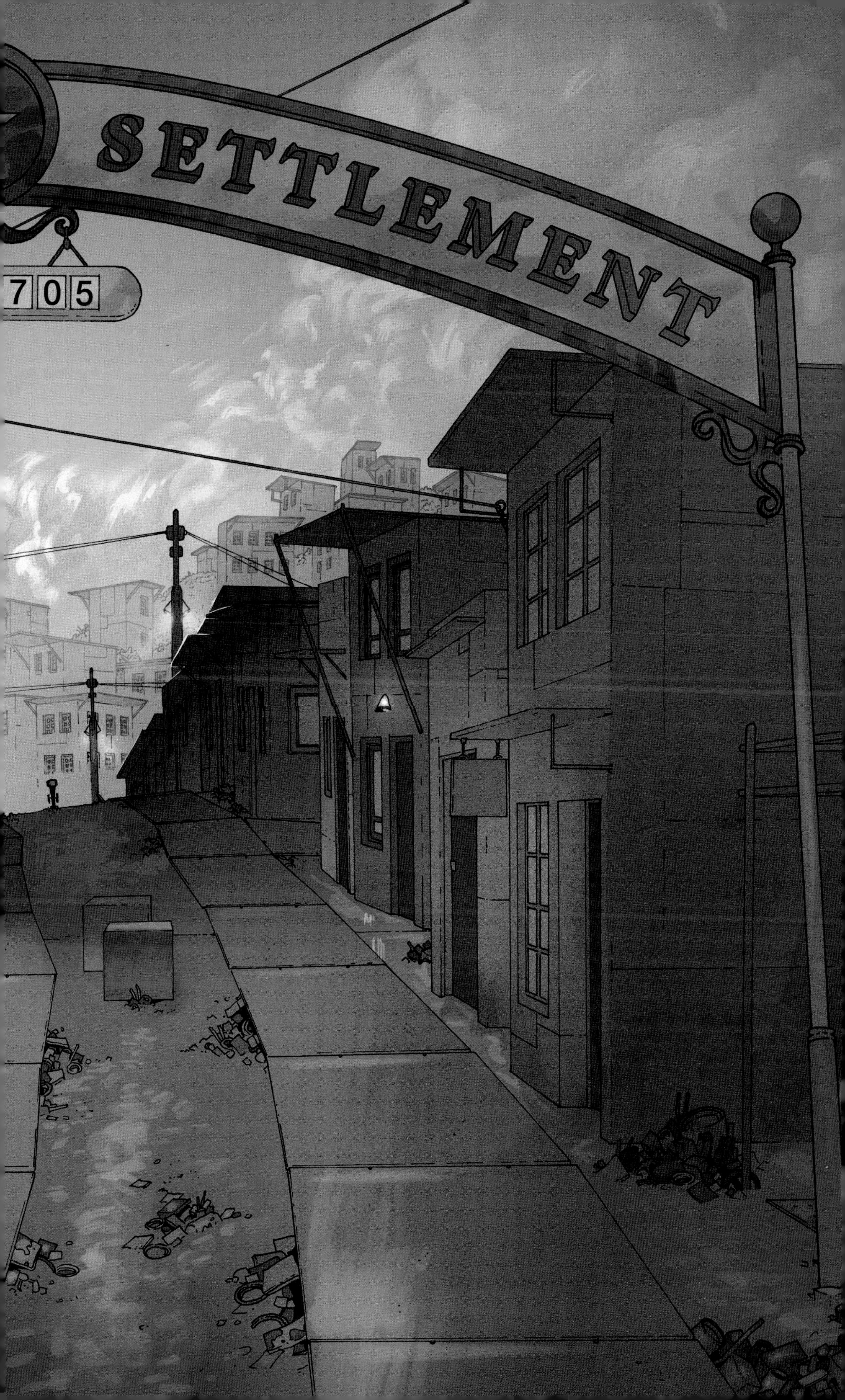
SETTLEMENT
705

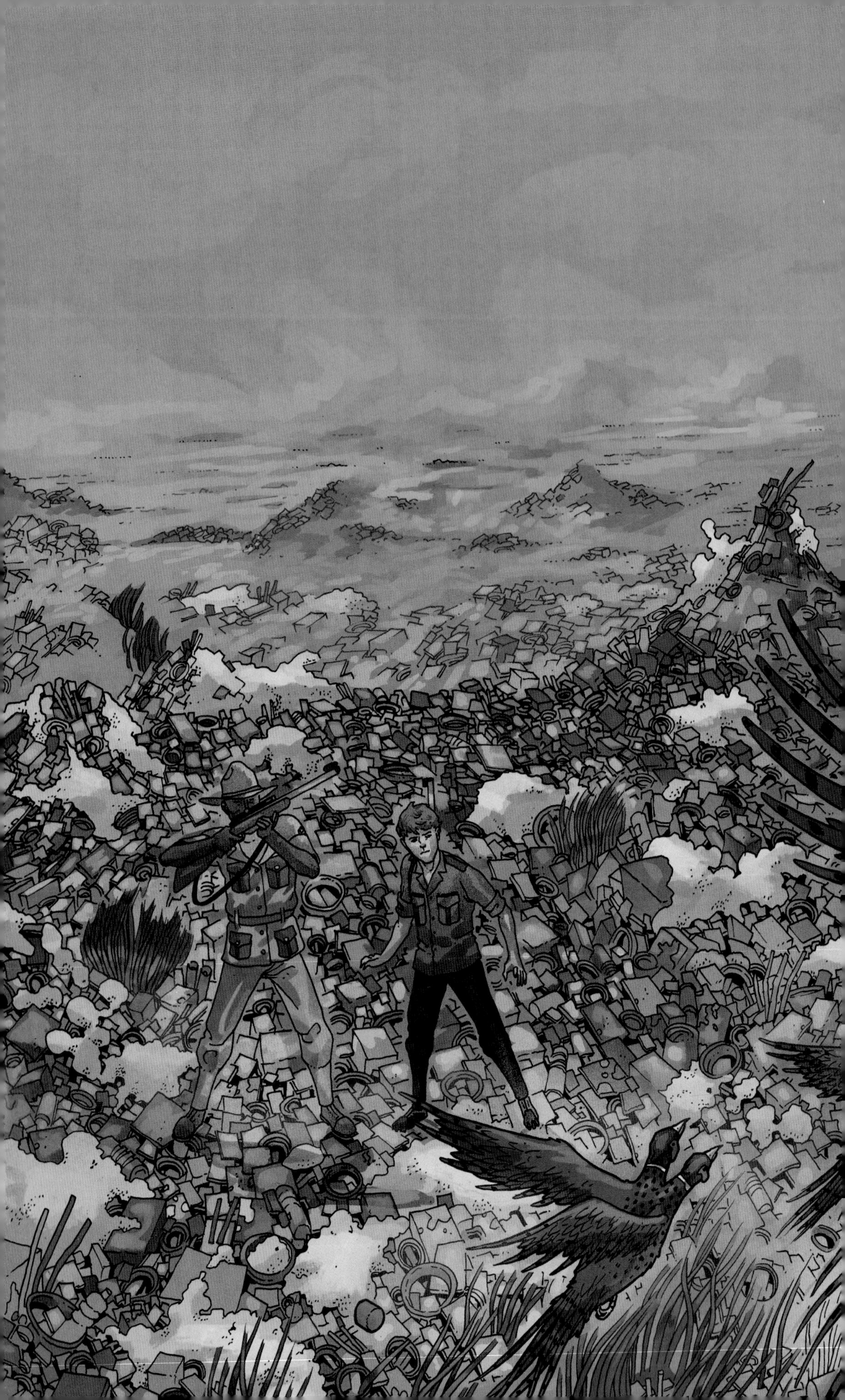